THE MAPPING OF

NORTH
AMERICA

Three centuries of map-making 1500-1860

THE MAPPING OF

NORTH
AMERICA

Three centuries of map-making 1500-1860

JOHN GOSS

THE WELLFLEET PRESS

WELLFLEET

Published 1990 by The Wellfleet Press
an imprint of Booksales Inc.,
110 Enterprise Avenue, Secaucus,
New Jersey 07094

Designed and produced by
Studio Editions Ltd.,
Princess House, 50 Eastcastle Street,
London W1N 7AP, England

ISBN 1-55521-672-2

Printed and bound in Italy

frontispiece
[Straet (Johannes van der) and Adriaen Collaert. *Christophorus Columbus Ligur terroribus Oceani superatis alterius pene Orbis regiones à se inventas Hispanis regibus addixit. An. Salutis M. VIIID*. 1592, this issue Theodor de Bry, Frankfurt am Main, 1594 and later.]

In 1592, one hundred years after the first landfall of Christopher Columbus in the New World, the engraver Adriaen Collaert produced a series of four plates after the Flemish artist Johannes van der Straet (or Stradanus, as he is otherwise known). The series bore the title *Americae Retectio* and was published at Antwerpen by Filips Galle in 1592.

Copies of the van der Straet plates were issued by several publishers elsewhere in Europe, but they became best known through the slightly reduced and reversed images published by Theodor de Bry of Frankfurt am Main to accompany his famous collection of voyages and travels, known collectively as the *Great Voyages*, which began publication in 1590.

The plate shown here is from the de Bry version—but the title given is that of the 1592 original. It shows Columbus standing on deck in full armour holding the banner of the Holy Cross, while Columbus's own arms may be seen on the pennant attached to the masthead above him. His vessel is depicted approaching land—seen in the upper right-hand corner—the ship itself being drawn through shallow waters by the allegorical figure of Diana.

The Latin caption, in translation, reads: 'Christopher Columbus, Ligurian, having overcome the terrors of the Ocean, assigned these regions, almost a second World discovered by him in 1492, to the kings of Spain.'

Contents

Introduction

The story of the discovery, exploration and settlement of North America is one of the most exciting in the age-long history of exploration and endeavour. From the first, tentative, toe-hold of Columbus in the autumn of 1492 in the West Indies, the general outline of a great landmass which we now call North and South America emerged from the ocean in recognizable form on printed maps within the short span of a mere half-century. Contrast this with the two or three millennia that it took for the revelation of the Old World. For the first time in the recorded history of western Europe, the unveiling of the continent was, as a modern commentator might put it, a 'media event'.

The discovery of America was, like the Renaissance, a new beginning, a revelation, comparable in scale with the unveiling of a neighbouring planet in our own corner of the Universe, the Solar System, by *Voyager* 2 during the 1970s and 1980s. The unveiling of the New World during the fifteenth and sixteenth centuries is an event as vital in human history as the *Voyager* expeditions of our own times. Indeed a curious parallel may be drawn between the discovery and exploration of the Americas and the *Voyager* programme today, for both were subject to political indecision and financial faint-heartedness.

The intention of this book is to present a sample of the range and types of mapping, richly varied in style, content, and price too, which are available to the modern collector of old printed maps. Manuscript maps have deliberately been left out, for by their very nature manuscripts are almost always unique or extremely rare, many surviving by good fortune in large libraries or institutional collections. Most of these can be examined by *bona fide* students with little difficulty. Printed maps, on the other hand, were often produced in quite large numbers, many of which have survived in a collectable condition to delight the late twentieth-century collector. Some are very rare, but all of the maps illustrated in this book are, with care, patience and sometimes a stroke of good luck, obtainable today.

As we approach 1992, an auspicious date which marks a new beginning for Europe, as well as the five-hundredth anniversary of that new beginning across the Atlantic, the attention of collectors and students of old maps is sure to be drawn to the wide range of maps available, and to their content in a historical context and their significance in a geographical sense.

In 1709, the London geographer and mapmaker, Herman Moll declared:

> The Art of making MAPS and Sea-Charts, is an Invention of such vast use to Mankind, that perhaps there is nothing for which the World is more endebted to studious Labours of Ingenious Men. For by the help of them geography is made plain and easie, the Mariners are directed in fetching us the Commodities of the most distant Parts and by the help of them, we may at home, with Pleasure, survey the several Countries of the World, and be inform'd of the Situation, Distance, Provinces, Cities and remarkable Places of every Nation. To do this with Exactness, was an Art (to be sure) not easily attain'd; it was not one Man, nor one Generation of Men, that could bring it to any reasonable Perfection (Herman Moll, in his introductory text to the *Atlas Manuale*, published in London from 1709 onwards).

Largely as a result of painstaking research and prolonged labours by the great collectors and researchers of the late nineteenth and early twentieth centuries, America enjoys the distinction of being better documented than any other continent. From the time of its first recorded discovery—the rival claims and counter-claims of the Hispanic, Italian, English or Scandinavian lobbies are best left to others as this is a book about printed maps—the continent has excited the imagination and interest of the European world ever since 1492, with a vast number of books on or about America, sufficient to fill a large library or a twenty-nine volume bibliography in the form of Sabin.

The same can be said of printed maps, the earliest known being the unique copy of the World map by Matteo Giovanni Contarini engraved by Francesco Rosselli in 1506, a fan-shaped map which shows the early discoveries in North America as part of the eastern extremity of Asia in the form of an elongated peninsula, with a similar connection to the south. The West Indies are hinted at, with a wide gulf shown between North and South America. As Columbus himself wrote in the dedication of his published log to Ferdinand and Isabella of Spain: 'Your highnesses ordained that I should not go eastward by land in the usual manner but by the western way which no one about whom we have positive information has ever followed'. But as the Contarini map showed, and as the near contemporary Ruysch map also showed, no one was quite sure what Columbus had found. Some sixty years after the land-fall of Columbus, Francisco López de Gómara described the discovery of the West Indies as 'the greatest event since the Creation of the World, excepting the Incarnation and Death of Him who created it' (dedication to Charles V in *Historia de las Indias*, Zaragoza 1552).

Even the very name AMERICA does not appear on any printed map until 1507, when it was used on the great Martin Waldseemüller woodblock map *Universalis Cosmographia*. This map, of which only one copy is known to have survived, was compiled in the tradition of Ptolemy and after the voyages of Amerigo Vespucci. Measuring 1370 by 2440 mm, it is the earliest printed map to sketch the discoveries of Columbus in the west as a distinct, unambiguous continent, entirely detached from the eastern mainland of Asia. It spawned a number of imitators and provided source materials for other mapmakers, as will be seen in the maps illustrated in this book.

The earliest *obtainable* map to show the Americas appeared shortly after the Contarini and Waldseemüller maps, in 1507–1508. Compiled by Johannes Ruysch, the *Universalior Cogniti Orbis tabula*, an engraving measuring 410 by 610 mm, is, like the Contarini map, on a fan-shaped projection. It was published as one of the group of so-called 'modern' maps added to the Rome edition of Ptolemy's *Geographia* in 1508 (although copies of 1507 edition are known to contain the map as an addition). Ruysch's map was the first modern World map added to Ptolemy. The northern extremity of North America stretches from Greenland to Newfoundland, but for the first time on such a map, Greenland itself is no longer joined to Europe by a polar landmass. *Terra Nova* is the name given to Newfoundland, which appears as a large peninsula of eastern Asia, or an extension of eastern Cathay.

When Christopher Columbus ventured out into the Atlantic, Europe stood on the periphery of the civilized world, at the edge of a Eurasian continent with the Ming Empire of China at the opposite extremity and the rising power of the Ottoman Empire between the two. The early European voyages of discovery from 1487, beginning with Dias's rounding of the Cape of Good Hope, presaged a new era in the history of the known World, an era which was brought neatly to a close in 1779 with the death of Captain Cook.

In those two hundred years, nearly all of the coastlines of the World had at least been seen or visited, if not totally explored, by Europeans—just as the Chinese had seen or visited the coasts of the Indian Ocean and southern Africa centuries before, let us not forget. The unveiling of the Americas from 1492 onwards was but a part of that great series of European discoveries. In the course of that two-hundred-year period, explorers from the major maritime nations of Europe linked ocean to ocean, ventured into the almost impassable frozen waters of the Arctic and Antarctic, and opened up the seas to European navigation, trade and empire. The Portuguese went eastwards to Asia, to India, the East Indies and

Introduction

beyond; the Spanish sailed west to the West Indies and their Spanish Main, as it later became known, eventually meeting up with the Portuguese in Southeast Asia in the 1520s by virtue of the first circumnavigation. That route was not practical for trading purposes, though—it was too long and dangerous, the Americas lay in the way—but the Pacific was shown to be the great ocean which lay between the New World and Asia, proving once and for all that the New World was not the East Indies, Cathay or any other dimly heard of part of Asia. Even so, the physical separation of the New World from Asia remained unproven until late in the eighteenth century, at the very end of that two-hundred-year period of the European voyages of discovery. So, the New World having been discovered, Spain set about the process of settlement and colonization, almost exclusively a Spanish endeavour, for about a century following Columbus.

To circumvent the Spanish- and Portuguese-dominated sea lanes west and east, other European nations attempted to reach Asia by a northern route, the Northwest Passage, beginning with Cabot in 1497, who rediscovered Newfoundland, and Verrazzano, who saw the eastern seaboard of North America in 1522, thereby revealing the continental nature of North America.

The Spanish and Portuguese discoveries showed that the oceans were interconnected and that the continents, the New World included, were essentially large islands in those oceans. Spain and Portugal effectively barred their claimed domains to anybody else, so that other Europeans—the English, the French and the Dutch—revealed other American coastlines in their searches for routes to Asia. Their voyages outlined the North American shores of the Atlantic from Florida to the Arctic, opening up the way to colonization of eastern North America and Canada. Among those who pursued these routes were Jacques Cartier, who travelled into Canada as far as Montréal in 1534–1535; Martin Frobisher, who reached Baffin Island in 1576; John Davis, who in 1587 explored the shores of western Greenland; Henry Hudson, who in 1610 sailed through the Hudson Strait into Hudson Bay, which he believed to be the Pacific; and William Baffin, who explored the coastline of Baffin Bay in 1616 and concluded that no navigable Northwest Passage existed in those parts after all.

At the turn of the century, the dominance of Spain in the Americas began to be challenged effectively by the rival European powers. True, France and England had attempted to establish colonies in Florida and Virginia in the 1560s and 1580s, but these were short-lived and doomed to failure. Later, Spanish and Portuguese settlements began to be challenged by privateers and raiders, particularly in the Caribbean, so that during the seventeenth century the English, the French and the Dutch had established a string of foothold colonies and settlements on the islands and coasts of the Atlantic seaboard extending from the Antilles to Canada, with flourishing sugar, tobacco and other cash-producing crop plantations.

On the mainland, Jean-Baptist Colbert, Minister of Finance to Louis XIV of France, laid the foundations of a state-controlled empire in Canada and eventually elsewhere, in Louisiana, by his creation of a French merchant fleet and by his active encouragement of settlement in North America through the granting of land in the St Lawrence region to emigrants from France. By contrast, the English set up their colonies by means of private companies, in Virginia for example. In North America, French power was considerable, despite the fact that the population of New France was only a fraction of that of the English colonies. The French forts on the Great Lakes and in the Ohio and Mississippi valleys blocked English westward movement over the Allegheny and Appalachian ranges, the 'Back country', as it were. English settlements were confined to the seaboard coastal regions, from Carolina northwards as far as Nova Scotia. The appearance of French explorers in the lower Mississippi valley and on the shores of the Gulf of Mexico sounded alarm to the Spanish in their empire in New Spain.

However, Spanish hold on its empire in New Spain, in the Southwest and in Mexico and beyond was never seriously threatened, its grip being relinquished

INTRODUCTION

only as a result of war or purchase in the first half of the nineteenth century. Spain owed the relative safety of its Empire to inaccessibility and to the English and Dutch fears of French power in Europe, which led to a series of political accommodations and compromises between Spain, Britain and the Netherlands.

Broadly speaking, by the end of the seventeenth century the colonial situation in North America was this: British territory consisted of Carolina, settled from 1663; Virginia, settled by the Virginia Company from 1607, becoming a crown colony from 1624; Maryland, settled as a proprietary colony from 1632; Pennsylvania, settled as a colony from 1681; New Jersey, formerly part of the New Netherlands, becoming a proprietary colony from 1664; New York, settled as the New Netherlands from 1623, becoming an English proprietary colony from 1664; Connecticut, settled from 1635 to 1638, incorporated in 1662; Massachusetts Bay Colony, settled by the Massachusetts Bay company from 1632; Rhode Island, settled by groups of colonists from Massachusetts Bay from 1636, incorporated from 1644; New Hampshire, part of Maine in 1622, becoming a separate province in 1698; Maine itself, settled from 1622, part of Massachusetts Bay from 1651, annexed in 1691. Delaware was a small Swedish foothold for a short period from 1638, becoming a proprietary colony of the English in 1704. Farther north, Nova Scotia, settled first by the French as Acadia from 1604, was ceded to Britain in 1713, and Newfoundland, claimed by Cabot for England as early as 1497, was formally recognized as being under British sovereignty in 1713, while Rupert's Land far to the Northwest was the trading area of the Hudson Bay Company from 1668–1670, the claim being recognized by France in 1713.

During the same period, French territories consisted of New France in the St Lawrence valley region, settled from about 1608 onwards, together with the vast but sparsely settled lands in Louisiana, with its forts and outposts established here and in the Great Lakes region from 1639 to 1703. After the explorations of La Salle in the Mississippi valley in 1682, France was encouraged to lay claim to all the area drained by the Mississippi River system, almost half a continent in extent.

Spain, for its part, maintained foothold settlements in the Florida region in addition to its vast empire to the south and west. During the seventeenth and eighteenth centuries, Spain began to adopt a vigourous policy of colonial government in New Spain in the wake of the miners who had come to search for precious metals to fill the royal treasury at home. Soldiers and soldier-priests moved into the hostile environment of the Southwest, establishing military governments in Texas in 1718, New Santander in 1746, and California in 1767, for example. By then Spanish control extended from California to the Mississippi and northwards to Monterey and San Francisco, with occasional attempts to establish posts in the Northwest on the Alaska shores halted only by the Russians, who were active here in their quest for furs and skins, venturing along the Pacific coast as they hunted.

By the eighteenth century, France was extending its North American territories from Acadia (later called Nova Scotia) on the cold Atlantic coast in a great crescent-like sweep down into Louisiana and the eastern banks of the Mississippi to the Gulf shore, effectively encircling the English colonies—now the Thirteen Colonies. To set a seal on their expansion, the French established the town of New Orleans in 1718. French interests were mainly in the trade for furs and skins, of which there was a ready and plentiful supply, bought up by traders from the Indians, as well as from European fur-trappers all over the Great Lakes region and the upper Mississippi valley. Missionaries, mostly Jesuit, ventured far into Canada, converting Indians as they went, having established firm settlements, for example Québec in 1608, Montréal in 1642, and Detroit in 1701.

The early failures on the Atlantic seaboard notwithstanding, English colonists were particularly active throughout the seventeenth and eighteenth centuries in North America. In 1607 Jamestown had been established in Virginia, and the Mayflower colonists had settled in Massachusetts Bay in 1620. By 1733, when

INTRODUCTION

Georgia became the Thirteenth Colony, the English Empire in North America was well established, with a prosperous agricultural, fishing and commercial economy.

Naturally, such a situation in North America could not, almost by definition, have come about without war and competition between the major colonial contenders. Anglo-French rivalry was long established, Québec for example had been attacked by the English as early as 1629. The English fur-trading empire to the Northwest of New France was a growing threat to French interests, based as it were on the seemingly as it was limitless hunting grounds of the Hudson Bay region. As in Europe there had been territorial wars between England, France, the Netherlands and Spain, so these conflicts were echoed in North America. By the Treaty of Utrecht of 1713, England was granted Acadia, and the Hudson Bay Company was confirmed in its territories in the Arctic north of Canada. The greatest and most serious Anglo-French conflict was the French and Indian War in 1754–1760, which effectively halted French North American ambitions, confirming English power—fairly short-lived over a great area, as it turned out—in North America. The Treaty of Paris of 1763 granted Britain, Canada and the lands east of the Mississippi, while the rest of Louisiana went to Spain as compensation for the earlier French transfer of Florida to Britain.

However, British colonial administration devised policies and acted in ways which led directly to the American Revolution, the loss of the Thirteen Colonies, and the birth of the United States of America in the 1770s. This is not the place to relate that history in detail, for it has been written by many others in far greater detail than is possible within these pages.

British (or Anglo-American) policy toward the native Indians had always been one of elimination or expulsion to make way for European settlers—in contrast to the Hispanic policy of assimilation, especially in Mexico. So, in 1763, the British government declared all land to the west of the Allegheny and Appalachian ranges, well away from the prosperous seaboard colonies, to be an Indian reserve, beyond the so-called Proclamation Line. Like all such vaguely defined lines and boundaries not delimited precisely on paper by survey or treaty, the Proclamation Line had no real geographical existence. Far from stemming the westward expansion of the colonists from the seaboard, it actually encouraged colonists to seek land and fortune within and beyond its purlieus, adding also to the growing list of grievances against the British government and its tax demands and fiscal controls. The Quebec Act of 1774 redrew the boundaries of the new colony far beyond those of the Royal Proclamation of 1763—a move seen by the Thirteen Colonies, and Virginia and Pennsylvania in particular, as a direct threat to them, especially as Virginia and Pennsylvania were claiming linear extension of their own territories in this region. Such moves on the part of the British helped spark off the American War of Independence, which lasted from 1775 until settled in the Treaty of Paris of 1783, by which Britain at last formally recognized the establishment and existence of the United States of America.

The War of Independence broke out at Lexington and Concord in Massachusetts in April 1775, and in June the Continental Congress of the Colonies created a Continental Army commanded by General George Washington. Despite early failures and defeats, Washington held on, and by December 1776, with the successful crossing of the Delaware, he began a series of successful campaigns which culminated at Saratoga in 1777, the military turning-point of the war. A Franco-American alliance in 1778, joined by Spain in 1779, assured victory for the Americans, with French troops and naval support. The British surrender finally came at Yorktown on 19 October 1781. The Paris Treaty in the autumn of 1783 established the boundaries of the young United States at the Great Lakes in the north, east bank of the Mississippi in the west, and Florida in the south.

The new republic had a population numbering barely three million, mostly in rural settlements and small towns, militarily weak after an exhausting war, its economy still dominated by Britain. But by the 1880s, the infant nation had grown

12

into a giant, economically and industrially, with an economy larger than any other in the world, a territory spanning the width of the continent, and with a strong, stable government. While European powers built their empires far overseas and spent huge sums in maintaining those empires and their life-lines, the United States, too, built its empire, but on its own territory, in its own backyard, so to speak.

In 1783, the United States covered 800,000 square miles, much of it fertile arable land. That was soon enlarged by even larger, more fertile tracts. The Louisiana Purchase in 1803 from France of some 827,000 square miles effectively doubled the land area of the republic. West Florida was annexed in 1812, and the lands of East Florida were purchased in 1819. The area of the contiguous United States was added to by further annexations and accretions in the 1840s and early 1850s. Negotiations with Britain over the contested Oregon Territory covering some 285,000 square miles in 1846, which meant that from the Lake of the Woods westwards to the Pacific shore opposite Vancouver Island, all land to the south of the Forty-ninth Parallel was now United States territory. The Republic of Texas, 390,000 square miles in extent, was incorporated into the Union in 1845, and 529,000 square miles of Mexican territory was awarded to the United States following the war of 1848 as the Mexican Cession, by which present-day California, Nevada, Utah, Arizona and New Mexico were taken over. A smaller purchase of land to the south for a railroad route, the Gadsden Purchase of 1853 from Mexico, set the southern boundary with Mexico as it exists today.

It did not take long to populate and develop these great expanses of territory as they were acquired by the United States. At the end of the colonial era in 1776, the 'Back-country', as the interior was then called, was sparsely settled. However, after about 1800, that country had become a historic frontier in the advance of westward expansion. By about 1810, the middle of the continent was occupied; by 1820, the settlement frontier of the Mississippi had been crossed, and the Trans-Mississippi West lay beyond to be settled. The hundredth meridian—a line running from just east of Fort St Pierre on the Missouri to the Rio Grande in Texas—had been reached, almost halfway across the continent.

Beyond the frontier lay the Great Plains, the Rocky Mountains and California. All this time and for decades afterwards, tides of emigrants from Europe were arriving on the eastern shore, the oldest frontier, landing, some staying in the East, others travelling westward as part of the march of settlement in the nineteenth-century United States. The plains were broken by the steel ploughshare and harnessed by barbed wire fences defended by the six-shooter of the Old West of popular imagination and legend. The railroads soon followed, bringing still more settlers to populate the continent, pushing forwards to the Pacific shore.

The maps illustrated in the following pages tell some of the story, from foothold colony to continental republic.

For ease of reference all the maps in this book have been given general headings which appear in the contents list and on each map page. The exact titles are given in precise detail in the captions. Please note that all information which appears in square brackets cannot be derived immediately from simply looking at the map and has been obtained from other sources.

MAP 1

The World

[Ruysch (Johannes)] *Universalior Cogniti Orbis Tabula ex recentibus confecta observationi.* [Rome, Bernadinus Venetus de Vitalibus, 1507 or 1508.]

For nearly four centuries this was held to be the first printed map to show any part of North America. Such claims have, in more recent years, been superseded, but Ruysch's map indisputably remains the earliest obtainable map to record the discoveries in the New World. It is the earliest indication of America in any edition of Ptolemy's *Geographia* and was the first modern World map added to an edition of that work.

Ruysch's map is especially important in the cartographic history of Canada, since Newfoundland appears for the first time, here in its Latin form *Terra Nova*. Indeed, the map represents Newfoundland and Cape Breton quite independently of any earlier known map. It has remained an unsolved mystery why later mapmakers did not follow Ruysch in this respect, despite the reasonably wide dissemination of his work at the time by means of the Rome edition of Ptolemy in 1507 and 1508.

Shown also is part of the Gulf of St Lawrence and Placentia Bay. Greenland (*Gruenlant*) is attached to North America rather than to northern Europe as part of a boreal continent, which in turn is depicted as a peninsula of Asia. South America and the eastern Caribbean appear hazily as if rising out of a sea mist, but to the west the Caribbean itself becomes part of the sea off the China coast.

Farther afield, Ruysch's map is important for its indications of Portuguese discoveries along the African coasts; and India and Ceylon appear correctly relative to each other, providing an early modern view of the Spanish, Portuguese and English discoveries in a form made available for the first time. In this respect, the map is a bridge between classical, medieval and early Renaissance geographical thought.

Almost nothing is now known of Johannes Ruysch himself, except that he was born in Antwerpen of German parentage and that he died in 1533. Some authorities believe that he sailed with Cabot from England to North America in 1497, while others hold that he participated in a voyage of a Bristol and Portuguese syndicate sometime between 1501 and 1505. Either of these theories supports the view that Ruysch's map is the first printed map showing America by a mapmaker who had himself visited the New World.

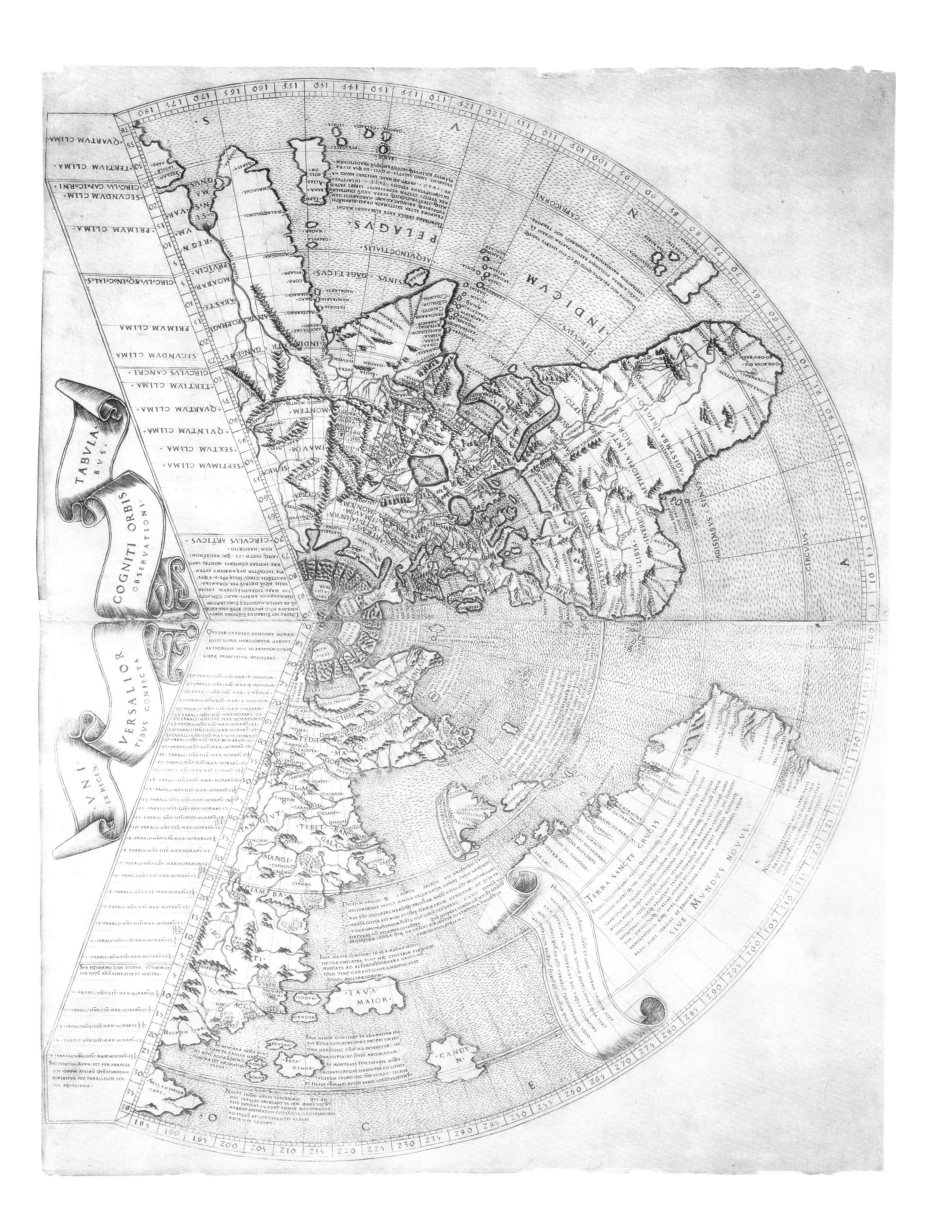

MAP 2

The World (The Admiral's Map)

[Waldseemüller (Martin)] *Orbis Typus Universalis iuxta Hydrographorum Traditionem.* [Strassburg, Johannes Schott, 1513 or 1520.]

This woodcut World map has sometimes been called 'The Admiral's Map', since it has been asserted by some commentators to have been partly compiled by Columbus himself. Whether that is true or not cannot be said with absolute certainty, but the New World is shown in the west—unnamed—as if it were some huge landmass slowly coming into view through clearing mists at sea.

Much of the northern coast of South America and of Brazil is shown, along with Hispaniola and Isabella (Cuba), and a vague indication of Labrador, the *Terra de Rey de portugall* of the manuscript navigational map of Alberto Cantino, drawn in 1502. It is odd that this, like the bulk of the New World, was left unnamed, for the 'modern' World map in the 1511 Venetian edition of Ptolemy had indeed named Labrador very prominently. Perhaps this was a simple error of omission. Note also that Greenland is shown as an elongated peninsula of Scandinavia.

The great commentator on editions of Ptolemy, N.A.E. Nordenskiöld, noted that Portuguese sources were used to compile this map, and that it 'scarcely shows any progress reached by the maps of Ruysch [1507], [or] Sylvanus [1511]'. It is interesting to observe that somewhat less of the New World appears on this map than on Martin Waldseemüller's own World map of 1507 (see notes to map 4), or indeed on his contemporary *Tabula Terre Nove* map (see map 3).

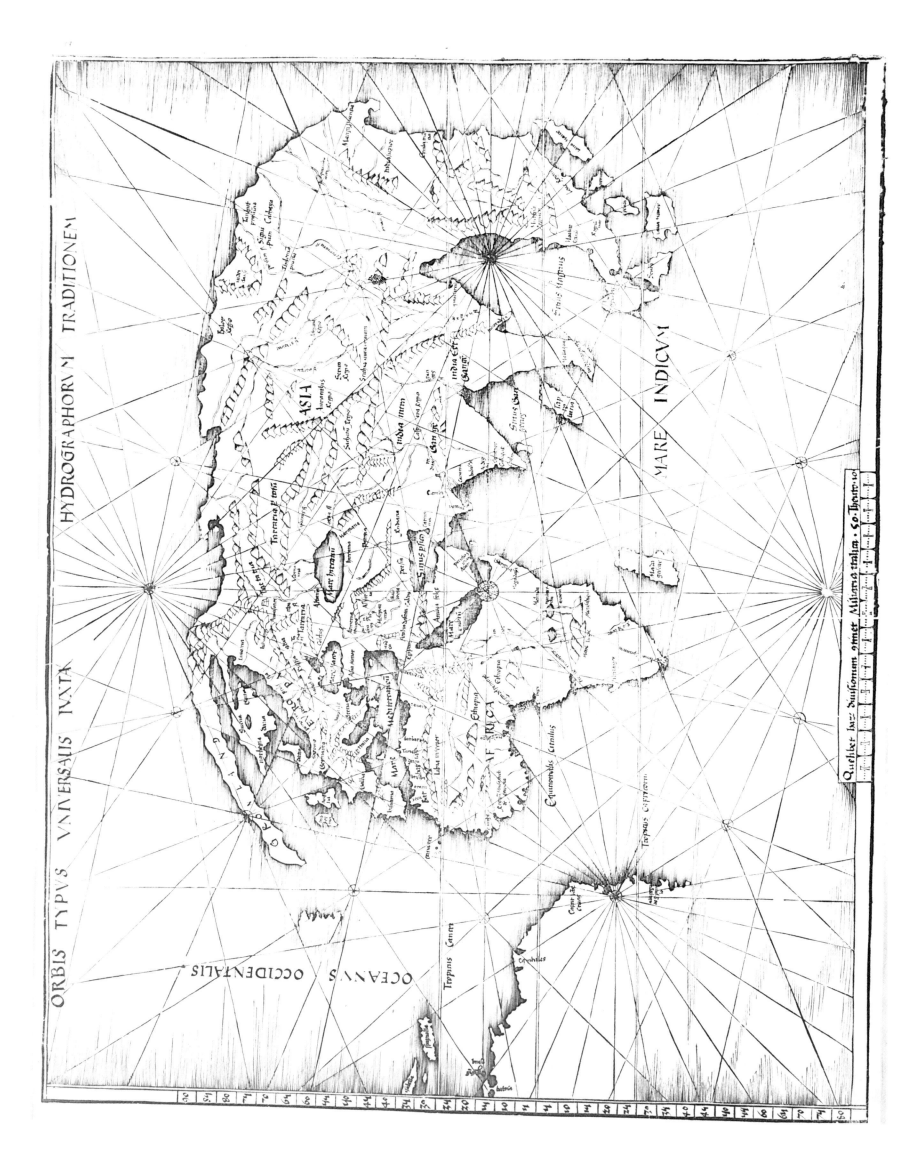

ORBIS TYPVS VNIVERSALIS IVXTA   HYDROGRAPHORVM TRADITIONEM

ASIA

India intra

India extra Gangem

AFRICA

EVROPA

MARE INDICVM

OCEANVS OCCIDENTALIS

Tropicus Cancri

Tropicus Capricorni

Equinoctialis Circulus

MAP 3

The New World

[Waldseemüller (Martin)] *Tabula Terre Nove*. [Strassburg, Johannes Schott, 1513 or 1520.]

As with the World map *Orbis Typus Universalis* (see map 2), this map, covering much of the middle eastern shores of the Americas, parts of western Europe and Africa, has frequently had Columbus cited as its originator. It shows the Atlantic in a sense linking, rather that dividing, the Old World and the New World.

However, Waldseemüller shows much more of the New World than on his contemporary map for his edition of Ptolemy, and he extends the coasts farther west (definitely joining North to South America in so doing) and farther north to show the results of the Columbus voyages of 1492–1493.

This Strassburg map of 1513–1520 is the first printed map devoted to the Americas, even though Waldseemüller appears to have used his own large world map of 1507 as his principal source. The world gave Amerigo Vespucci credit for the discovery of the Americas—the 'fourth part of the Globe', as it were—but now Waldseemüller nails his colours to the mast by stating 'Hec terra cum adiacentib[us] insulis inuenta est per Columbu[m] ianuensem ex mandata Regis Castelle' ('This land with the adjacent islands was discovered by Columbus the Genoese by Order of the Kings of Castille'), just below the Equator in what we now call South America.

In other words, Martin Waldseemüller had rejected the name *America*, calling it simply *Terra Incognita*. But the name *America* stuck in the minds of men.

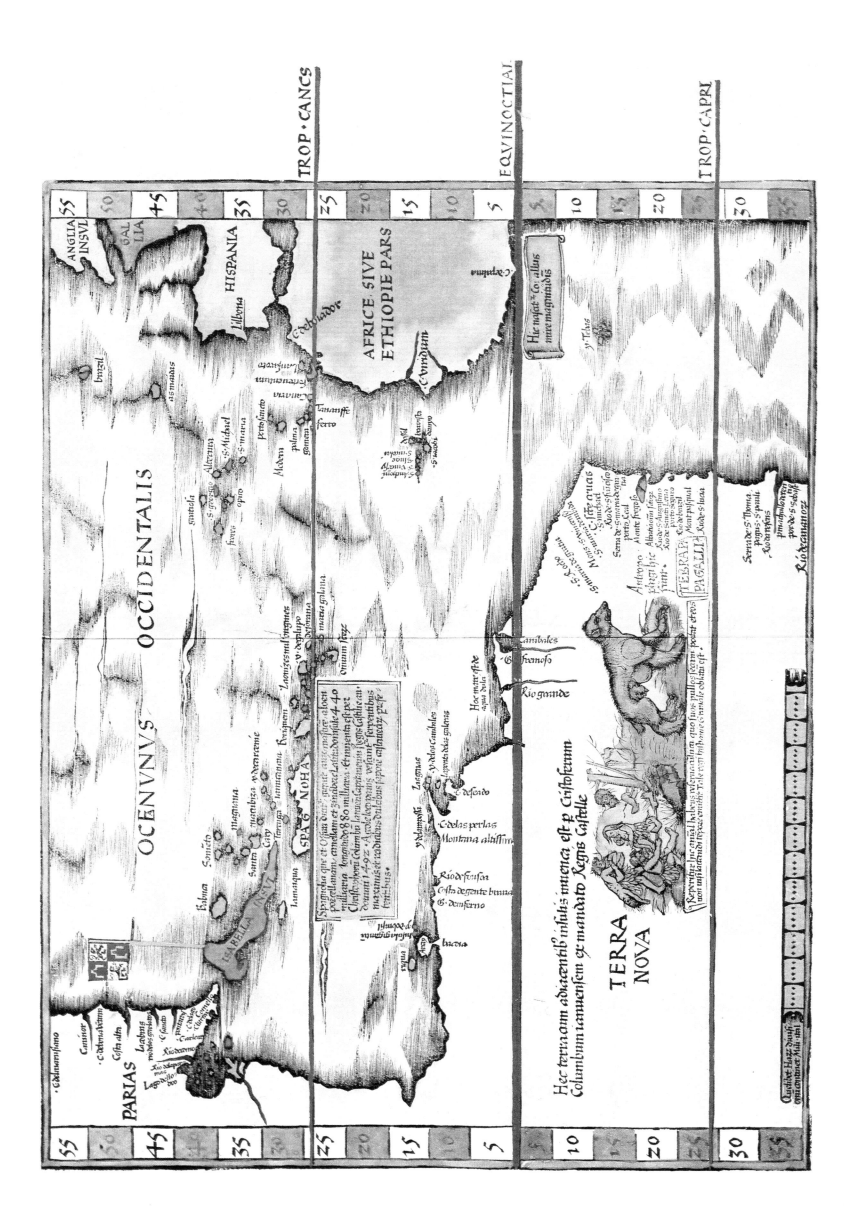

MAP 4

The World

Apian (Peter) *Tipus Orbis Universalis iuxta Ptolomei Cosmographi traditionem et Americi Vespucii alior[um]que lustrationes . . . Anno M.DXX.* [Vienna, Luc Alantse, 1520 and later.]

Published as a 'modern' illustration of the world in a sixteenth-century edition of the early mythology of Caius Julius Solinus's *Polyhistor*, revised and edited by Johannes Camers in 1520, this plate shows a relatively new kind of map: the World on a *cordiform*, or heart-shaped, projection, thought to have been perfected by Peter Bienewitz (better known, perhaps by the Latinized form of his name as Apianus).

Seen as a narrow strip along the left-hand, or western, margin of this woodcut map are two large islands labelled *America*—the two continents being separated by a non-existent strait, with notes relating to Christopher Columbus's voyage of 1497 attached to the more southerly of the two. Much of the detail is reduced from the large World map of 1507 by Martin Waldseemüller of St Dié, in the Vosges region of eastern France. Only one example of the 1507 map now survives.

Therefore, as far as the map-collector is concerned, Apian's map is one of the earliest World maps available on which the name *America* appears. Indeed, until the discovery as recently as 1901 of the unique example of the 1507 map, Apian's map was widely regarded as the oldest printed map to show the name.

In many senses, although it is dwarfed by the 1370 by 2348 mm dimensions of the Waldseemüller map, this is a cornerstone reduction of the 1507 map surviving in a number of copies of Solinus's work, based, as the title has it, partly on the Ptolemaic tradition of classical geography and partly on the voyages of Amerigo Vespucci, the accounts of which appeared in print in 1504 describing, as Vespucci himself expressed it, 'the fourth part of the globe'—in other words, America.

ORIENS

SEPTENTRIO

MERIDIES

OCCIDENS

TIPVS ORBIS VNIVERSALIS IVXTA PTOLOMEI COSMOGRAPHI TRADITIONEM ET AMERICI VESPVCII ALIORVQVE LVSTRATIONES A PETRO APIANO LEYSNICO ELABRA AN·DO· M·DXX

LONGITVDO
LATITVDO

INDIA SVPERIOR
INDIA
INDIE MERIDION
TARTARIA
SCITHIA
SERICA
INDIA INTRA GANGEM
MARE INDICVM
OCEANVS INDICVS MERIDIO
OCEANVS INDICVS
CAPRICORNVS
MADAGASCAR
ZANZIBAR
MARE PRASSODVM
TOTA ISTA PARSA FRICE PTOLEMEO ERAT INCOGNITA

AFRICA
ARABIA FELIX
SABA REGIO
ELEPHAS
LIBIA INTERIOR
AEGYPTVS
AETHIOPIA
AEQVINOCTIALIS
SINVS MAGNVS AFRICA
TROPICVS CANCRI
TROPICVS CAPRICORNI
MONS LVNE

EVROPA
MEDITERRANEVM

ISABELLA
AMERICA
TROPI

CLIMA 8
CLIMA 7
CLIMA 6
CLIMA 5
CLIMA 4
CLIMA 3
CLIMA 2
CLIMA 1

CIRCVS
ZEPHIRVS
AVSTER
FAVONIVS
BOREAS

SEBASTIAN
CHOROGRAPHIA

JAVA MAIOR

GRAD 144

MAP 5

The World

[Waldseemüller (Martin)], and Laurens Fries] *Tabu[la] Nova Orbis. Diefert situs Orbis Hydrographorum ab eoquem Ptolomeus posuit.* [Strassburg, 1522, this issue Lyon, 1535 and later.]

This impressive woodcut map shows the general conception of the World in the sixteenth century, with merely a brief length of coastline to the Southwest indicating Brazil, with a shadowy coastline in the Northwest to indicate the early discoveries on the Atlantic seaboard. In the traditional manner, a long peninsula extends outwards from northern Europe marked *Gronlandia*.

The map itself is reduced from Martin Waldseemüller's World map 1513 in his edition of Ptolemy published at Strassburg, and is one of the earliest maps of the World generally available to the modern collector. It is one of the most popular early maps, despite the fact that it actually shows less of the Americas than its earlier models (see map 3), but does, more by accident of design than anything else, indicate that the Americas were indeed separated from the Old World.

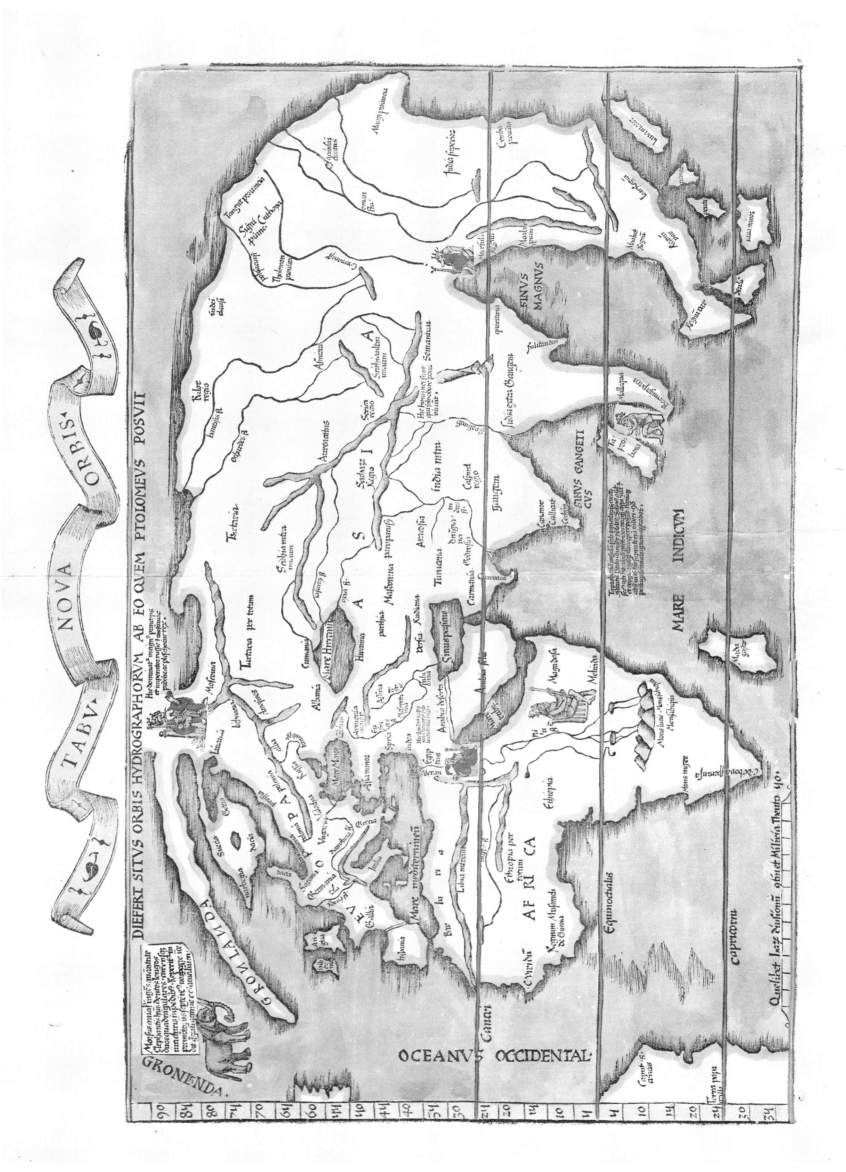

MAP 6

The Americas

[Münster (Sebastian)] *Tabula nouarum insularum, quas diverses respectibus Occidentales & Indianas uocant.* [Basel, Heinrich Petri, 1540 and later.]

This is the earliest separate map of the Americas. It is one of the most remarkable of its kind in that it shows the New World as a distinct landmass in its own right, thereby emphasizing the continuity of North and South America. It was this view of America which held sway for thirty or so years until the publication of Abraham Ortelius's map in 1570 (see map 11).

Sebastian Münster shows the Portuguese standard off the west coast of Africa, the Spanish standard in the West Indies above established colonies there, and Magellan's flagship, the *Victoria* in the Pacific. South America is well defined, showing clearly the estuaries of the Rio del Plata and the Amazon. North America, however, does not fare quite so well: Canada, marked *Francisca*, is joined to *Terra Florida* by the narrow isthmus at the Carolinas, reflecting the beliefs of Verrazzano who, in 1524 when in the service of François I of France, having reached what are now known as the Outer Banks of North Carolina, mistook Pamlico Sound for the Pacific Ocean.

The west coast trends north-south, with a large island off-shore called *Zipangri* (Japan) located approximately where later generations of mapmakers were to place their beloved 'island' of California. Between this island and Asia—here called *Asia Superior*, in outline similar to Münster's own map of the continent published contemporary with the present map—is placed *Archipelagus 7448 insularu[m]*, a distant echo of Marco Polo's travels in the East.

The Caribbean region is depicted accurately in general outline, but with Yucatan (*Iucatana*) shown as an island and *Temistitan* to indicate Mexico. The legend *Novus orbis insula Atlantica quam uocant Brasilij & Americam*, together with the German name *Die Nüw Welt*, appears in South America. Nearby is a gruesome reminder of earlier reports of cannibalism among the Tupinamba Indians of Brazil.

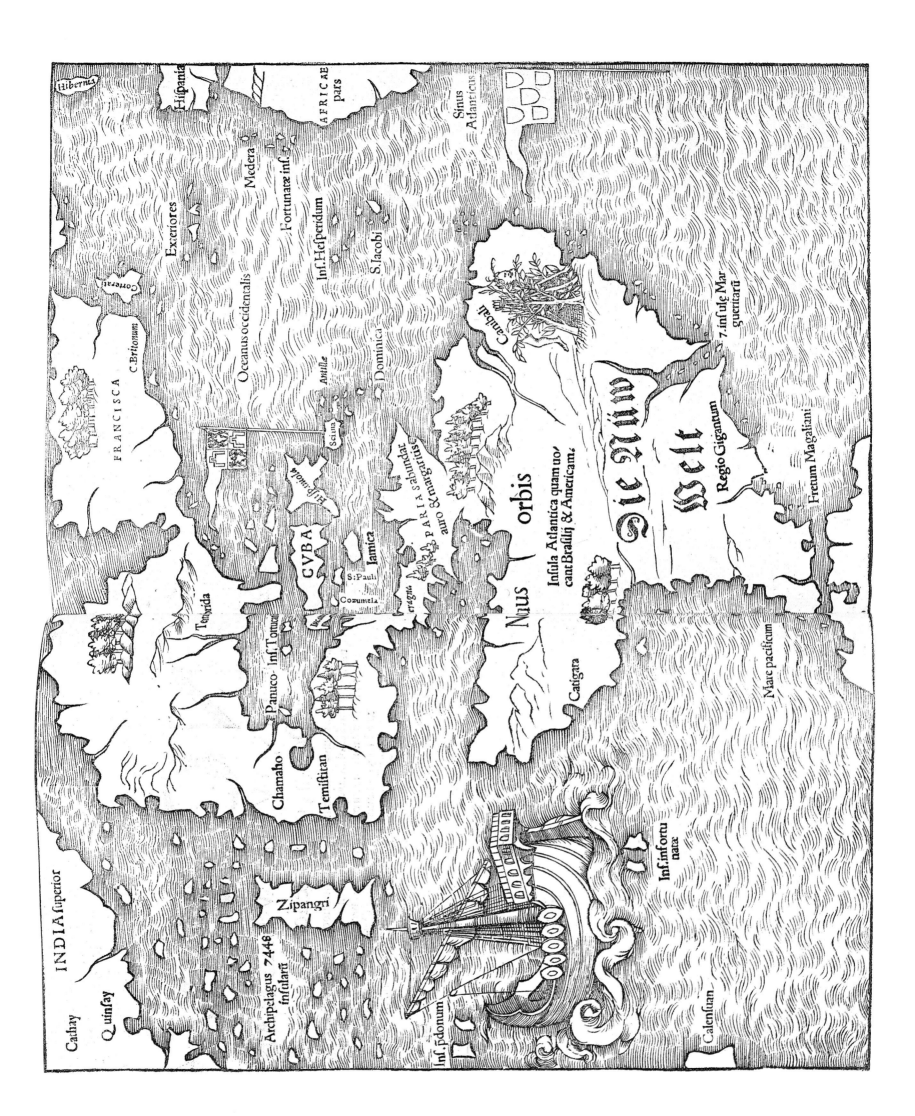

MAP 7

The Land of Hochelaga

[Ramusio (Giovanni Battista)] *La Terra de Hochelaga nella Nova Francia*. [Venice, Giunti, 1556 and later.]

Published in volume III of Ramusio's famous collection *Delle navigationi et viaggi* in 1556, this woodcut is the first printed plan of a settlement in North America. It is based on the description of Hochelaga by Jacques Cartier during his visit there in 1536.

Hochelaga was a fortified Iroquois Indian village near *Monte Real*: it was seen as lying near 'a great mountain, tilled round about, very fertile, from the top of which you may see very far; we called it Mont Réal'. On the way to Hochelaga, Cartier observed 'as goodly and pleasant a country as possibly can be wished for, full of all sorts of goodly trees . . . Okes, Elmes, Walnut-trees, Cedars, Firres, Ashes, Boxe, Willows, and great store of Vines, all as full of grapes as could be, so that . . . our fellowes . . . came home laden with them'.

The plan shows some fifty bark-covered longhouses within a timber palisade, with what appear to be cornfields nearby. The Iroquois and their children welcomed Cartier and his men, squatting before them in rows, awaiting a reply to their request that Cartier might heal their sick.

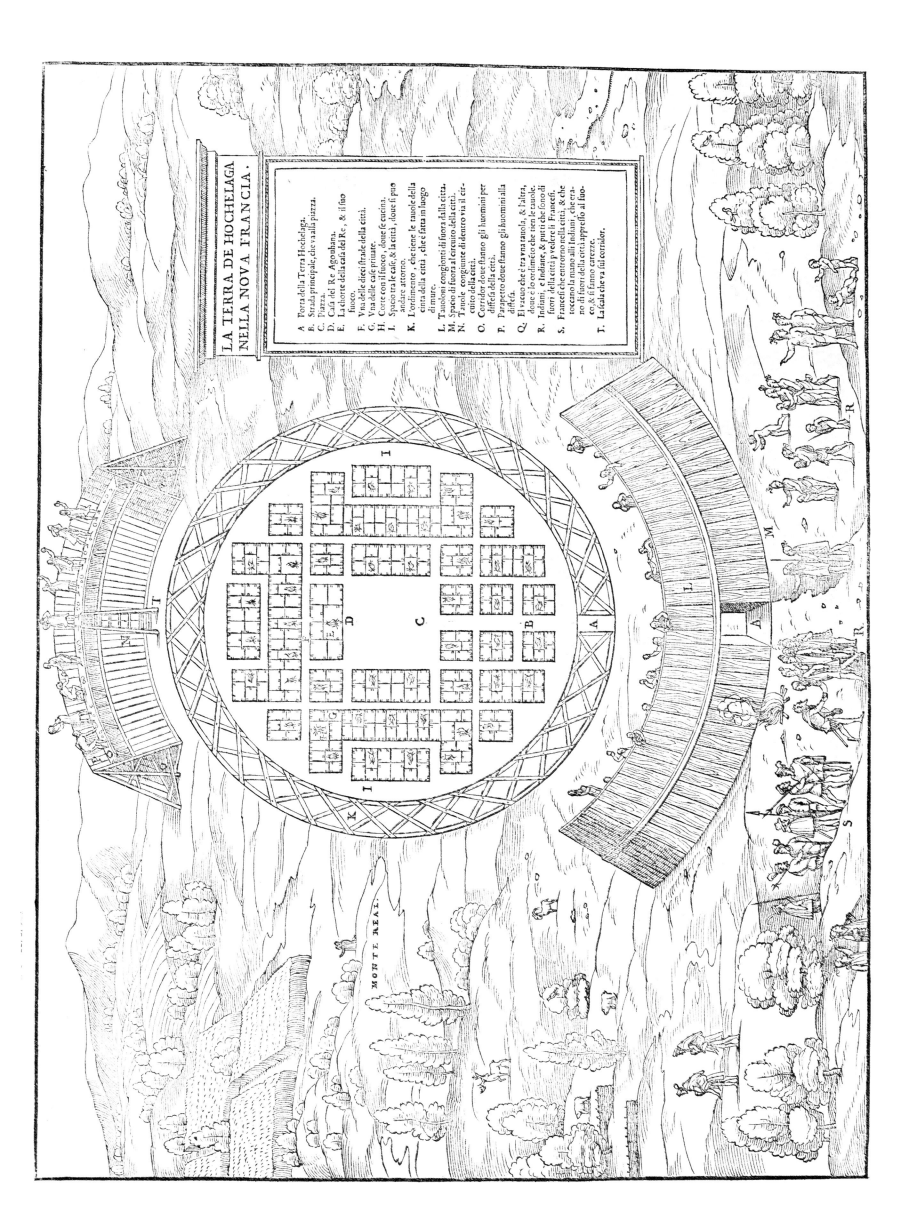

LA TERRA DE HOCHELAGA
NELLA NOVA FRANCIA.

A Porta della Terra Hochelaga.
B Strada principale, che va alla piazza.
C Piazza.
D Cafa del Re Agohana.
E La forte della cafa del Re, & il fuo
   fuoco.
F Vna delle dieci ftrade della città.
G Vna delle cafe priuate.
H Corte con il fuoco, doue fe cucina.
I Spacio tra le cafe, & la città, doue fi puo
   andare attorno.
K L'ordinamento, che tiene le tauole della
   cinta della città, che è fatta in luogo
   di mure.
L Tauoloni congionti di fuora dalla città.
M Spacio di fuora al circuito della città.
N Tauole congiunte didentro via il cir-
   cuito della città.
O Corridor doue ftanno gli huomini per
   diffefa della città.
P Parapetto doue ftanno gli huomini alla
   diffefa.
Q El vacuo che è tra va tanola, & l'altra,
   doue c'lo ordimeéo che tien le tauole.
R Indiani, e Indiane, & putti che fono di
   fuori della città p̃ vedereli Franceft.
S Francefi che entrorno nella città, & che
   toccano la mano alli Indiani, che era-
   no di fuori della città appreffo al fuoco, & fi fanno carezze.
T La fcala che va fu'l corridor.

MONTE REAL.

MAP 8

New France

[Ramusio (Giovanni Battista)] *La Nuova Francia*. [Venice, Giunti, 1556 and later to 1606.]

From Ramusio's *Delle navigationi et viaggi*, volume III, first published in 1556.

Although the text of Ramusio's great collection of voyages and travels was carefully and meticulously edited, so that he included a precise account of Jacques Cartier's voyage to the Gulf of St Lawrence in 1534, his map, which was designed by Giacomo Gastaldi in woodcut, shows nothing of the Frenchman's discoveries, except the name *La Nuova Francia*. The source for this map appears to be the voyage of Giovanni da Verrazzano in 1524. Verrazzano was a Florentine sent by François I of France in the vessel *Dauphine* out of Dieppe to explore the western passages to Asia—such passages as were then thought to exist.

This map covers approximately the area from Narragansett Bay to Labrador by way of Cape Breton and the collection of islands in the eastern part equating to Newfoundland. Two features to note are the name *Terra de Nurumbega* (New England), shown also on Wytfliet's map of 1597 (see map 21), which is thought to be an early rendering of the Abnaki Indian name *norumbega*, meaning 'quiet waters between two rapids', which Verrazzano learned during his voyage, and the long stippled marking running parallel to the coast. While this last has been drawn in a manner representing shoals and shallows, namely, the Grand Banks, it could also be taken as representing the Gulf Stream or North Atlantic Drift.

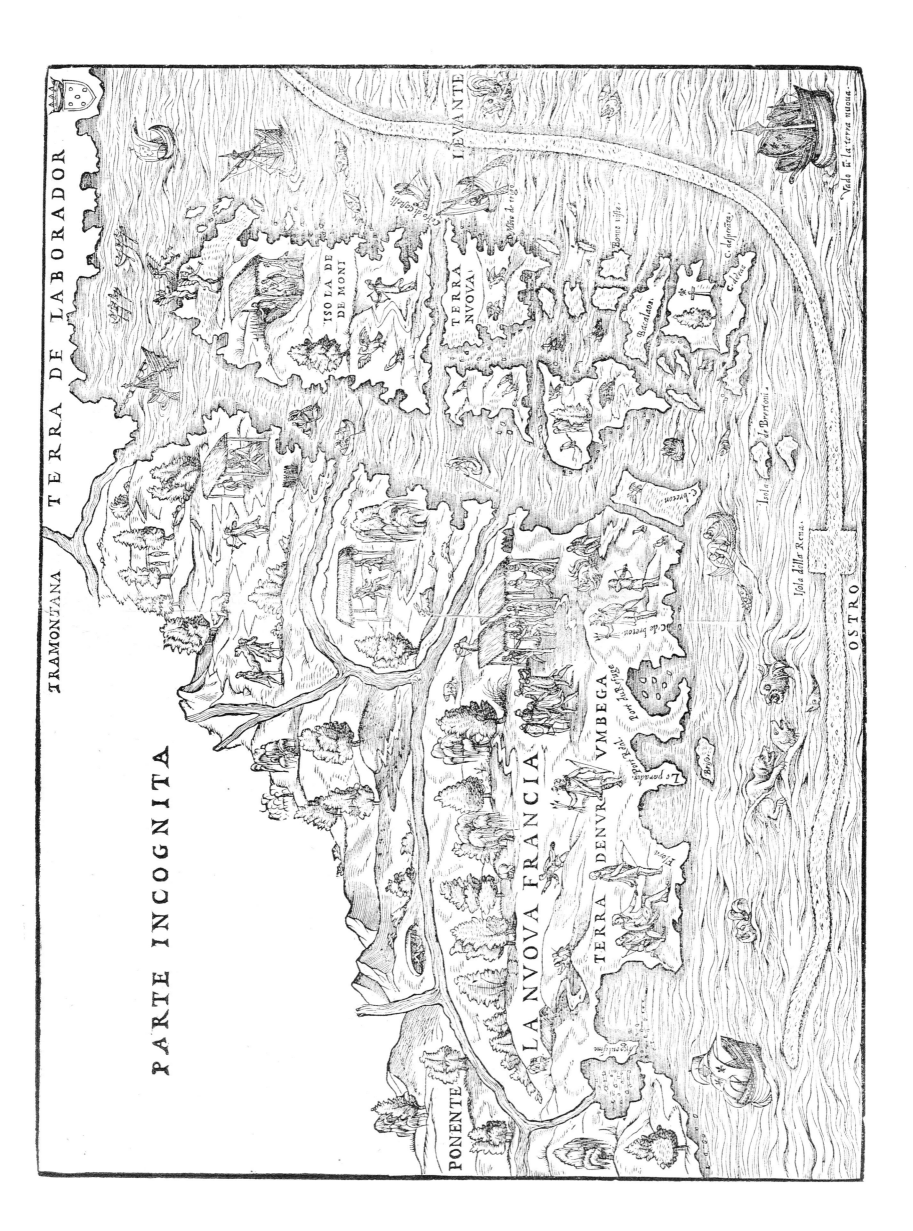

MAP 9

The New World

[Gastaldi (Giacomo)] *Tierra Nueva*. [Venice, Giordano Ziletti, 1561 and later to 1574.]

This map saw publication in Venetian editions of Ptolemy's *Geographia*, first of all in 1548 in the now very rare small-format edition with maps by Gastaldi, and later in another edition with Gastaldi's maps recut for Girolamo Ruscelli's editions issued from 1561 onwards.

Essentially this map shows the shores seen by Jacques Cartier on his first voyage to the Canadian coast in 1534, beginning at the northern entrance to the Gulf of St Lawrence, the Strait of Belle Isle—here marked as *Baye Das Chasteaulux*—already known to some Breton fishermen who ventured across for the cod off Newfoundland. Cartier coasted the Gulf, but missed the strait between Nova Scotia and Newfoundland, now called Cabot Strait, and actually missed the St Lawrence itself, although he crossed from Gaspé to Anticosti, probably as a result of the many fogs in these waters.

Other names to note on this map, some of which will also be found on Ramusio's map (see map 8), are *Larcadia*, *Angoulesme* within *Tierra de Nurumberg*, also *Tierra del Bacalaos*, more usually given to one of the islands in the vicinity of Newfoundland on account of the rich cod-fisheries.

Sometimes, entirely fictitious names appear, one such being *Orbellanda*, one of many mythical islands with which the North Atlantic was liberally sprinkled.

TIERRA NVEVA TIERRA

OCEANO SEPTENTRIONALE

TIERRA DEL LABORADOR.

TIERRA DEL BACALAOS.

TIERRA DE NVRVMBERG.

ISOLA DE DEMONI.

S: Iuan.

C. Hermoso.

TERRA NOVA.

Baye.

Daf Chafteaulux

Monte de Trigo

Buena Vista

C: de spoir.

C. Breton. C. de Raf.

B Breton

Orbellanda.

y verde

Maida.

Gratiofa. Trecera.

Y de laf Flores.

Fayal

s iorge s. migel

Pico

S. Maria.

P: Refuge

Le Para. dif.

Tierra de los Broton.

Flora

Angoulefine

P. Rial.

Brifa-1

Larcadia

C. def Maria

LA FLORIDA

La Bremuda

OCEANO OCCIDENTALE

MAP 10

New France

Zaltieri (Bolognini) *Il disegno del discoperto della nova Francia . . . Anno. M.D.LXVI.* Venice, 1566.

Zaltieri's handsome map is one of the earliest printed maps—in this case separately published rather than originating in an atlas—to show the entire continent of North America, despite the wording of the title. However, many French names are indeed given, for example, *R.S. Lore[n]zo* (St Lawrence River), *Larcadia*, and, well to the west, *La Nova Franza*, together with Spanish names in Florida and on the west coast, such as *Tigua. f.* (Colorado River), *Quivira Pro:*, and *Sierra Nevada* (Snowy Mountains), a name still in use today, of course, and appearing here for the first time on any printed map.

However, a particularly important feature of this map lies farther afield, to the northwest, for Zaltieri's map is the first printed map to show and name the broad strait which separates North America from Asia—the *Streto de Anian*—linking the unknown northern sea, or *Mare Setentrionale incognito*, with the Bering Sea in the North Pacific, which is named here as *Golfo Chinan.* The notion of such a strait originated in the work *La universale descrittione del mondo* of Giacomo Gastaldi, published in Venice in 1562, reflecting the concept of Marco Polo who, however, first recorded the name *Anian* as a kingdom of northeastern Asia. Most sixteenth-century mapmakers followed Zaltieri in locating Anian in the American Northwest (see map 12 as a derived example).

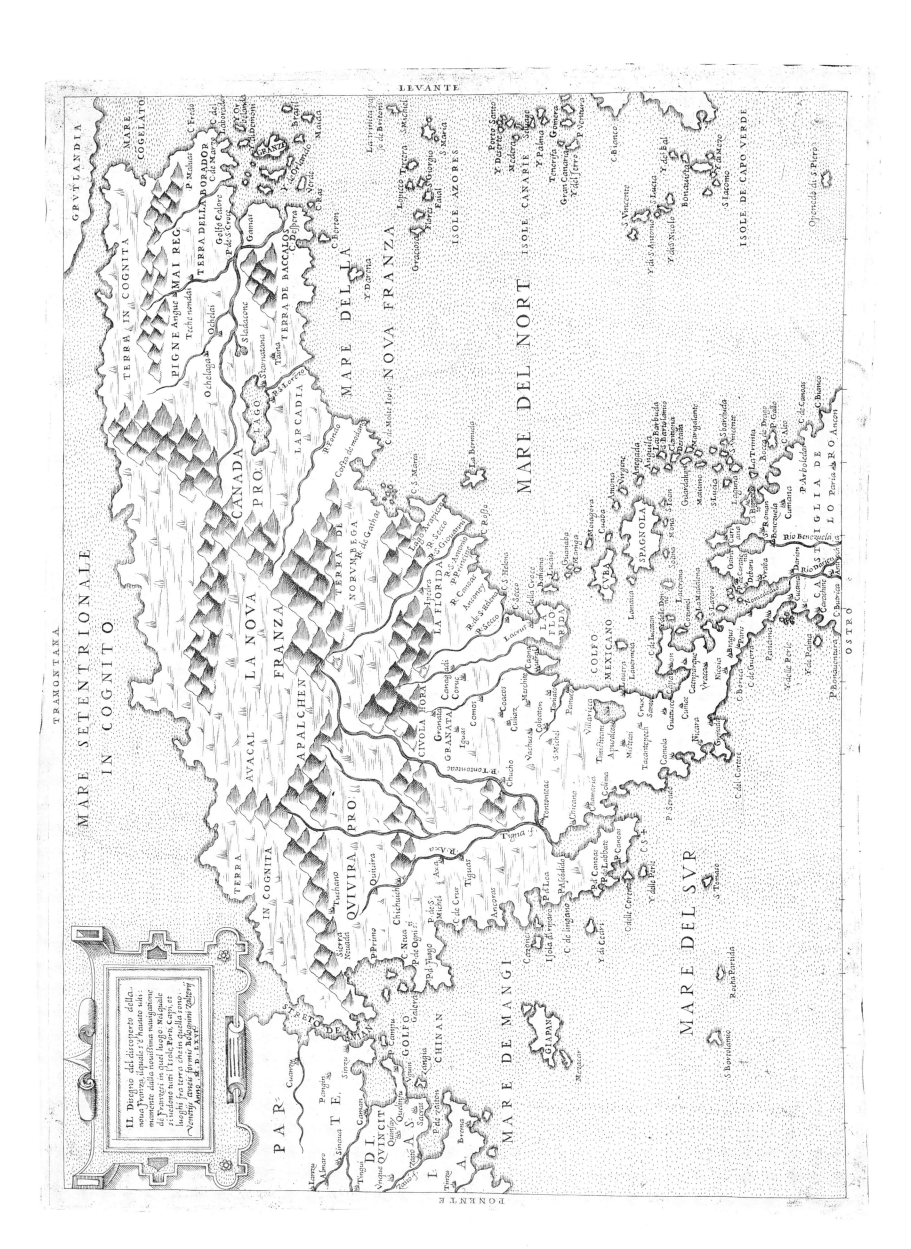

MAP 11

America

[Ortelius (Abraham)] *Americae sive Novi Orbis nova descriptio.* [Antwerpen, 1570 and later to 1587.]

Until Abraham Ortelius included a map of New Spain in the 1579 edition of his atlas, the *Theatrum Orbis Terrarum*, this highly decorative general map of the Americas was the only depiction of the New World in that work. It is in direct line of descent from the map by Sebastian Münster of 1540, and it replaces that map as the most important general map of the Americas published in any sixteenth-century atlas.

South America in this version, issued before 1587, shows a great bulge at the southwestern coast, copied from the 1569 World map of Gerard Mercator, Ortelius's fellow mapmaker.

Ortelius's map, regarded as a 'keystone map', provides the best general picture of the settlement of the New World in the latter part of the sixteenth century: it is, in effect, the Renaissance view of America.

It shows Ponce de Leon's penetration of the Southeast in 1521, the Gulf coast explorations of Navaez in 1521 and Cabeza de Vaca in 1528, as well as de Soto's expedition in 1539. Information gleaned from Cortés in Mexico in 1518, Fr de Nizza in the Southwest in 1539, Coronado going into the interior from Mexico in 1540, and Cabrillo along the California coast in 1542, all add significantly to the detail of Ortelius's map.

To fill what would otherwise be a large expanse of unknown land to the southeast of New Guinea, Ortelius has strategically located his title-cartouche astride the coastline of the great southern continent.

Following the revision of the South American coastline in 1587, this map continued to be included in Ortelius's atlas, with minor alterations, for a further twenty or so years, until the final edition of the *Theatrum* in 1612.

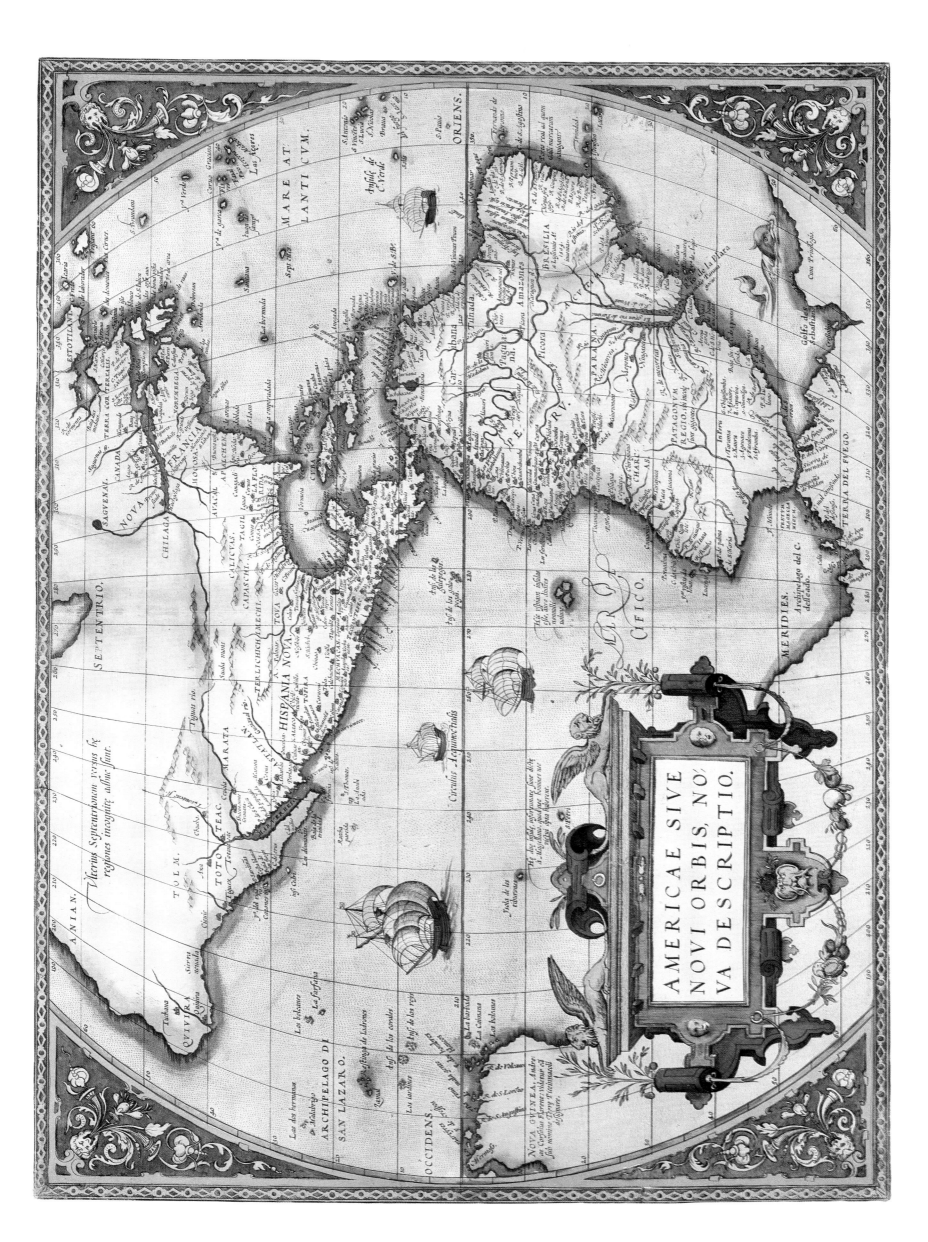

MAP 12

The New World

[Porcacchi da Castiglione (Tomaso)] *Mondo Nuovo*. [Venice or Padua, 1572 and later to 1620.]

From Porcacchi's island book *L'isole più famose del mondo*, which treats the continents, logically enough, as a series of islands, this little map—measuring barely 105 by 145 mm—is based on the Zaltieri map of 1566 (see map 10). It is, therefore, a readily available version of the first printed map to show the narrows between Asia and America, the *Stretto de Anian*, so marked.

The concept of this map, despite its small size, is more accurate than that of many later productions, for the relative positions of Florida and California are reasonably well placed, although the region called *Quivira* is here well to the northeast of California. Verrazzano's sea persists as the large lake—*Lago*—to the north of *S. Lorenzo* in Canada, between *Larcadia* and *Labrador*.

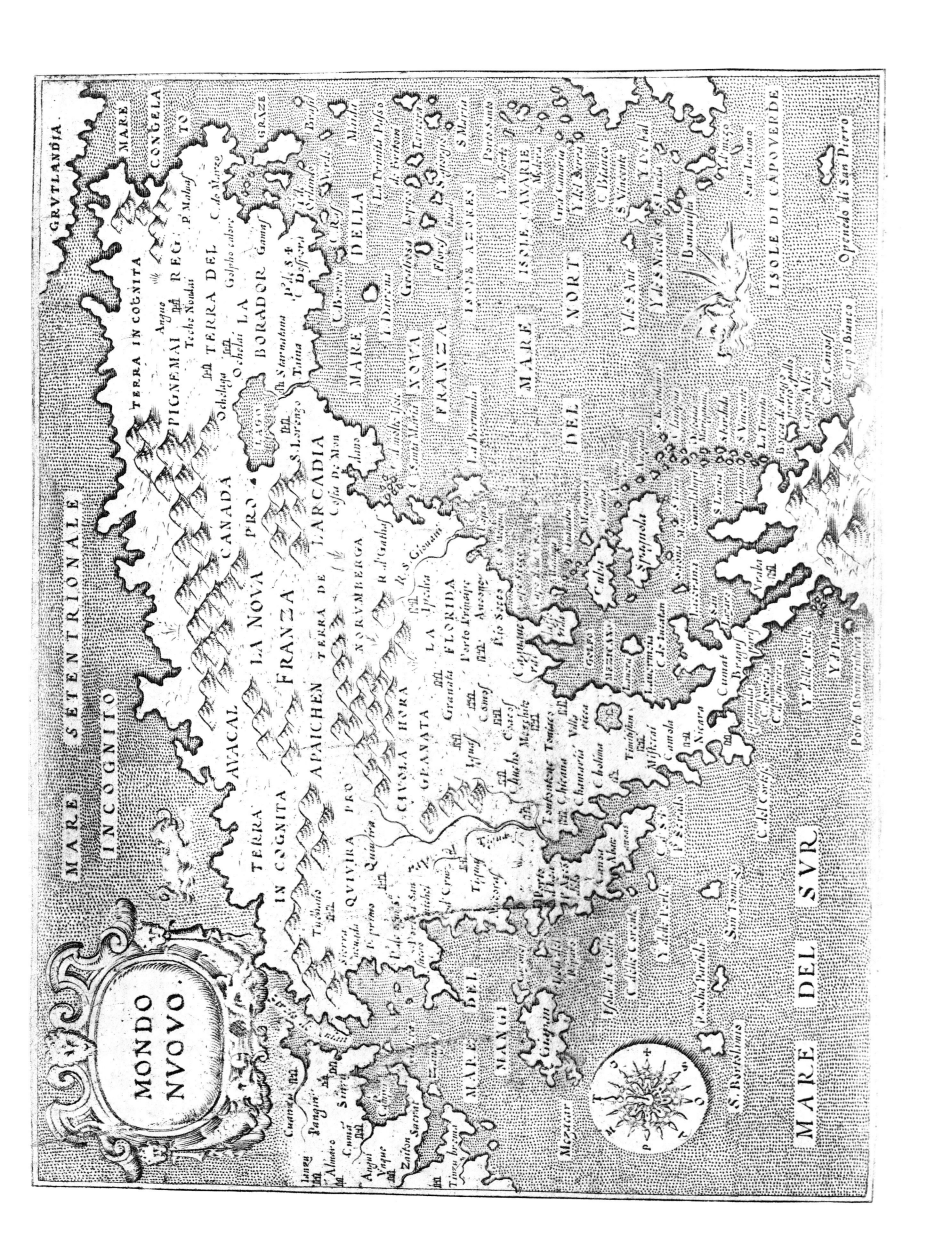

MAP 13

Florida, Guasteca and Peru

[Ortelius (Araham)] *La Florida; Guastecan; Peruviae auriferae regionis typus.*
[Antwerpen, 1584 and later, to 1612.]

Published in editions of his *Theatrum Orbis Terrarum* from 1584 onwards, Abraham Ortelius here shows the three main areas of Spanish colonial interest in America in the sixteenth century: Florida, Guasteca, and the gold-rich regions of Peru.

Ortelius's version of Hieronymo Chaves's map of Florida provides the first atlas depiction of the region and it shows some of the interior detail recorded by Hernando de Soto during his expedition in 1539–1542. The anonymous map of Guasteca continues the coastline of the Gulf of Mexico to the south of the Rio de las Palmas, and Diego Hurtado de Mendoza's map of Peru shows the regions taken by the Spanish invasion of 1531–1533. The fabled kingdom of El Dorado is marked as *Aurea Regio.*

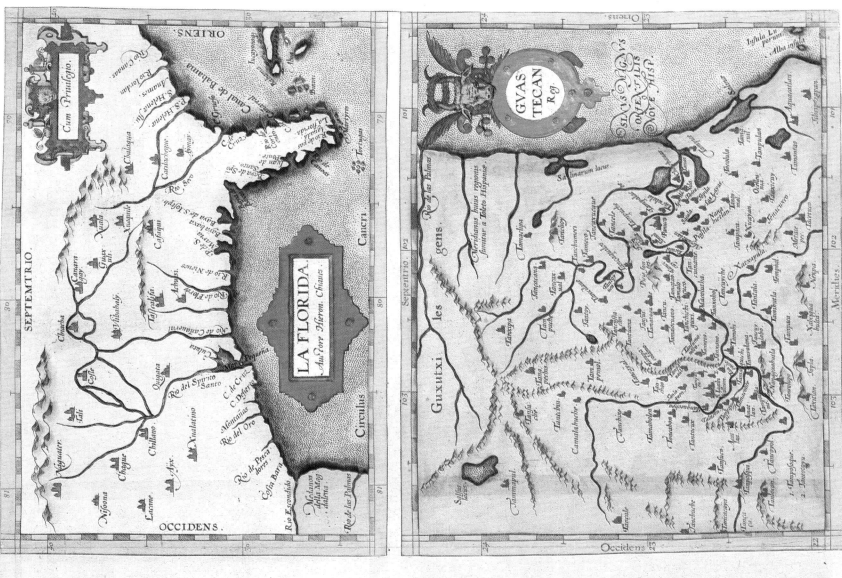

Cum Priuilegio.

SEPTEMTRIO.

LA FLORIDA.
Au Core Hieron. Chiaus.

Rio de Canaas

Rio de Iordan

S. Helene flu.
P. S. Helene

Canal de Bahama

M. Chalaqua

Canauera
Buxula
Guaxule
Chiaha
Costa
Xati
Xoguater
Nysoona
Lacane
Choque
Chillano
Ayx
Tuscalosa
Tassaluza
Culata de Canaueral
Rio de Canaueral
Vualatino
Montanas
Rio del Oro
Rio del Spirito Sancto
C. de Cruz
C. Deserto
Rio de Pescadores
Costa baxa
Melanos della Magdalena
Rio de las Palmas

Nueua de Spo
Rio de Canto
S. Cruz
Baya de S. Iosiph
Archusi
Rio de Flores
Rio de Nieues

OCCIDENS.

Cancri

Circulus

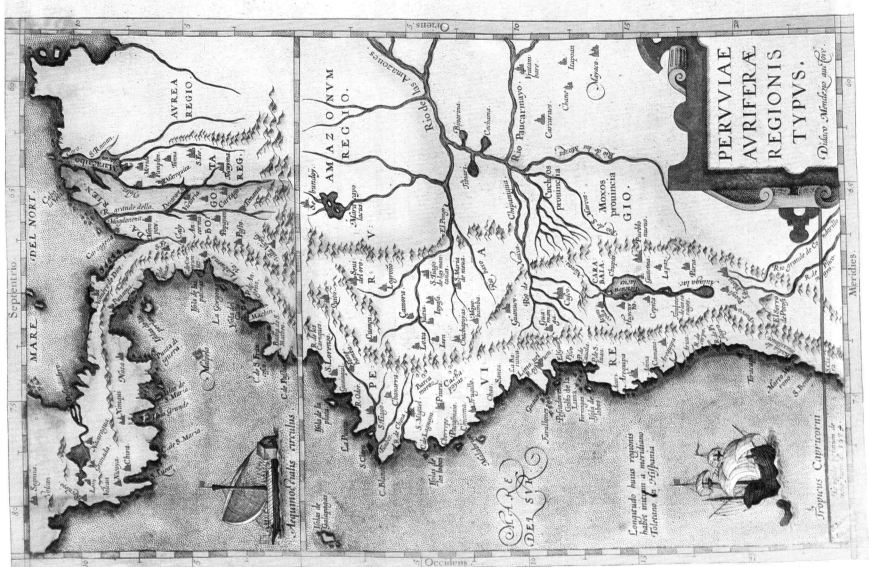

GVAS-TECAN Reg.

COSTVS MARIS ORIENTALIS à NOVÆ HISP.

Insula Luporum

Alba insula

Salinarum lacus

Septentrio

Guxutxi
les gens

Rio de las Palmas

Meridianus huius regionis sumitur a Toleto Hispaniæ.

Tampico
Tanchipa
Panuco
Tanchuser

Occidens

Meridies

PERVVIAE AVRIFERÆ REGIONIS TYPVS.

Didaco Mendezio auCore.

Septentrio

MARE DEL NORT.

AVREA REGIO.

BOGOTA REG.

DARIEN

AMAZONVM REGIO.

Rio de las Amazones

AVREA REGIO.

Rio Paucarnayo

Moxos prouincia GIO.

Chichos prouincia

CARABAIA

PERVVIA REGIO.

MARE DEL SVR

Longitudo huius regionis habet initium a meridiano Toletano in Hispania.

Tropicus Capricorni

Aequinoctialis circulus

Occidens

Meridies

MAP 14

The Pacific Ocean

Ortelius (Abraham) *Maris Pacifici (quod vulgò Mar del Zur) . . . novissima descriptio.*
Antwerpen, 1589 [and later].

One of the most striking and popular of the maps in Ortelius's *Theatrum* atlas, first
issued in 1589, and long a great favourite of the collector.

This is the first printed map devoted to the Pacific Ocean, and the first in which
North America and South America are separately named: *Americae Septentrionalior
pars* and *Americae Meridionalior pars*, respectively.

The Pacific is mapped with remarkable accuracy, showing Japan and the
Philippines much closer to Asia than usual on maps of the period, and California—
note that it is correctly drawn as a peninsula, despite the efforts of later mapmakers
(see map 24)—is placed close to North America. To the north, in the American
Northwest, Ortelius added new information not shown on any previous map, but
what his sources were, we do not now know. The Gulf of California is entirely new
in shape here also.

The outstanding design is complemented by the strapwork cartouches typical of
Flemish ornamentation of the period, one of which fills a large expanse of the
great southern continent—*Terra Australis*. In the South Pacific, Ortelius pays
tribute to the circumnavigator Magellan by inserting his flagship, the *Victoria*, to
celebrate his achievement in navigating the unknown South Sea, or *Mare del Zur* as
it was called in the common tongue.

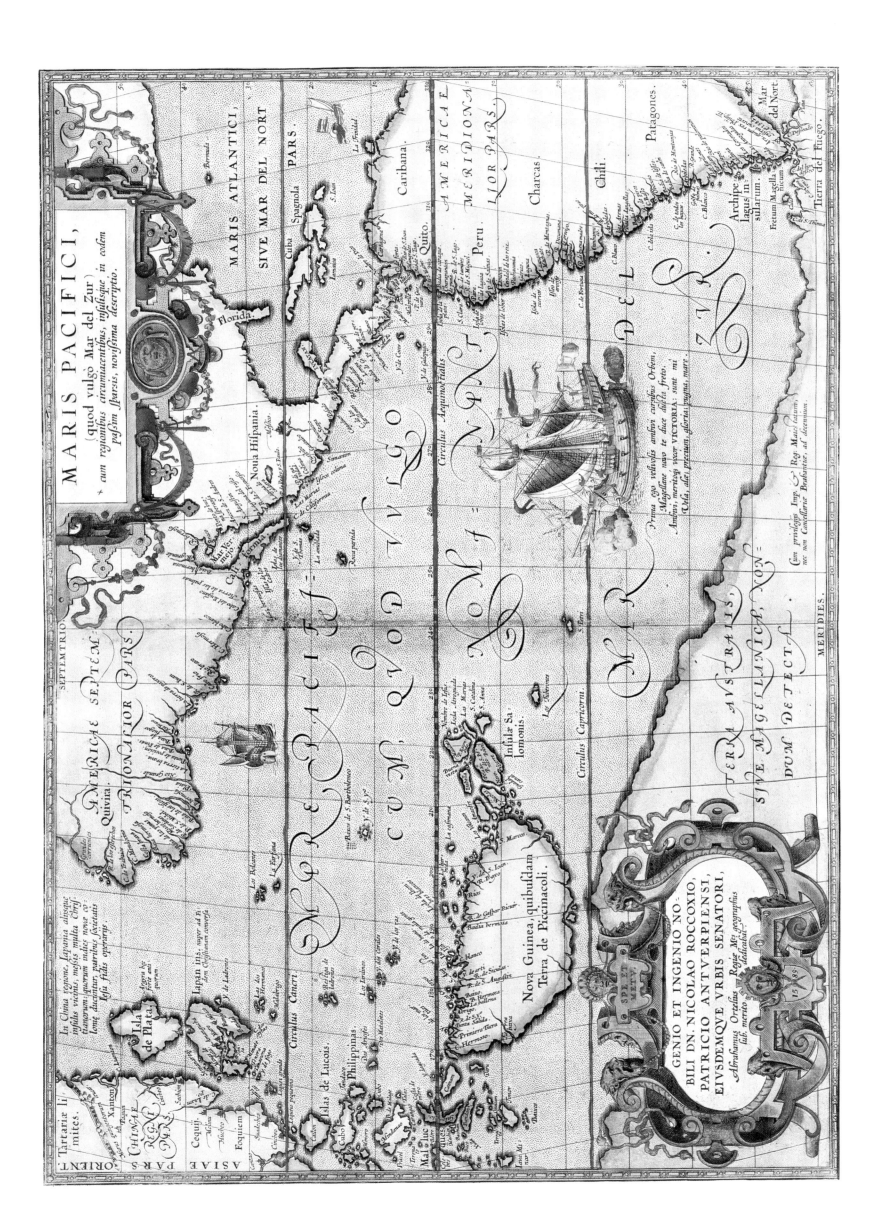

MARIS PACIFICI,
(quod vulgo Mar del Zur)
cum regionibus circumiacentibus, insulisque in eodem
passim sparsis, novissima descriptio.

MARIS ATLANTICI,
SIVE MAR DEL NORT PARS.

AMERICAE MERIDIONALIS PARS.

MAR DEL ZVR.

MORE PACIFICVM DICTVM CVM QVOD VVLGO

SEPTENTRIO

AMERICAE SEPTEM= TRIONALIOR PARS.

ASIAE PARS ORIENT

MERIDIES.

TERRA AVSTRALIS, SIVE MAGELLANICA, NONDVM DETECTA.

Prima ego velivolis ambivi cursibus Orbem,
Magellane novo te duce ducta freto.
Ambivi, meritoque vocor VICTORIA: sunt mi
Vela, alae; precium, gloria; pugna, mare.

Cum privilegio, Imp. & Reg. Maiestatum,
nec non Cancellarie Brabantiae, ad decennium.

GENIO ET INGENIO NO-
BILI DN. NICOLAO ROCCOXIO,
PATRICIO ANTVERPIENSI,
EIVSDEMQVE VRBIS SENATORI,
Abrahamus Ortelius Regiae Mtis geographus
sub. merito dedicabat.

1589

Tartariae li= mites.

In China regione, Iapana absque insulis vicinis, messis multa, Christianorum; quorum inites nova co= lonie ducantur, paribus societatis Iesu fidis operariis.

CHINAE REGNI PARS.

Cequij.

Iapan ins. nuper ad Fi= dem Christianam conversa.

Isla de Plata.

Philippinae.

Islas de Lucois.

Circulus Cancri.

Quivira.

Florida.

Noua Hispania.

Cuba
Spagnola

Caribana.

AMERICAE

Quito.

Peru.

Charcas.

Chili.

Patagones.

Circulus Aequinoctialis

Insula Sa= lomonis.

Circulus Capricorni.

Nova Guinea, quibusdam
Terra de Piccinacoli.

Tierra del Fuego.

Freturm Magella= nicum.

Archipe= lagus in= sularum.

Mar
del Nort

MAP 15

Virginia

White (John) *Americae pars, Nunc Virginia dicta, primum ab Anglis inventa : . . Autore Ioanne With.* [Frankfurt am Main, Theodor de Bry, 1590 and later.]

Engraved by de Bry after John White's manuscript map of 1585, this is the first printed map of the first English colony in North America. Accurate and carefully drawn, it has been called the most meticulous and detailed map of any part of North America made during the sixteenth century.

John White's map accompanied de Bry's printed account (in Part I of his *Great Voyages* series) of Thomas Hariot's *A briefe and true report of the new found land of Virginia*, published in 1590. White travelled with Sir Walter Ralegh to Virginia in 1585 as surveyor and 'Skilfull painter', and served as governor of the ill-fated settlement at Roanoke (*Roanoac* on the map). White's other claim to fame was as grandfather to Virginia Dare, the first child born to English colonists in Virginia. He produced a series of highly detailed and accurate pictures and sketches of Indian life, manners and customs, many of which still exist today. Like those of Le Moyne de Morgues (see map 16), Theodor de Bry managed to acquire the drawings for publication along with the map, since when they have provided us with a vivid and unparalleled view of life in North America at the end of an era of Indian isolation and on the eve of an era of European colonization. The publication of White's and Le Moyne's drawings probably did more to open up North America to Europeans than any number of voyages. Shown on White's map is the region between present-day Cape Lookout (*Promontorium tremendum*) and just north of Chesapeake Bay, with the inlets along the Outer Banks, Albemarle and Pamlico Sounds, together with the Chowan, Roanoke and Neuse Rivers.

White returned to England after a year, but went back to Roanoke in 1587 as governor of a fresh colony there. But soon afterwards, he found it necessary to leave for England again to seek out additional supplies. The region around present-day Pamlico Sound had a considerable Indian population at the time who were initially friendly; but the English colonists later found themselves not particularly welcome there because of their constant demands for food and labour. Unfortunately, it turned out to be quite the wrong time to seek help from home: England was under threat of invasion by a Spanish armada and no effort could be spared to help the infant colony in Virginia. White had left behind in Virginia his daughter, her husband and their child; on his eventual return in 1590, he found that the colony had perished, leaving hardly a trace.

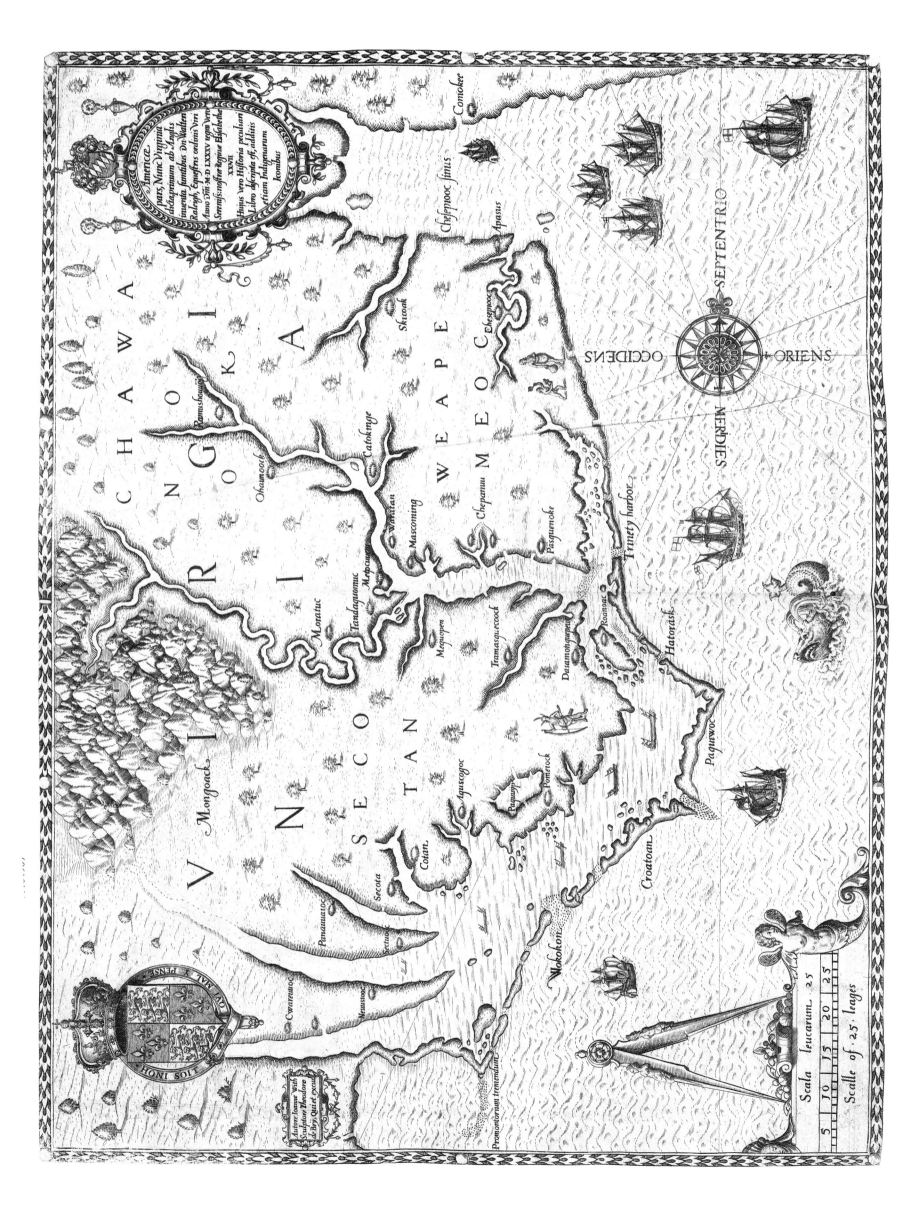

America.
pars, Nunc Virginiæ
dicta, primum ab Anglis
inuenta, sumptibus Dn. Walteri
Raleigh, Equestris ordinis Viri
Anno Dñi. M·D·LXXXV regnante Virgine
Serenissima nostra Regina Elisabetha
XXVII
Huius vero Historia peculiari
Libro descripta est, additis
etiam Indigenarum
Iconibus

CHAWANOOK

VIRGINIA

WEAPEMEOC

SECOTAN

Ohanoock

Ramuskonong

Catokinge

Waratan

Mascoming

Metaquem

Moratuc

Trandaquomic

Skicoak

Chepanoc sinus

Comokee

Apasus

Chesepiooc

Pasquenoke

Pasquenoke

Roanoac

Dasamonquepeuc

Hatorask

Trinety harbor

SEPTENTRIO

OCCIDENS   ORIENS

MERIDIES

Mequopen

Tramasquecooc

Tomtetock

Paquippe

Pomeiooc

Paquiwoc

Mongoack

Secota

Pomanuac

Aquascogoc

Cotan

Croatoan

Wokokon

Cwareuuoc

Newasiooc

Scala leucarum   25
5   10   15   20   25
Scalle of .25. leages

HONI SOIT QUI MAL Y PENSE

Promontorium tremendum

Autore Iacono Witi
Sculptore Theodoro
de Bry, Qui et excud.

MAP 16

Florida

Le Moyne de Morgues (Jacques) *Floridae Americanae Provinciae Recens & exactissima descriptio*. [Frankfurt am Main, Theodor de Bry, 1591 and later.]

This is one of the most attractive maps of North America. It was produced by Theodor de Bry in 1591 to illustrate the account of the ill-fated French Huguenot colony in Florida led by Jean Ribaut and René de Laudonnière between 1562 and 1565. Jacques Le Moyne de Morgues travelled as official artist on that expedition. The manuscript draft of this map, together with the drawings of the Florida Indians made on the spot, were acquired by de Bry after the death of Le Moyne in 1588, de Bry having previously attempted to obtain them in 1587 when Le Moyne and he met in London. Le Moyne was then in the service of Sir Walter Ralegh and had refused to part with the manuscripts.

De Bry engraved this map for publication in Part II of his *Great Voyages* series, entitled *Brevis Narratio eorum quae in Florida Americae Provincia Gallis acciderunt* in 1591. Although the map is somewhat less than accurate, it does show Port Royal (*Portus Regalis*) for the first time on a printed map, together with the French Fort Caroline (*Carolina*) on the St John River, a probable indication of Lake Okeechobee in the south of the peninsula (*Lacus & Insula Sarrope*) and Lake George farther north (*Lacus aquae dulcis*), from which flows the river *Maij* (St John River). Many of the place names shown on this map were derived from Indian sources; many are no longer extant, having been superseded by names given in the seventeenth century by English colonists. De Bry's version of Le Moyne's map was later adapted, errors and all, by Hondius in 1606 in his edition of Mercator's *Atlas* (see map 23).

An interesting historical echo of earlier explorations may be seen at the top of the map. It is tempting to think that the sea shown there may represent Verrazzano's sea. It is also possible that it may represent the Great Lakes, for there are references on the map nearby to an enormous waterfall which may be an allusion to Niagara, heard about from Indian legends.

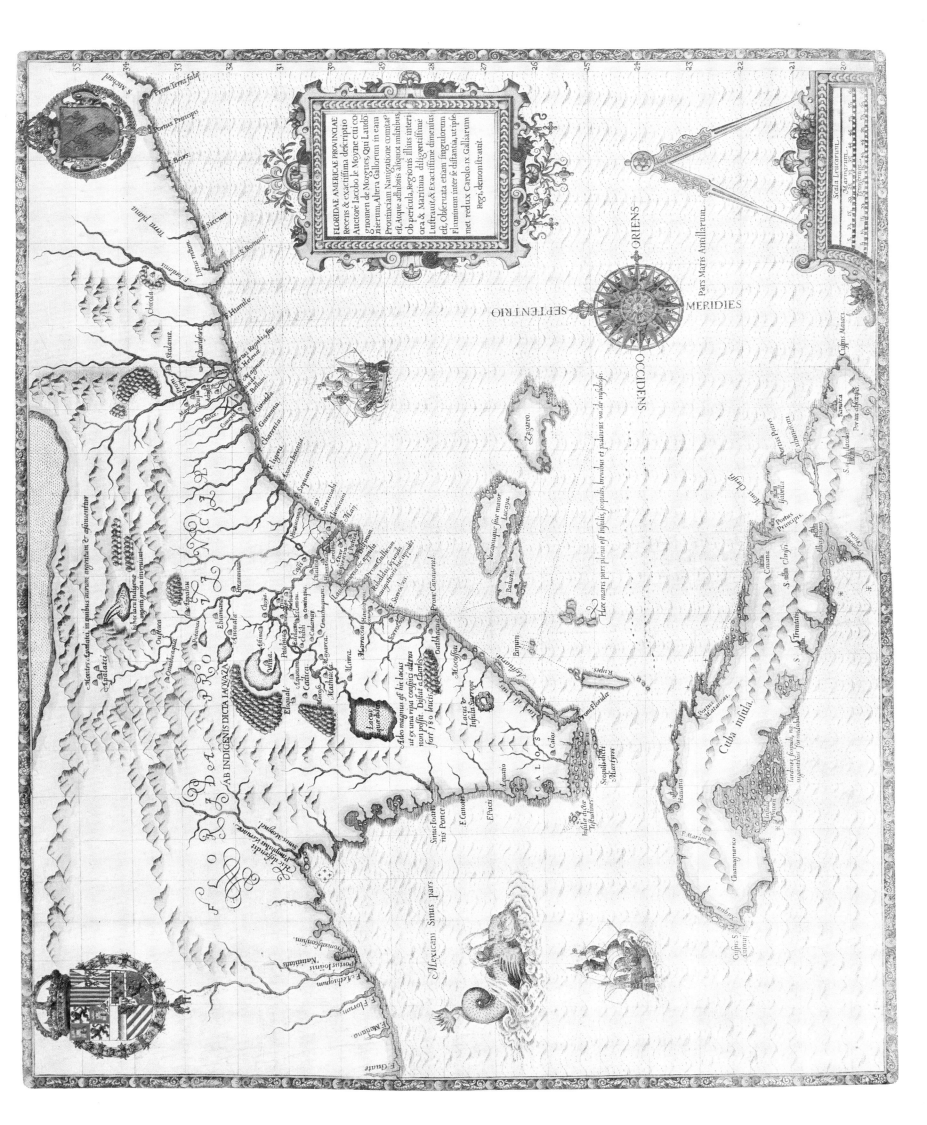

FLORIDAE AMERICAE PROVINCIAE Recens & exactissima descriptio Auctore Iacobo le Moyne cui cognomen de Morgues, Qui Laudonnierum, Altera Gallorum in eam Provinciam Nauigatione comitat' est, Atque adhibitis aliquot milidibus ob pericula, Regionis illius interiora & Maritima diligentissime Lustrauit, & Exactissime dimensus est. Observata etiam singulorum Fluminum inter se distantia, ut ipse met redux Carolo IX Galliarum Regi, demonstrauit.

SEPTENTRIO
ORIENS
OCCIDENS
MERIDIES

Pars Maris Antillarum.

Scala Leucarum.

S. Michael
Prom. Terræ fala
Portus Principis
Bays.
Siccum
I. Iordanis
Littus rectum
Prom. S. Roman.
terra plana
Chicola
I. Stalame
Charefort
Humle
Portus Regalis, siue Helma.
Magnum et Bellum.
Garonda
B. Garunna
Charentia
F. Lypera
Aquæ Ioannæ
F. Sequana
Sarauahi
Moloua
Edisto
Hiouacara
Casti
Enecaque
Conthua
Eçetou
Onatheaqua
F. Somma
Coya
Onachaqua
Potanou
Eloquale
Cadica
Matiaca
Aquouena
Apalou
Molona
Mocoso
Oathkaqua
Lacus Aquæ dulcis
Adeo magnus est hic lacus ut ex una ripa conspici alteru non possit. Distat a Charts fort 180 leucis.
Lacus de Insula Serrope
E. Canoe
E. Pacis
Prom. Carnaueral

FLORIDA PROVINCIA AB INDIGENIS DICTA IA YAZA

Montes Apalatci, in quibus aurum, argentum & æsinuentur.
In hoc lacu Indigenæ argenti præda inuenium.
Montes Apalatci.

Mexicani Sinus pars

the defensibi amplissi feruat
F. Florion
F. Medano
F. Gaute

Haec maris pars plena est insulis, scopulis, breuibus et plaisiris vade insulosis.

Zagaro.
Vacacuque siue maior
Baham.

Bariana
Buana fluuius
Rupes
Prom. Floride
Calos
C A L O S
Scopuli de Martyres
Insulæ dictæ Testudinis
Sinus Iouanne ris Ponce

Cubam insula.

Portus Mataliza.
Hauana
Cubana
F. Marien
Guanaguanico
Cassus S. littori
Angua

Mont Christi
S. dela Christi
Iubella
Portus Principis
Portus Patres
S. Iohannes
Isabellam
S. Michael
Xaraca
Portus Macaei
Cupus Macaei

Iardines, scopuli, nec nauigantibus formidabiles.

MAP 17

Northwest America

[Jode (Cornelis de)] *Quivirae Regnu[m], cum alijs versus Borea[m].* (Antwerpen, Cornelis de Jode, 1593.)

This most unusual map was published in the 1593 edition of the very rare de Jode atlas, *Speculum Orbis Terrarum*.

It was the first of its kind published in the Netherlands, and it is interesting to note that not even Abraham Ortelius, who was a contemporary of de Jode, ever included such a map in his own comprehensive *Theatrum Orbis Terrarum* atlas.

De Jode's map is one of the earliest regional maps of the American Northwest, extending from the Tropic of Cancer to north of 80°N. The Northwest Passage and the Strait of Anian (*El Streto de Anian*), together with the fictitious tribes and kingdoms of the regions, are named. Note, however, that California is conspicuous by its absence here. Compare this with Ortelius's near-contemporary map of the Pacific, for example (see map 14).

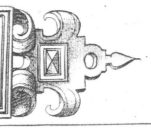

MAP 18

Canada

[Doetecom (Jan van)] *Nova Francia, alio nomine dicta Terranova, anno 1504. à Britonibus primum detecta circa sinum S. Laurentij, & anno 1524. à Ioanne Verrazano Florentino, qui ex portu Diepensi 17. Martij, solvens nomine Francisci Regis Galliarum ibidem appulit ad gradum 34. circiter latitudinis sive altitudinis Polus, plenius recognita usque ad promontorium dictum Cabo de Breton.* [Amsterdam, Cornelis Claesz, probably for Pieter Plancius, 1594?]

Formerly attributed to the English mapmaker Gabriel Tatton, this extremely rare map is here shown in its first issue with the title and the label of the whaling scene on letterpress slips pasted onto the face of the engraving. Later, the names of van Doetecom and of David de Meyne (engraver of the vignette) were added.

This beautiful map has been described as a summary of all that was known about Canada at the end of the sixteenth century, so far known only in a very few examples. This example of state 1 shows the map title and the legend to the vignette in letterpress; in state 2, these texts are engraved directly onto the plate.

Neither the mapmaker's name nor that of the engraver appears on this state, but we know from state 2 that the engraver of the map itself was Jan van Doetecom, while the whaling scene was engraved by David de Meyne. The publisher was Cornelis Claesz.

This remarkable map belongs to a small group of charts believed to be the earliest nautical charts used by the Dutch on their voyages outside Europe, voyages which enabled them to challenge the supremacy of Portugal overseas. This chart of the North Atlantic, southern Greenland, Labrador, New France and Newfoundland is perhaps the oldest printed map to show the Elizabethan discoveries in the Canadian Arctic according to information first depicted on a globe by the Englishman Emery Molyneux of Lambeth, in 1592–1593.

These voyages, of Martin Frobisher (1576–1578) and John Davis (1585–1587), did not find a Northwest Passage, but some of the coasts they did find are included on this map: in Greenland a misplaced bay on Baffin Island, is marked as *S.ͭ Martin Forbosshirs straijtes*, which is repeated on the western part of Davis Strait, following Davis's own voyage into the same waters.

The shape of Newfoundland and the Canadian-New England coast is probably derived from Portuguese charts and named *Ilha dos Bacalhos* after the Portuguese name for cod, of which a long shoal is shown, probably indicating the Grand Banks (see also map 8).

The importance of whaling, even in these early years, is vividly depicted in the vignette which shows whales—*Balenae*—being driven towards the shore and taken by whalers in their longboats.

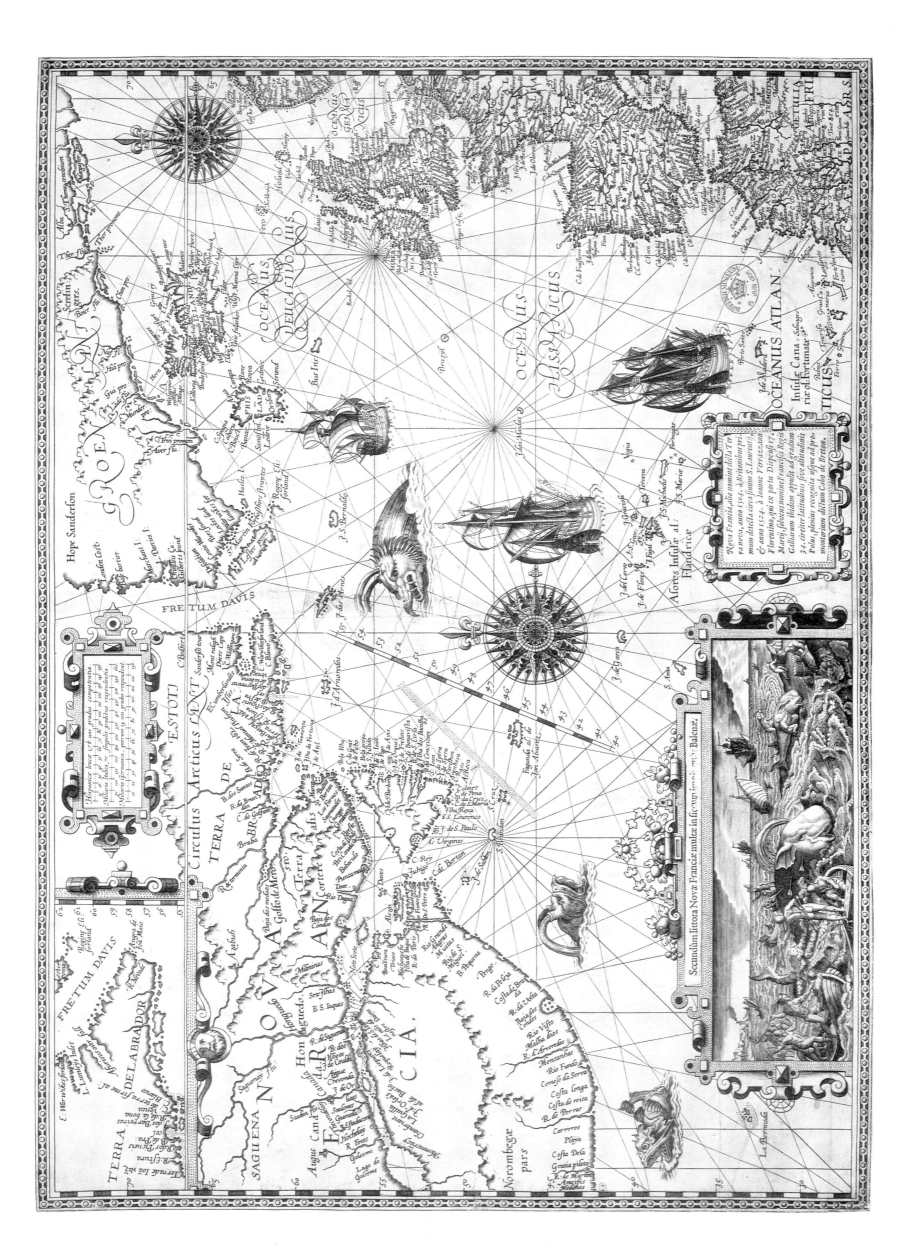

MAP 19

The Western Hemisphere

Mercator (Michael) *America sive India Nova. ad magnae Gerardi Mercatoris avi Universalis imitationem in compendium redacta.* [Duisburg, 1595; later editions at Amsterdam to 1636.]

This beautiful map of the western hemisphere was based on the great World map of 1569—so acknowledged in the Latin title—of Gerard Mercator included by the cartographer's grandson Michael (*c*.1567–1600) for publication in the *Atlas* of 1595. It is the only known map published by Michael Mercator.

The spandrel inset roundels contain maps of Cuba, Hispaniola and the Gulf of Mexico. The main map includes a large portion of *Terra Australis*, the great unknown southern continent, a Northwest Passage, a host of mythical islands in the Atlantic and the Strait of Anian separating America from the Asian mainland. In the north part of America appears a large freshwater body labelled *Mare dulcum aquarum*—perhaps an early hint, from the Indians, of the Great Lakes beyond the coasts. A river corresponding to the St Lawrence appears emptying into a broad gulf called *Sinus S. Laurentis*, together with a probable Hudson River in *Norumbega*, equating with Gerard Mercator's acceptance of the accounts of Verrazzano's voyage. No Mississippi appears, but instead there are shown several rivers flowing from de Soto's east-west mountain range in the north of his Florida.

Altogether, this map is a remarkable achievement, for it must be remembered that when Gerard Mercator first published his outline in 1569, America was barely sixty years old, cartographically speaking.

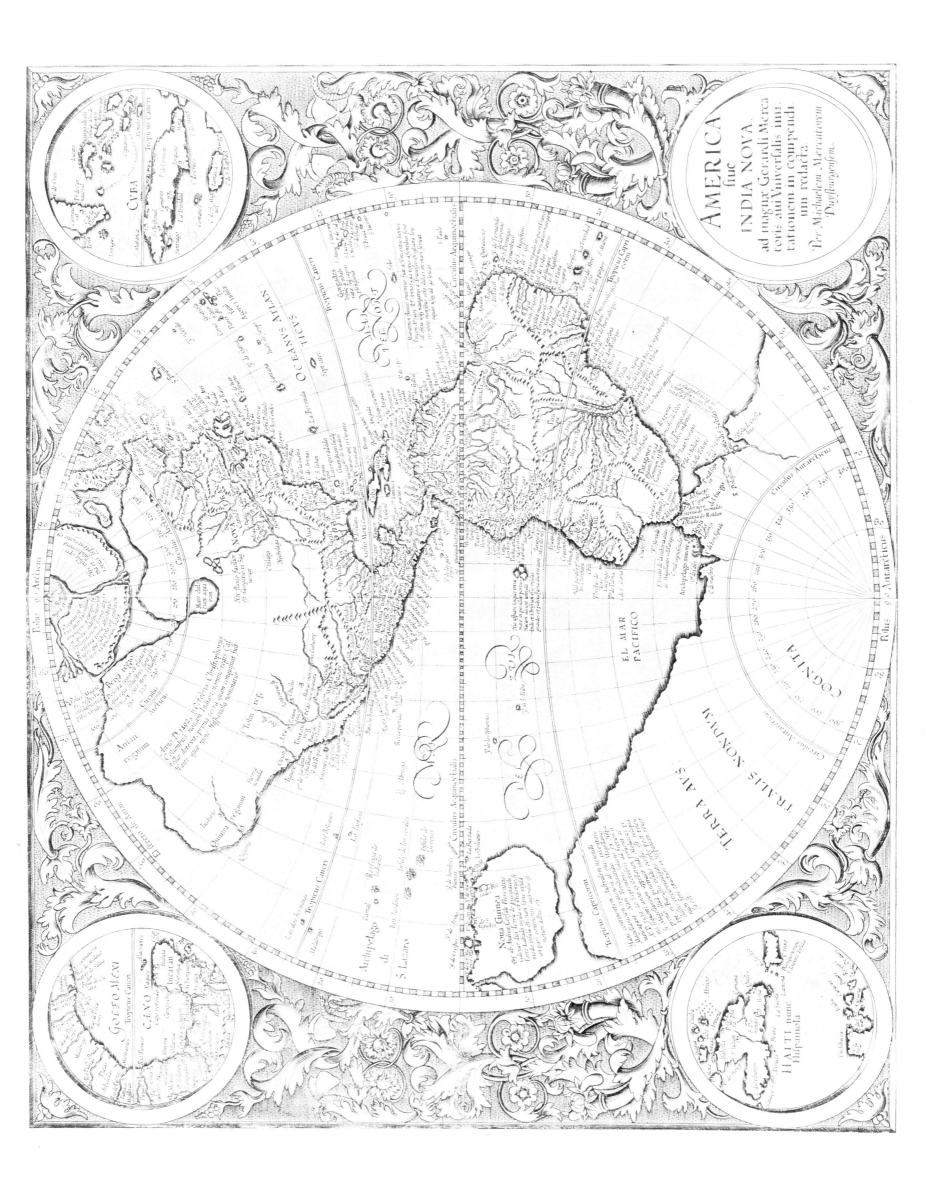

MAP 20

Florida

[Wytfliet (Cornelis van)] *Florida et Apalche*. [Leuven, Johannes Bogaerts, 1597; or Douai, François Fabri, to 1611.]

Published in *Descriptionis Ptolemaicae augmentum, sive Occidentis notitia brevi commentario illustrata*.

When Cornelis van Wytfliet, secretary to the Council of Brabant, wrote a supplement to the geographical text of Ptolemy, he in effect produced the first atlas devoted entirely to the Americas. Barely a century after Columbus's first landfall in the autumn of 1492, an atlas was published covering the entire New World in a series of nineteen maps. Given the difficulties and problems encountered by the early discoverers and explorers in the Americas, the very long lines of communication and the length of time that elapsed between individual discoveries and their announcement, the appearance of Wytfliet's work at all was no small achievement and a testament to the remarkable abilities of those early pioneering explorers. In other words, what took a century in the revelation of the geographical outline of the New World took at least one-and-a-half millennia for the Old World.

To be sure, not all of Wytfliet's map showed the very latest geographical information. Here, in this map of the Southeast, the first separate atlas map of Florida and its hinterland, Wytfliet used the small map of 1584 by Ortelius as his source, albeit with some alterations and showing a somewhat wider area. Essentially therefore, Wytfliet's map depicts the information gathered during Hernando de Soto's travels in 1539–1542, but note that the latitudinal mountain ranges are rather less prominent on this map than on either Ortelius's map or Jacques Le Moyne de Morgues's map of 1591 (see maps 13 and 16).

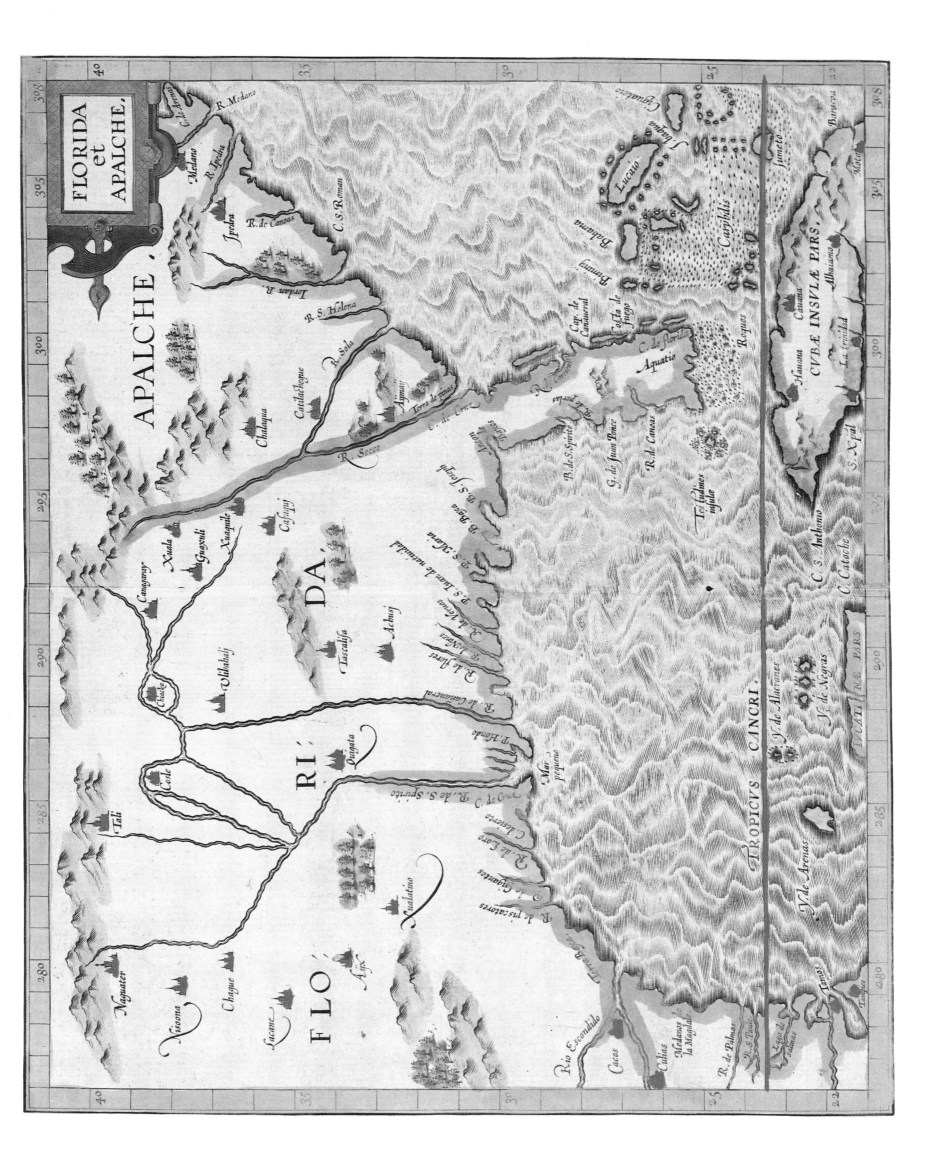

FLORIDA
et
APALCHE.

APALCHE.

FLO' RI' DA'

Naguater
Ysoona
Chaque
Sucame
Ayr
Tali
Coste
Onigata
Xualatino
Chiaha
Sahabaij
Tascaluja
Achusi
Canagazuy
Xuala
Guazuli
Xuaquile
Cafaqui
Chalaqua
Cutlachequi
Torra de pinas
Ajmay
R. Secco
R. Sola
R. S. Helena
Jordan R.
C. S. Roman
R. de Canoas
Ipedra
R. Ipedra
Medano
R. Medano
C. de Arenas

Aicon
Bra?a
B. de S. Maria
B. de S. Mec
R. de Nieves
R. de Iures
R. la Canaveral
P. Hondo
R. de S. Spirito
C. de Cruz
C. desierta
R. de Oro
R. de Gigantes
R. de Pescadores
Rio de Palmas
Tierra Baxa
Rio Escondido
Cacas
Culias
Medanos de la Magdalia
R. de Palmas
R. S. Pab
Mar pequeno

B. de S. Spirito
G. de Juan Ponce
R. de Canoas
Los Martires insula
Cap. de Cañaveral
Costa de fuego
C. de florida
Aquatio
R. de Corrientes
R. de perlas
Roques

Lucaio
Bahama
Guanaio
Bimini
Cuyilibis
I. Lagua
Cigatao

CVBÆ INSVLÆ PARS.
Hauana
Canaria
Albaiamo
La trinidad
Jureto
Barcan
Matela
S. N. pal
C. S. Anthonio
C. Catoche

TROPICVS CANCRI.
Y. de Alacrones
Y. de Negras
Y. de Arenas
Tonos
Tanque
YVCATANÆ PARS.

MAP 21

Virginia and the Northeast Coast

[Wytfliet (Cornelis van)] *Norumbega et Virginia. 1597.* [Leuven, Johannes Bogaerts, 1597; or Douai, François Fabri, to 1611.]

From *Descriptionis Ptolemaicae augmentum.* Here, Wytfliet depicts the Atlantic seaboard northwards from Virginia to Cape Breton by way of Cape Hatteras (*Hatarask*), Chesapeake Bay (*Chesipooc*), and Roanoke (*Roanoac*), with a compression of coastal detail between Chesapeake and Cape Breton itself, omitting any hint, as yet, of Long Island and the mouth of the Hudson River. It is the first detailed atlas map of the region.

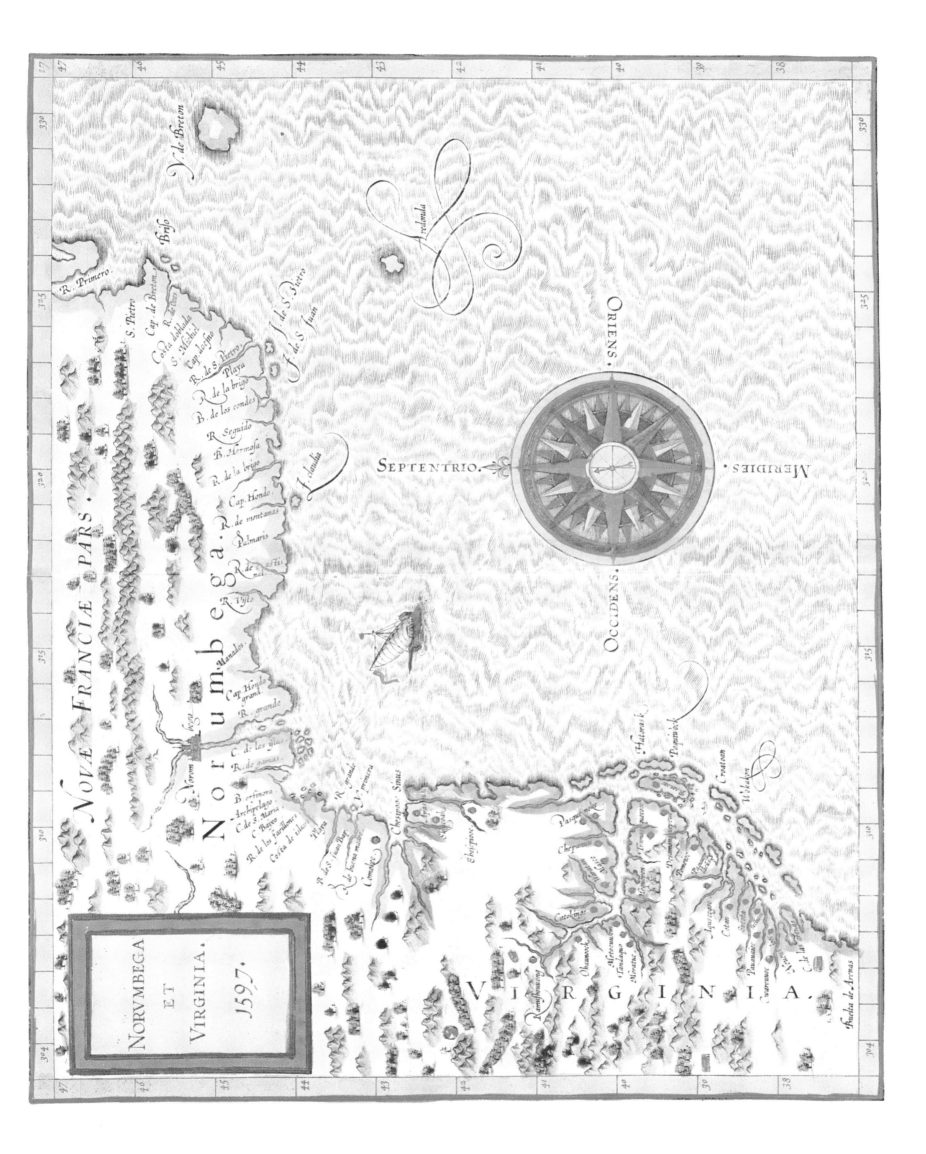

NORVMBEGA
ET
VIRGINIA.
1597.

MAP 22

North America

[Quad (Matthias)] *Nova Orbis pars Borealis, America scilicet, complectens Floridam, Baccaleon, Canadam, Terram Corterialem, Virginiam, Norumbecam, pluresque alias provincias.* [Köln, Johann Bussemecher, 1600 and later.]

This general map of North America, one of the earliest available, in contrast to the several general maps of the two continents, is based on the now very rare map by Cornelis de Jode of Antwerpen, published in 1593. Quad's version was issued in his scarce atlas, the *Geographische Handtbuch.*

The map itself has its rather squashed appearance as a result of a translation of the detail of Gerard Mercator's World map of 1569—on the now familiar projection named after the great mapmaker—onto a cylindrical projection, which has the effect of squeezing geographical information at the northern extremities.

Nevertheless, Quad's copy (itself now relatively rare) is a compendium of late sixteenth-century thought on the geography of North America, including that of John White in Virginia, Jacques Le Moyne de Morgues in Florida, and so on. Some remarkable errors creep in, among them *Virginia* being placed at the same latitude as Cape Cod (marked as *C. de las arenas*), Chesapeake Bay (or its equivalent) being shown level with Boston, and a double promontory of Florida being drawn in the south. The map also contains a very prominent Northwest Passage, with the mythical lake *Lago de Conibas* (taken by some commentators as an early hint of either the Great Lakes or perhaps even Hudson Bay) to its south. Despite these 'errors', Quad's map is one of the earliest obtainable, reasonably accurate outlines of the North American continent.

NOVI ORBIS PARS BOREALIS, AMERICA SCILICET, COM-PLECTENS FLORIDAM, BACCALAON, CANADAM, TERRAM CORTE-

rialem, Virginiam, Norombecam, plureséque alias prouincias. America, siue India noua, Anno D. 1492. à Chrystophoro Columbo Genuensi, nomine Regis Castellæ primùm detecta fuit: Nomen autem sortita sicut est ab Americo Vespucio Florentino, qui prima nauigatione cum Columbo emissus erat, iamque nauigandi artem edo-ctus, elapsis aliquot annis proprias instituit nauigationes, atque anno 1497. terram hanc quæ priùs insulæ esse nomine detexit. Regio est tam à Continente Orientali, quàm nos inhabitamus. Eam porrò regionem quam hodie Virginiam appellamus, anno 1585. Gualtero Raleigh nobili Anglas Reginæ suæ nomine detexit. Regio est Athenuis, tùm Ferris, Aeris, Cedri, ominuméque necessariorum feracissima, Frumenti incredibilis prouentu; gens mediocri statura, cÆmangue è ceruina pelle tecta, armas fani arcus et lapites ligneis, oppida exigua. Mari vicina sani, denarij aut duodenarum ædium, raro plurium, pænæ certæ. Capo de Breton à Ioanne Verrazano Florentino anno 1529. nomine Regis Galliæ detecta est; verùm inter Canadam et Floridam a barbaris capti; occiditur, assatur, et denoratur. Virginiæ et Floridæ historiæ libri Francof. apud Bryæos imprimuntur.

Coloniæ laminæ sunt typomechæri.

MAP 23

Virginia and Florida

[Hondius (Jodocus)] *Virginiae Item et Floridae Americae Provinciarum nova Descriptio.*
[Amsterdam, 1606 and later.]

First published in the Hondius editions of Gerard Mercator's *Atlas* from 1606
onwards, this highly decorative map influenced mapmakers throughout the
seventeenth century. Even so, it was based on sixteenth-century sources—the
observations of the Englishman John White in Virginia in 1585, and those of the
Frenchman Jacques Le Moyne de Morgues in Florida in 1564, published in 1590
and 1591 respectively.

   Shown here are the gold deposits of the Appalachians, the great lake at the foot
of those mountains, the far shores of which could not be seen ('ut ex una ripa
conspici altera non possit', a distant echo in time of Verrazzano), the French fort at
Port Royal on the Virginia coast, and so on. The cartographic historian, the late
William P. Cumming, commented: 'by putting the great lake and the direction of
the flow of the river May to the northwest of its mouth and changing the
accompanying topographical features and Indian settlements, Hondius created
geographical misconceptions of the region which lasted for nearly a century and a
half.

   Hondius's title is flanked by vignette illustrations of Floridan and Virginian
Indian villages taken from the illustrations in de Bry's *Great Voyages* series.

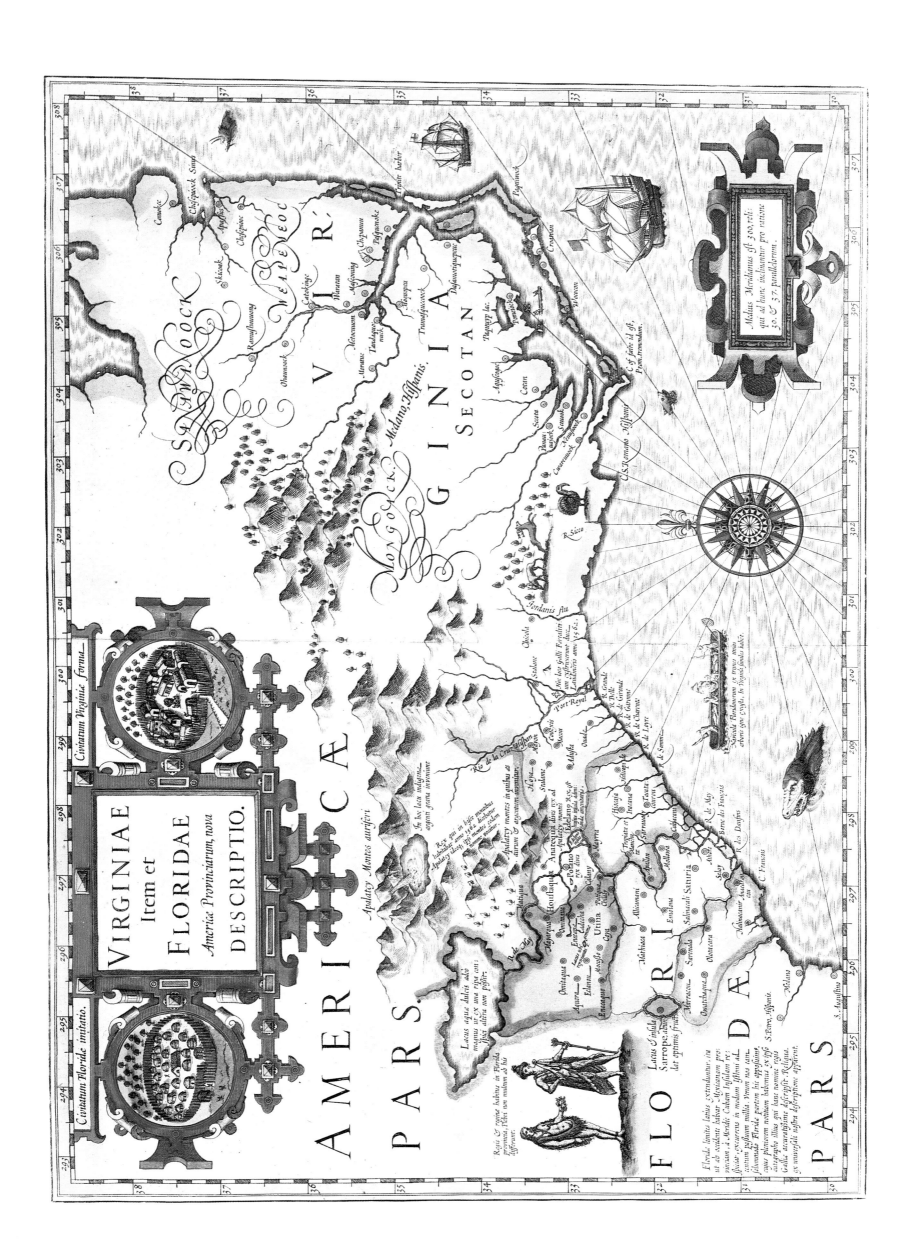

MAP 24

North America

[Briggs (Henry)] *The North Part of America . . . and upon y^e West the large and goodly Iland of California.* [London, William Stansby, 1625.]

'California sometymes supposed to be a part of ye westerne continent but scince by a Spanish Charte taken by ye Hollanders it is found to be a goodly Ilande: the length of the west shoare beeing about 500 leagues from Cape Mendocino to the South Cape there of Called Cape St Lucas: as appeareth both by that Spanish Chart and by the relation of Francis Gaule whereas in the ordinairie Charts it is sett downe to be 1700 Leagues.'

The first printed map of North America to show California as an island, it was engraved by Reynold Elstracke and issued in London in 1625 in an edition of *Hakluytus Posthumus* by the travel writer Samuel Purchas.

This is one of the most notorious maps in the history of North American cartography. It was compiled from information collected by Sebastian Vizcaino and Antonio de la Ascensión from the Spanish expedition to the west coast in 1602 for the purpose of locating a safe haven for the fleets out of the Spanish colony of the Philippines. Henry Briggs wrote his *Treatise of the Northwest Passage to the South Sea* in 1622 based on the Spanish account, stating that California was 'found to be a goodly Ilande', after having claimed to have seen a map captured by Dutch navigators which showed the peninsula separate from the American mainland.

Briggs's map initiated one of the most famous of all cartographical misconceptions—a remarkably persistent one at that—for California was still being depicted as an island in atlas maps issued in Amsterdam as late as the 1790s!

Briggs's map is also the earliest printed map to include the name *Hudsons bay* even though it is appended to the southern extension known today as James Bay in the north of Canada. The western reaches of Hudson Bay are here called *Buttons Baie*, with perhaps just a faint hint of a Northwest Passage nearby.

OCEANVS IAPONICVS

The North part of
AMERICA

Conteyning Newfoundland new England
land Virginia Florida new Spaine and
Nova Francia: wth y^e rich Iles of Iapan China
ba Iamaica and Porto Ricco wth y^e South.
and upon ye West ye large and goodly Countrye
of California. The lands of it are ye largest Ilande
i^t Ocean on ye South and w^e North Fretum Hudson
sea on ye west side and wth North w^ere entrance is found a
and Butons baye a sure entrance passage to Iapan & China.
and most temperate passage to Iapan & China.

AMERICA SEPTENTRIONALIS

NOVA BRITTANNIA

PARTE OF GRONELAND

Hudsons bay

BVTTONS BAIE

CANADA

New England

Virginia

Florida

GRANADA

NEWE
SPAINE

REALNE DE
MEXICO

PVEBLOS DE
MOQVI

EL REY COROMEDO

CALIFORNIA

CVBA

Summers Ilands

R. Elstracke sculpsit

MAP 25

America

Speed (John) *America with those known parts in that unknowne worlde—Both people and manner of buildings Discribed and inlarged by I.S. Ano 1626.* [London], George Humble [1627 and later to 1676].

Issued in the editions of John Speed's *Prospect* from 1627 onwards, this fine general map of the Americas was engraved by Abraham Goos. It is the first English map of the Americas.

The side borders show costumed figures taken from illustrations published by de Bry and others, while the upper border is a frieze of town views showing La Habana, Santo Domingo, Cartagena, Mexico, Cuzco, Rio de Janeiro and Olinda (see map 26 for a comparison with Blaeu's map).

Speed's map is also the first general map of the Americas to show California as an island, based on Henry Briggs's prototype (see map 24). The North Atlantic contains also the persistent mythical islands of *Brasil* and *Frisland*, which seemed to wander across the map of the North Atlantic through the decades like Flying Dutchmen, as it were.

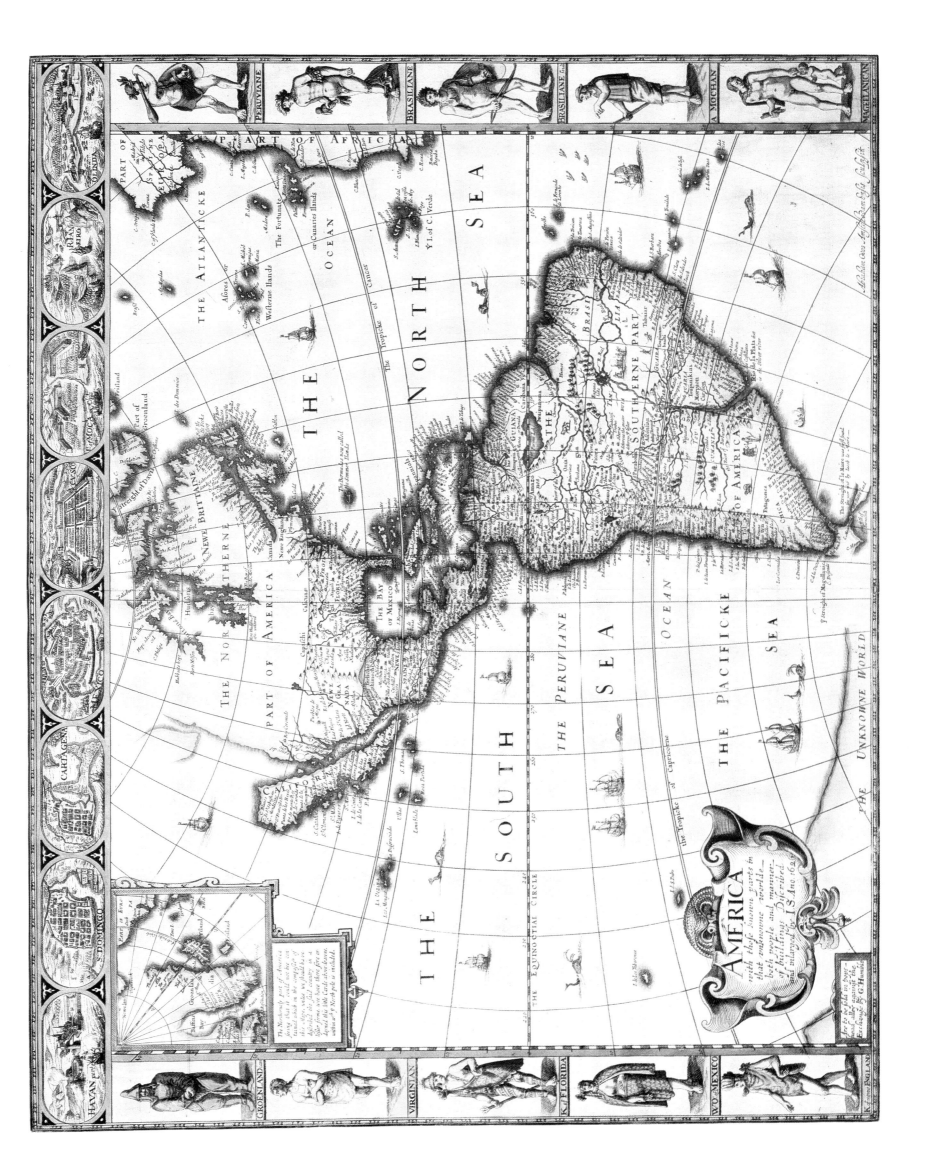

MAP 26

America

Blaeu (Willem) *Americae nova tabula*. [Amsterdam, 1630 and later.]

This magnificent map sums up the general European view of the western hemisphere in the early seventeenth century: the delineation of the coasts and the nomenclature of the Pacific and Atlantic coasts are basically Spanish in origin and follow the maps of Abraham Ortelius (see map 11) and those of his countryman Cornelis van Wytfliet (see map 20). To these, Willem Blaeu added the English names given by the Roanoke colonists in Virginia, and by Martin Frobisher, John Davis and Henry Hudson in the far North. In Florida and along the St Lawrence, Blaeu added the names given by the French settlers (see map 16), almost the only memorials of that ill-fated venture during the latter part of the sixteenth century.

When Willem Blaeu first made his map, Europeans still had no real knowledge of the nature of the Mississippi system. From the expedition journals of Hernando de Soto (1539–1543), they had inferred an extensive range of mountains trending eastwest to the north of the Gulf coast in *la Florida*, apparently precluding any great river system. The Great Lakes were, as yet, unknown, although by the time that Blaeu issued this map in his atlases of the 1630s, Samuel de Champlain's travels in the Huron region of Canada, together with his hearsay accounts from Coral Indians were becoming more widely known through his now extremely rare 1632 map of the region. The same can be said of Manhattan and Long Island as well, despite the fact that only a short distance from Amsterdam, the Leiden academic Johannes de Laet had published the first edition of his great work on the Americas, which provided source materials for any number of maps of the Americas throughout the remainder of the century.

To complete his picture of America as a whole, Blaeu provided perspective plans or views of important settlements there: La Habana, Santo Domingo, Cartagena, Mexico, Cuzco, Potosi, Rio de Janeiro and so on, as well as the side-border vignettes showing native figures, taken from the accounts of John White in Virginia, Johann von Staden in Brazil, and others.

MAP 27

America

Hondius (Hendrik) *America noviter delineata*. [Amsterdam], 1631 [and later].

Superficially, this general map resembles the continental map by Willem Blaeu (see map 26), but without the decorative borders.

Appearing initially in 1631, this plate was issued first by Hondius and later by the great rival of the Blaeus, Johannes Jansson. As on the Blaeu map, the early or peninsular form of California is shown. But by contrast, inset maps of both the Arctic and the Antarctic are included in the design, the latter still preserving the long-held notion of the mythical southern continent, while the Arctic inset still retains Martin Frobisher's illusory strait across southern Greenland.

Incidentally, this map affords a good example of how rival map publishers copied from each other: while the decorative detail on Hondius's map may be quite different from Blaeu's map, the topographical and toponymical information, even down to the positioning of individual words and letters, is almost identical!

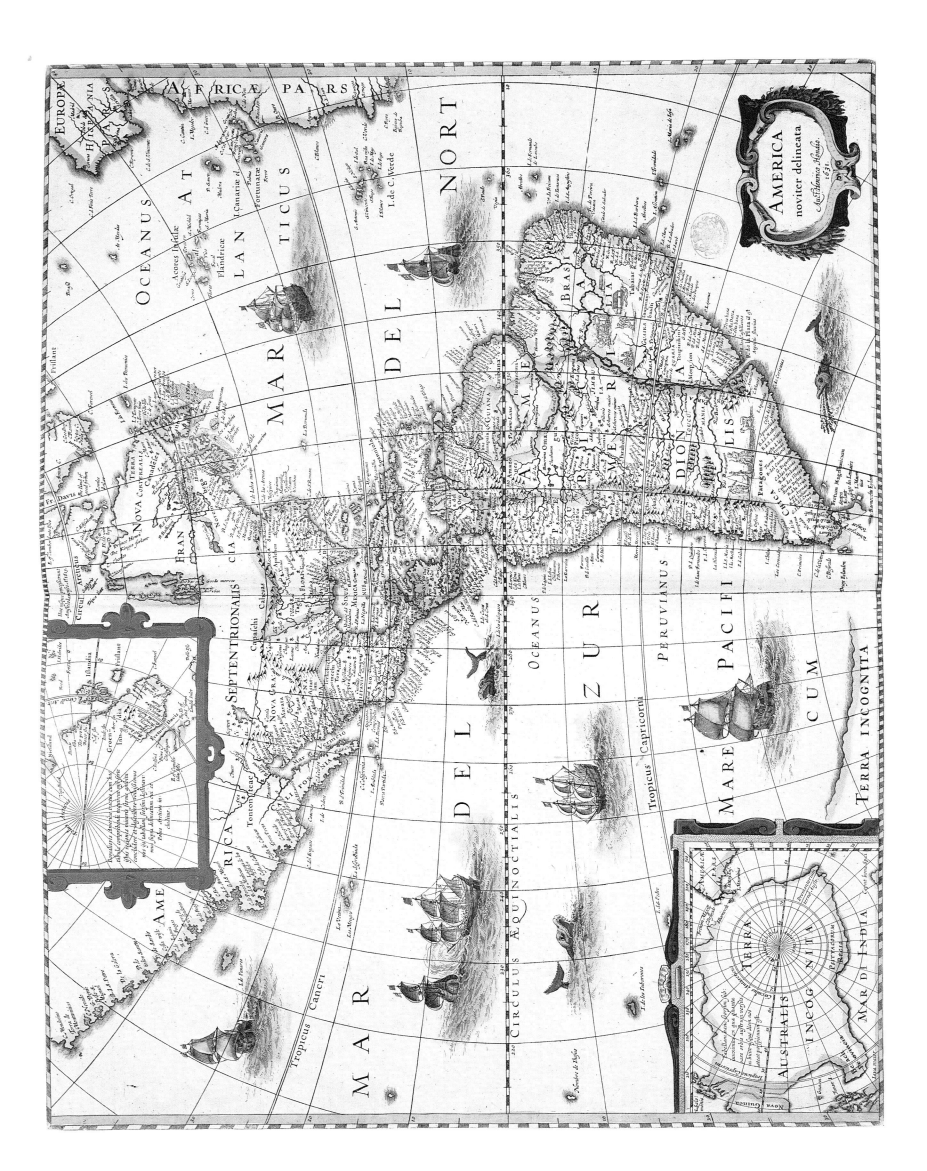

MAP 28

The New Netherlands and New England

Blaeu (Willem) *Nova Belgica et Anglia Nova*. [Amsterdam, 1635 and later.]

This beautiful map of New England and the New Netherlands is one of the earliest maps to include that part of North America colonized by the Dutch, and is the first printed map showing Indian canoes and several kinds of North American fauna, such as turkeys, beavers, polecats and otters.

First produced by Willem Blaeu in 1635, the map exercised considerable influence for many years. The geographical details were derived mostly from a manuscript map of the region drawn in 1614 by the Dutch explorer Adriaen Blockx, and from a map in Johannes de Laet's *Nieuwe Wereldt* of 1630.

Note the location of *Lacus Irocoisiensis* (Lake Champlain), placed in New England in error, after Samuel de Champlain's map of 1613.

Adriaen Blockx, a fur-trader as well as an explorer, first arrived in North America in 1611 and set out on a coasting voyage in 1614. His ship, the *Onrust*, was the first vessel built on Manhattan Island by Europeans. He sailed through the *Hellegat* (East River) into *De Groote bay* (Long Island Sound) exploring the shores and noting the locations of the various tribes of Indians, such as the *Manhattans*, *Morhicans*, *Pequatoos*, and others.

On the map, note also the detailed small illustrations of pallisaded Indian villages, reminiscent of Hochelaga in the north of Canada (see map 7), and dug-out canoes, and the male and female figures decorating the title-cartouche.

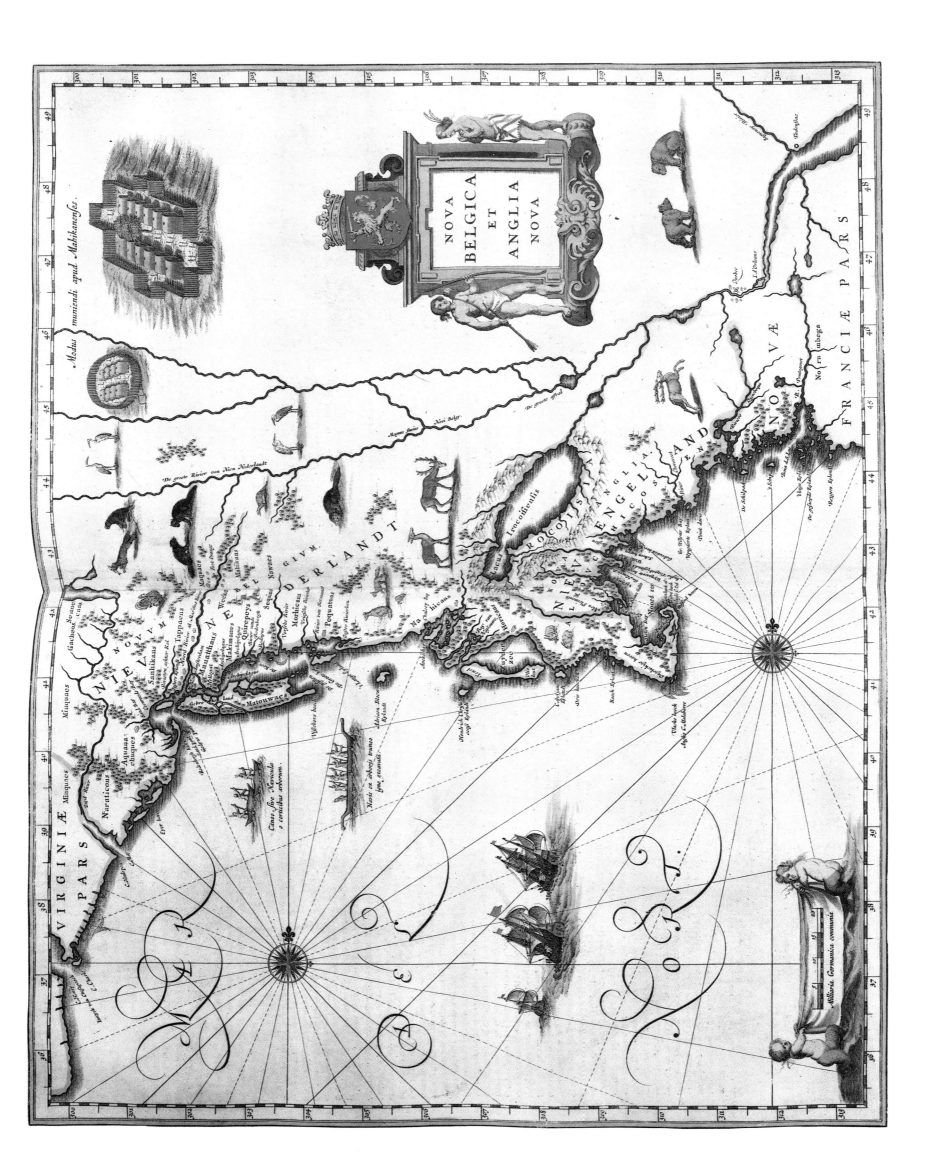

NOVA
BELGICA
ET
ANGLIA
NOVA

Modus muniendi apud Mahikanenfes.

FRANCIÆ PARS

NO RVM BEL GIVM

DER'LANDT

NIEVC ENGELAND

NOVA SCOTIA

Lacus Iroconien ſis

VIRGINIÆ PARS

NIEV

Matouwacs

Milliaria Germanica communia.

MAP 29

New England, The New Netherlands and Virginia

[Jansson (Johannes)] *Nova Anglia Novum Belgium et Virginia*. [Amsterdam, Hendrik Hondius, 1636 and later.]

This fine map is the first atlas rendering of a map first published in 1630 by Johannes de Laet in his *Beschrijvinghe van West-Indien*. Jansson shows the coast from Virginia to Nova Scotia, a greater extent than the corresponding map by Blaeu (see map 28), but unlike the rival map, Jansson shows the more familar northward orientation.

Of particular importance here is the inclusion of the place names *N. Amsterdam* and *Manbattes*, among the first appearances of these two names in a printed atlas. Also given is the extent of New Netherlands, sandwiched between the rival English colonies of New England and Virginia, also Fort Orange (built in 1624 on the west bank of the Hudson River) near present-day Albany, and the early appearance (on an atlas map) of *Noordt Rivier* (the Hudson River) and *Zuydt Rivier* (the Delaware River).

This map is, therefore, an important early cartographic record of the Dutch West-India-Company's colony of the New Netherlands, established in 1628.

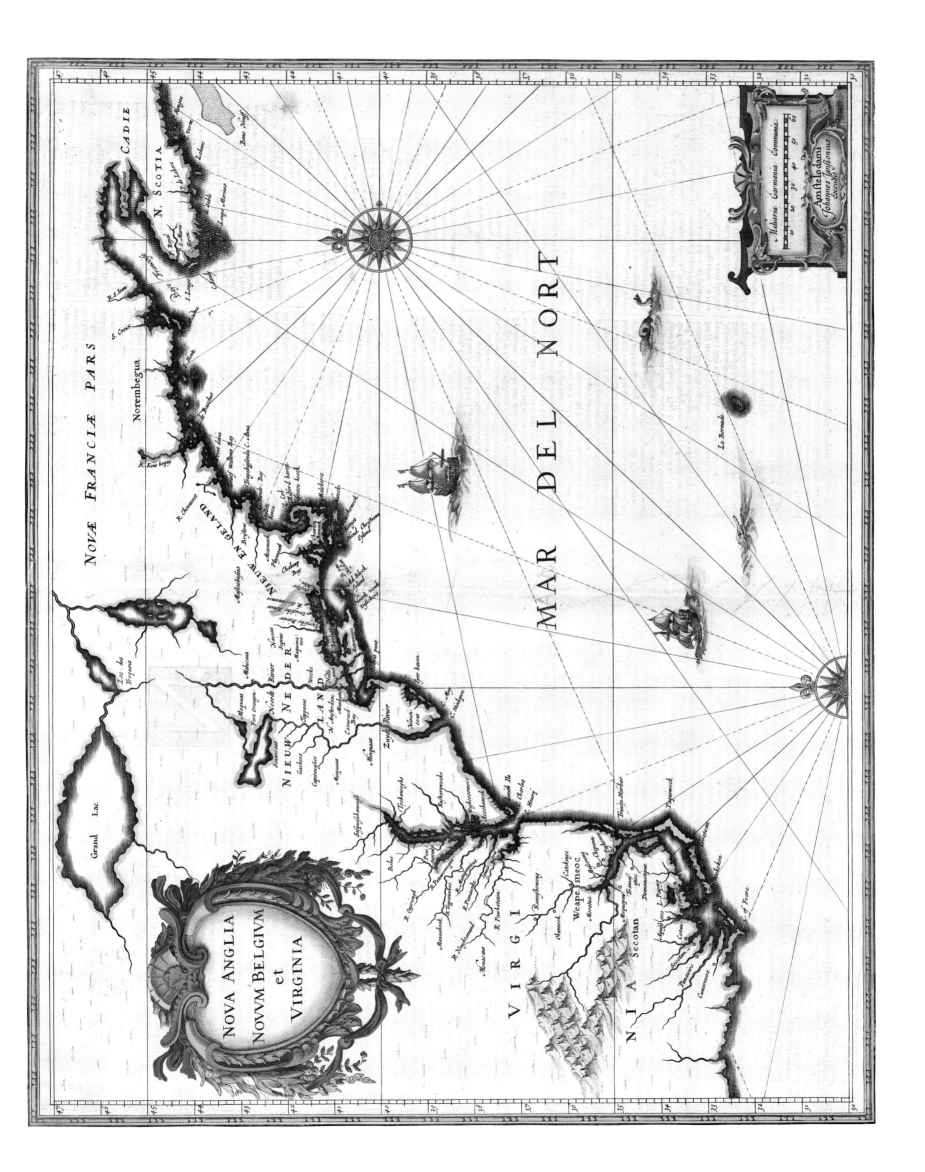

NOVA ANGLIA
NOVUM BELGIUM
et
VIRGINIA

MAP 30

North America

Jansson (Johannes) *America Septentrionalis*. Amsterdam [Hendrik Hondius, 1636 and later].

The first Dutch atlas map of North America, and the first Dutch atlas map to show California as an island. In this instance, the model is the outline published on Henry Briggs's map of 1625 (see map 24). It saw publication in this form in the later editions of Mercator's *Atlas* as published by Hondius, shortly before the business passed into the hands of Johannes Jansson himself, rivalling the firm of Blaeu in later years. Curiously, although Blaeu himself claimed the leadership of the Amsterdam map publishing business in the middle years of the seventeenth century, unlike Jansson he never included a separate map of North America in his series of atlases.

Jansson's map shows detail of Canada borrowed from Samuel de Champlain's map of 1613, indicating the St Lawrence and Lakes Ontario, Oneida and Champlain, but omitting those lakes which would later appear on maps as Lakes Huron and Erie. Hondius's map of Virginia and Florida (see map 23) published in 1606 provided the detail for the Southeast, while the Gulf region shows a vast network of rivers foreshadowing the Mississippi-Missouri system, a notion copied in later years by Sanson in 1650 (see map 33).

Important as this map is in its cartographic detail, the decorative appeal of Jansson's work is heightened by the inclusion of numerous small illustrations of native fauna: buffalo, caribou, Arctic foxes, polar bears, to take a few examples, while the title-cartouche shows the figures of Floridan and Virginian Indians drawn from the de Bry *Great Voyages* series of the 1590s.

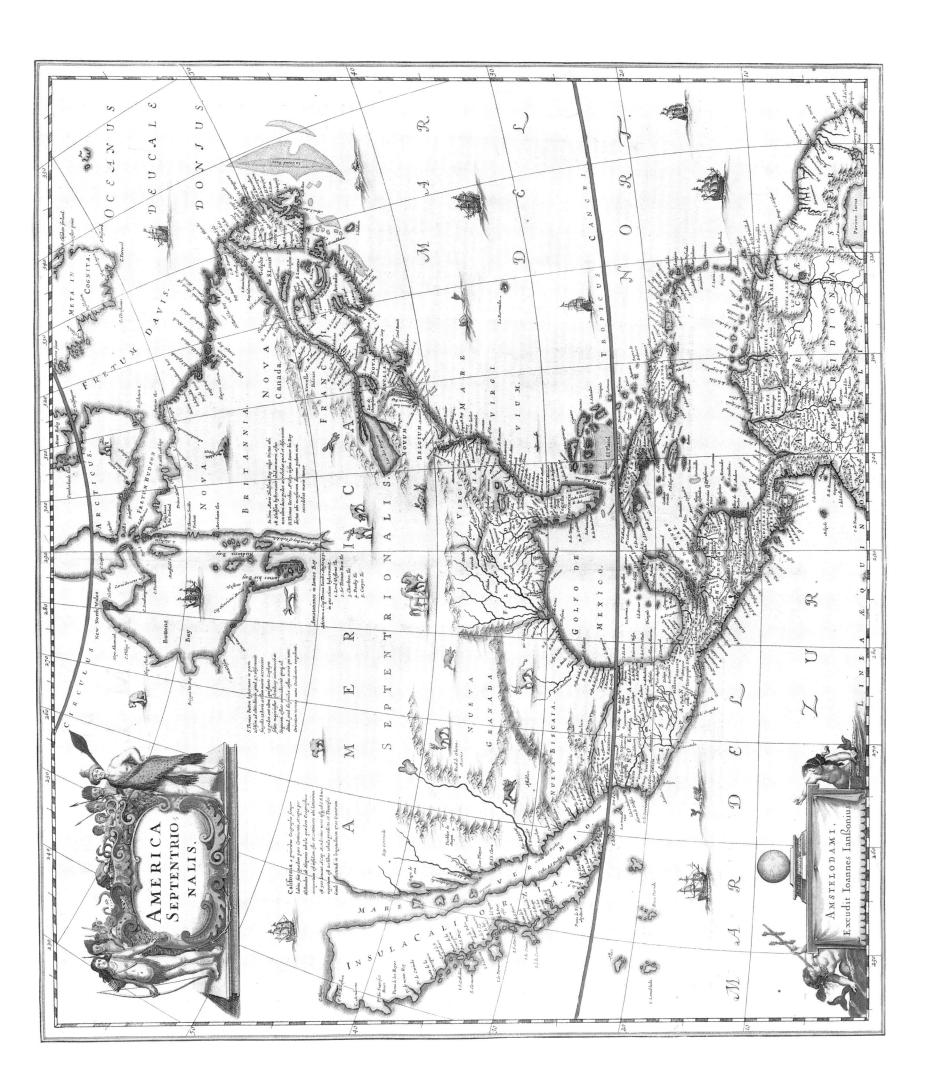

AMERICA SEPTENTRIONALIS.

AMSTELODAMI,
Excudit Ioannes Ianßonius

MAP 31

Virginia and Florida

Blaeu (Joan) *Virginiae partis australis, et Floridae, partis orientalis, interjacentiumq[uae] regionum nova descriptio.* [Amsterdam, 1638 and later.]

This map of the Southeast is based on Jodocus Hondius's version (published in 1606) of the surveys of the Englishman John White in 1590, and the Frenchman Jacques Le Moyne de Morgues in 1564–1565, with respective areas of English and French colonization shown by the royal arms of the two nations in Virginia and in Florida.

Blaeu shows a region at the southern end of the Appalachians where gold and silver were to be found: 'Apalatcy Montes in quibus aes aurum et argentum invenitur', in reference to the sixteenth-century accounts of panning for these precious metals by the Coral Indians.

Blaeu has attempted to incorporate more recent information, such as the settlement by the Irish at Newport News on the shores of Chesapeake Bay, and also at Jamestown upstream on the James River (here marked as *Powhatan flu.*). The general outline of the Carolina coast is another improvement on the older model, being mapped here with two cuspid bays now called Onlsow Bay and Long Bay.

An almost identical map was issued by Johannes Jansson, Blaeu's greatest rival publisher in Amsterdam.

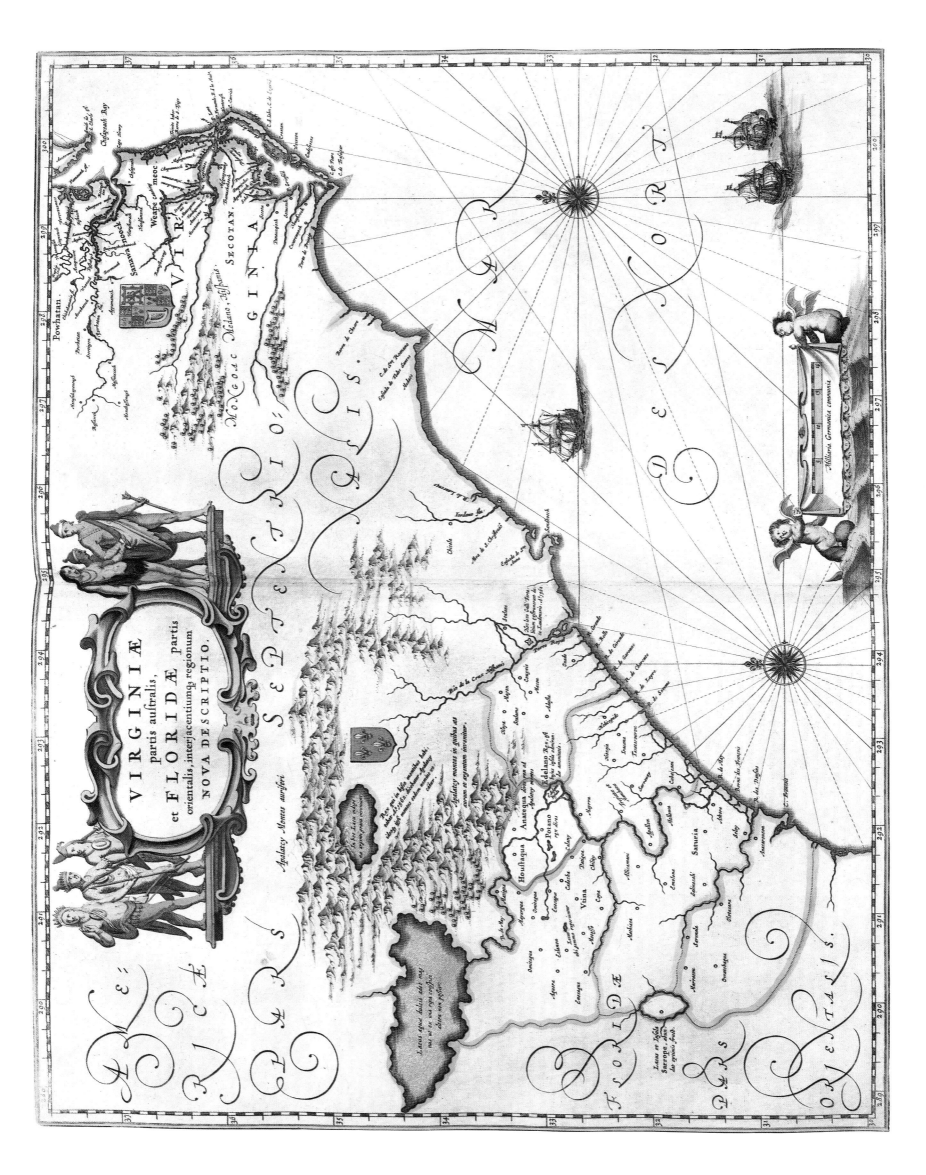

MAP 32

The Southwest Coast of America

[Dudley (Sir Robert)] *Carta particolare della parte occidentale della nuova Spagnia, è del la California*. [Florence, 1646 or 1661.]

Published in the rare chart atlas *Dell' arcano del mare*, the first atlas of sea charts compiled and published by an Englishman (albeit expatriate), this chart shows the southern part of the California peninsula and the northwestern coast of Mexico.

Apart from a few scattered place names along this stretch of coast there is little apparent evidence of any permanent Spanish settlements in this distant region of the Spanish American empire. A brief note appended to coastline, to the northwest of Acapulco at *Porto della Naciunta* states that here, every April the ships return from the Philippines run.

Here, at 'the rim of European civilization', Jesuit missionaries were busily establishing their missions in an attempt to tame the local Indians and their desert. Attempts farther north in the region shown on this map by Isidro Arondo y Antillón in the 1680s were to prove fruitless, largely as a result of the Jesuits' failure to come to terms with the harsh environment of northwestern Mexico in the Sonora Desert. Even into the nineteenth century, attempts to open up the region met with only very limited success.

Carta particolare della parte occidentale della nuoua Spagna, è del la California.
La longitudine Comincia da l'Isola di Pico de l'Azores.
D'America Carta XXXI.

IMPERIO DI MESSICO, O LA NVOVA SPAGNA.

AMERICA

Valle di S.Bartolomeo

Mexuacan

Mecoacan

Mexico Citta Metropolitana

Il Tropico di Cancer

NVOVA SPAGNA

Coatalpanecas.

Colima.

Colima.

Nuoua Galizia.

Nuoua Granada.

Sacatala.

Nuoua Bifcaia.

Culicana.

Massatlan

Mexico.

MARE DELLA NVOVA SPAGNA VERSO AVSTRALE.

Los Montes

LA CALIFORNIA

MARE VERMIO di Colore Bianco.

Il Tropico di Cancer

Par poco

Cor per Scirocco

I.S.Tommaso.

Anablada.

Rocco Partido.

Corrente Verso Ponente

Corrente Verso Ponente

MARE DEL ZVR

Corrente Verso Ponente

I das Mc. Scaperada

I.S.Camuilin

Correnti

Var. Cor di Grecale.

Var. Cor. di Grecale.

MAP 33

Canada

Sanson d'Abbeville (Nicolas) *Le Canada, ou Nouvelle France*. Paris, Pierre Mariette, 1656 [and later].

This is the most influential record of the French establishments in North America in the middle of the seventeenth century. It is based on the Jesuit Relations and shows an accurate course of the St Lawrence and the Great Lakes in more or less their proper locations. Another source was Sanson's own map of North America, published in 1650.

The discoveries and observations of Samuel de Champlain and the Jesuit fathers Jogues and Raymbault are shown, as well as much information gleaned from the reports of the many fur-traders in Canada at the time, together with hearsay information supplied by travellers among the Indians.

Note, however, the unusual orientation of Lake Michigan, probably gathered from Barthélemy Vimont's travels of 1642 in an east to west direction along the northern shores of the lake. Many other names here are Indian in origin.

MAP 34

New Mexico and Florida

Sanson d'Abbeville (Nicolas) *Le Nouveau Mexique, et la Floride: Tirées de diverses Cartes et Relations*. Paris, Pierre Mariette, 1656 [and later].

Sanson's map is the first printed French atlas map to emphasize California and New Mexico; it became the model for maps of the 'island' of California for more than fifty years. It appeared in Sanson's *Cartes générales de toutes les parties du Monde*.

Note that the outline of California is quite different from that presented by Henry Briggs in 1625 (see map 24). Much of the detail is adapted from Sanson's own general map of North America published in 1650, and shows additional information in New Mexico, and also names Lakes Ontario and Erie in far northeast, thereby subsconciously defining the extent of French pretensions to an empire in North America.

Other features appear here for the first time: the collected rivers of the Mississippi valley region emptying into a small sea called *Mar Pequeno* and place names in the Iroquois lands gathered from Jesuit Relations in 1649 and 1654. The indentations on the northern shore of California are new here also, shown above *C. Blanco* in *Nouvelle Albion*, whereas Sanson's 1650 map of North America showed the 'island' in a way more akin to the outline of Briggs.

The indentations and other features are now named *Talaago* and *R. de Estiete*, and the facing peninsula on the mainland is labelled *Agubela de Catu*. Other information in the region is revised here, so that fictitious names, such as *Cibola*, are now eliminated, but note that the widely-travelled name *Quivira* now appears in the area of present-day Texas. Compare this with de Jode's map of 1593, for example (see map 17). Other names appear now in Spanish rather than in their French equivalents, as shown on the earlier map of 1650.

In Florida, Sanson resurrects briefly the French Huguenot settlement of some hundred years before under Ribaut and Laudonnière: note the river names *Gironde, Charente, Loire,* and *Seyne* on the east coast of *Floride Francoise*. The colony lasted only a few years, from 1562 to 1568, until it was expelled by the Spanish (see map 16).

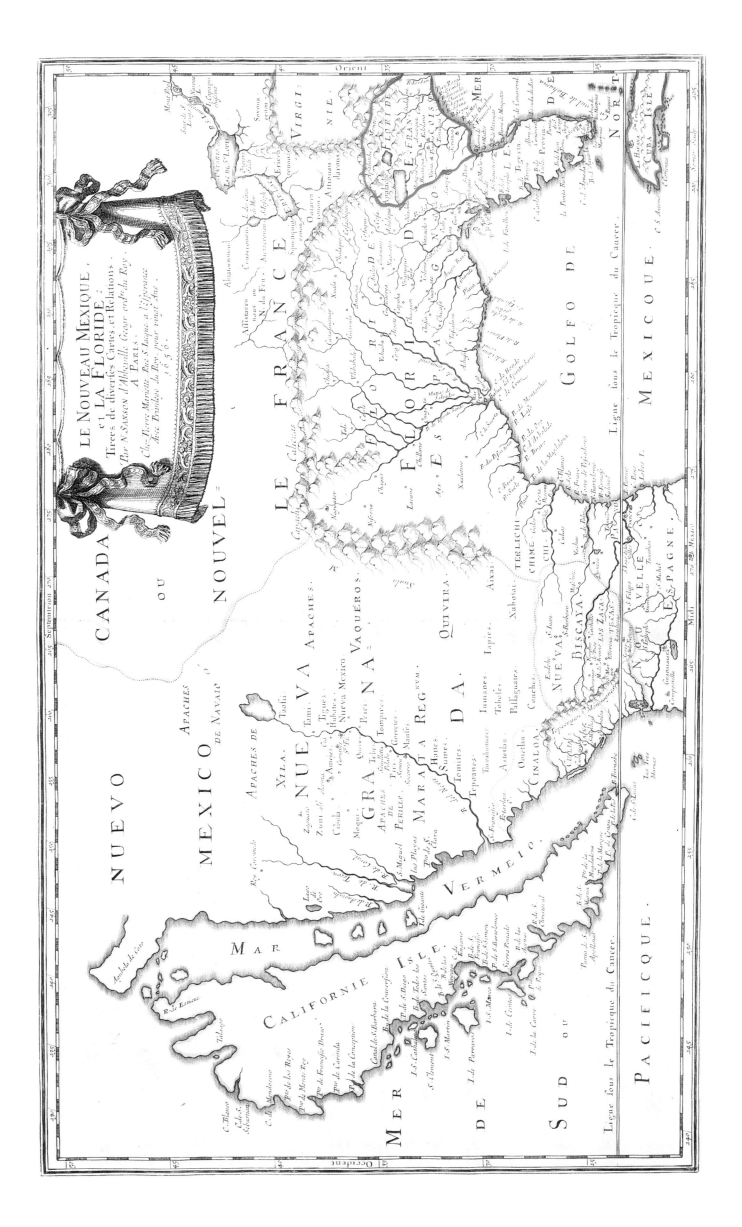

LE NOUVEAU MEXIQUE, et LA FLORIDE :
Tirees de diverses Cartes, et Relations.
Par N. SANSON d'Abbeville, Geogr. ord. du Roy.
A PARIS
Chez Pierre Mariette, Rue S. Jacque à l'Esperance.
Avec Priuilege du Roy pour vingt Ans.
1656.

MAP 35

The Pacific Coast

Doncker (Hendrik) *Pascaart vertoonende de Zeecusten van Chili, Peru, Hispania Nova, Nova Granata, en California. 't Amsterdam by Hendrik Doncker Boeckverkooper inde Nieuwe brugh Steegh in 't Stuiermans gereedtschap.* [1659 and later.]

Covering not only a substantial part of the Pacific by means of insets, Doncker's chart shows California as an island based for the most part on Sanson's famous outline of 1656 (see map 34), a small part of New Zealand after Abel Jansz. Tasman, and parts of northern Japan after Maarten de Vries.

Doncker specialized in marine atlases and charts in Amsterdam in the middle of the seventeenth century and, as with many other charts—both by himself and by his fellow publishers—many of his products are quite sparse in their decorative details, apart from small decorated title-cartouches. In other words, such charts as this were intended for practical navigational use rather than for show or ostentation.

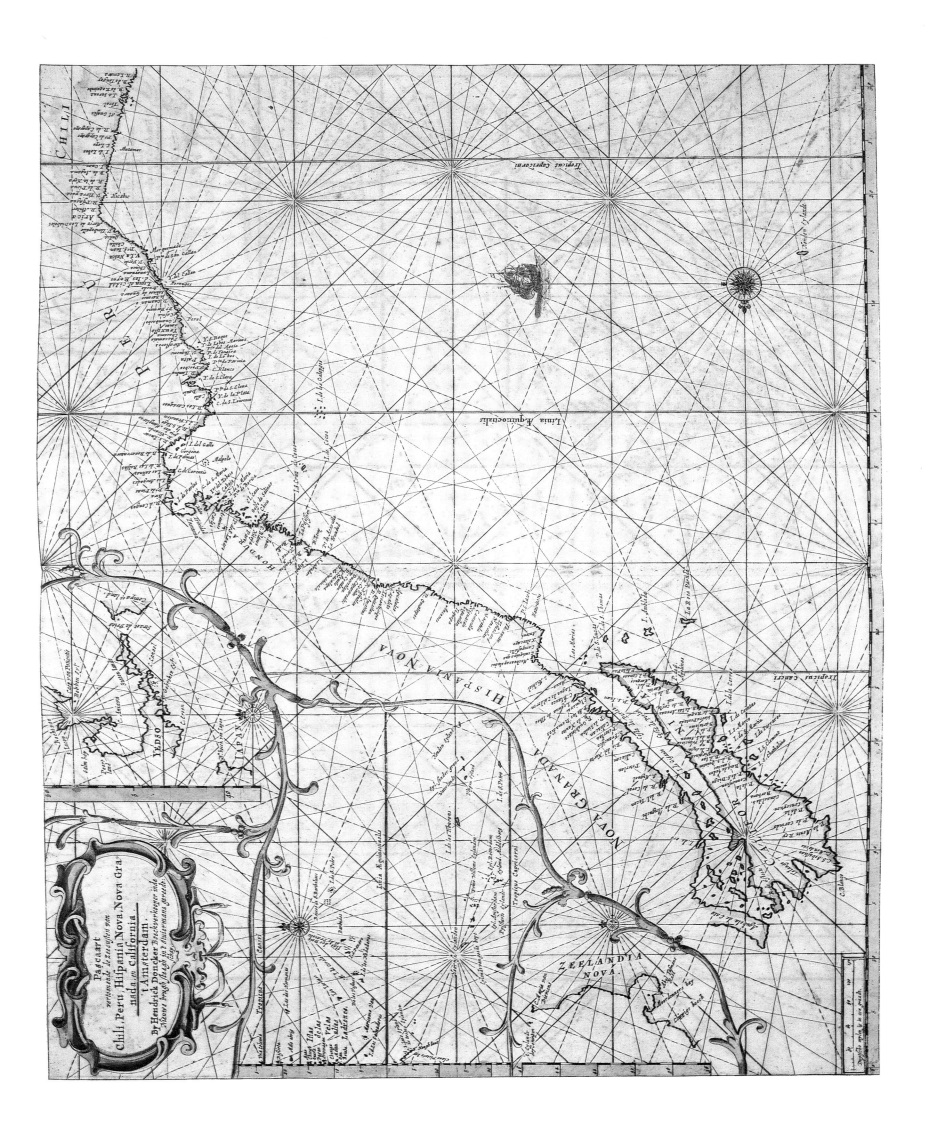

Pascaart
vertoonende de Zeecusten van
Chili, Peru, Hispania Nova, Nova Granada, en California.
t'Amsterdam.
By Hendrick Doncker Boeckverkooper inde
Nieuwe brugh Steegh in d'Stuurmans gereedtschap.

MAP 36

Eastern Canada and Labrador

Blaeu (Joan) *Extrema Americae versus Boream, ubi Terra Nova Nova Francia, Adjacentiaq(uae)*. [Amsterdam, 1662 and later.]

From the 1662 *Atlas Major*, Joan Blaeu's map of eastern Canada and Labrador, first published in 1662, appears to have been based on the eastern sections of Samuel de Champlain's extremely rare map of 1632, for many years the most extensive and accurate portrayal available, published in his history of New France, together with information taken from Nicolas Sanson's map of 1656 (see map 33).

Here, Joan Blaeu shows Nova Scotia, Newfoundland, the Gulf of St Lawrence, Labrador, and the Davis and Hudson Straits as well as the southern tip of Greenland. Forts and other settlements are named at Cape Sable, Port Royal, Quebec, St Croix, Tadousac, and, on the Penobscot River, Pemtegouet.

The title-cartouche gives an indication of the continuing and growing, importance of the Grand Banks fisheries, the Banks themselves being shown in an accurate outline off Newfoundland. Compare this with shoals presented by Jan van Deutecom on his map of *c.*1594 (see map 18).

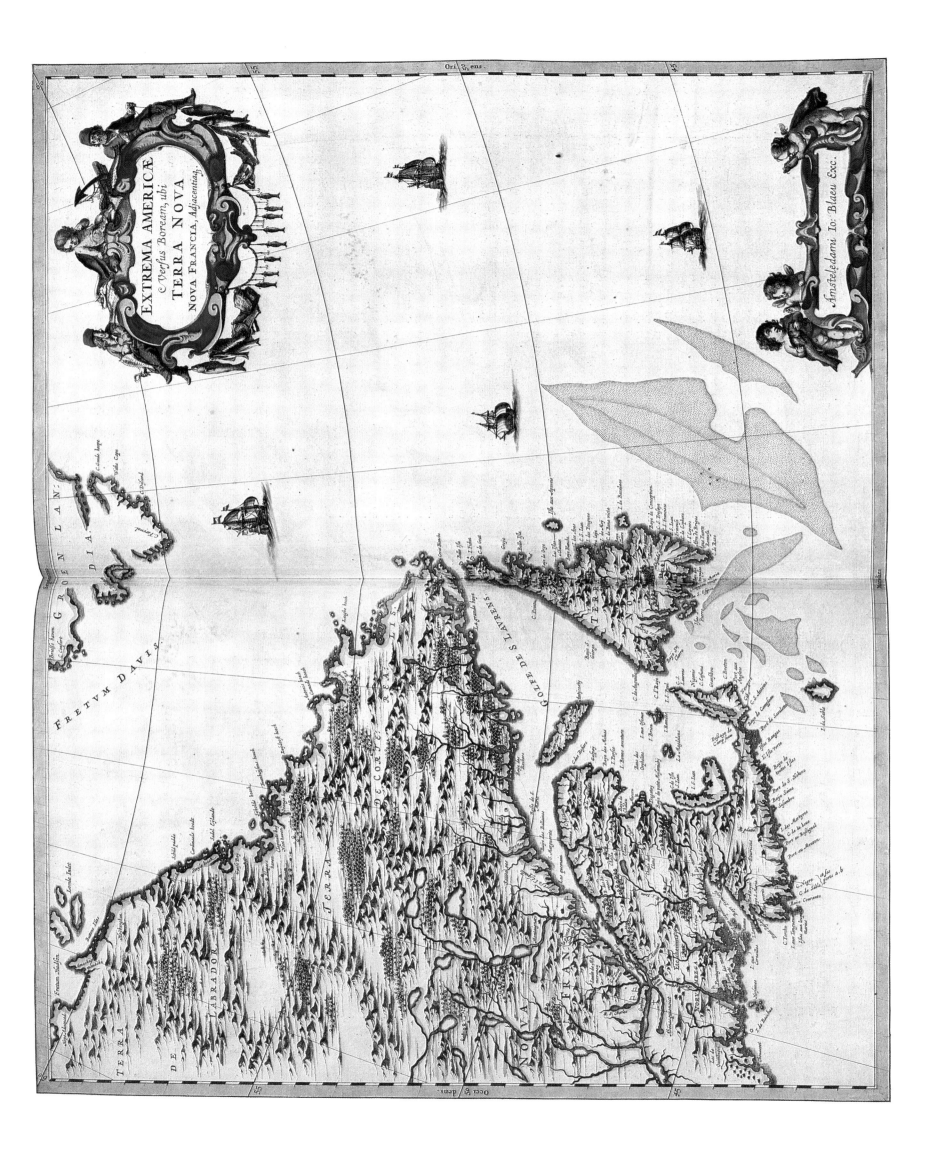

EXTREMA AMERICÆ
& versus Boream, ubi
TERRA NOVA
NOVA FRANCIA, Adjacentiaq.

Amstelodami Io: Blaeu Exc.

MAP 37

California

Goos (Pieter) *Paskaerte van Nova Granada en t' Eylandt California*. Amsterdam, 1666 [and later].

This is perhaps the finest map of the 'island' of California. Indeed, it is the only atlas map devoted to the 'island' alone.

Based on Sanson's 1656 outline, it shows the indented northern coastline, the facing promontory on the mainland coast and the unknown land to the north, here marked as *Terra Incognita* or *Onbekent Landt*. California is, in effect, the 'raison d'être' of the map, doing full justice to Henry Briggs's claim of it as a 'goodly Iland'.

Most of the place names are from Sanson's map, omitting *Pta. de Roque* but adding the names *Costa del Perles* and *B.S. Iuan* on the eastern, or gulf coast of California.

Goos's map is one of the most definite and aesthetically pleasing representations of California as it was thought to be during the second half of the seventeenth century and is a particular choice of many collectors.

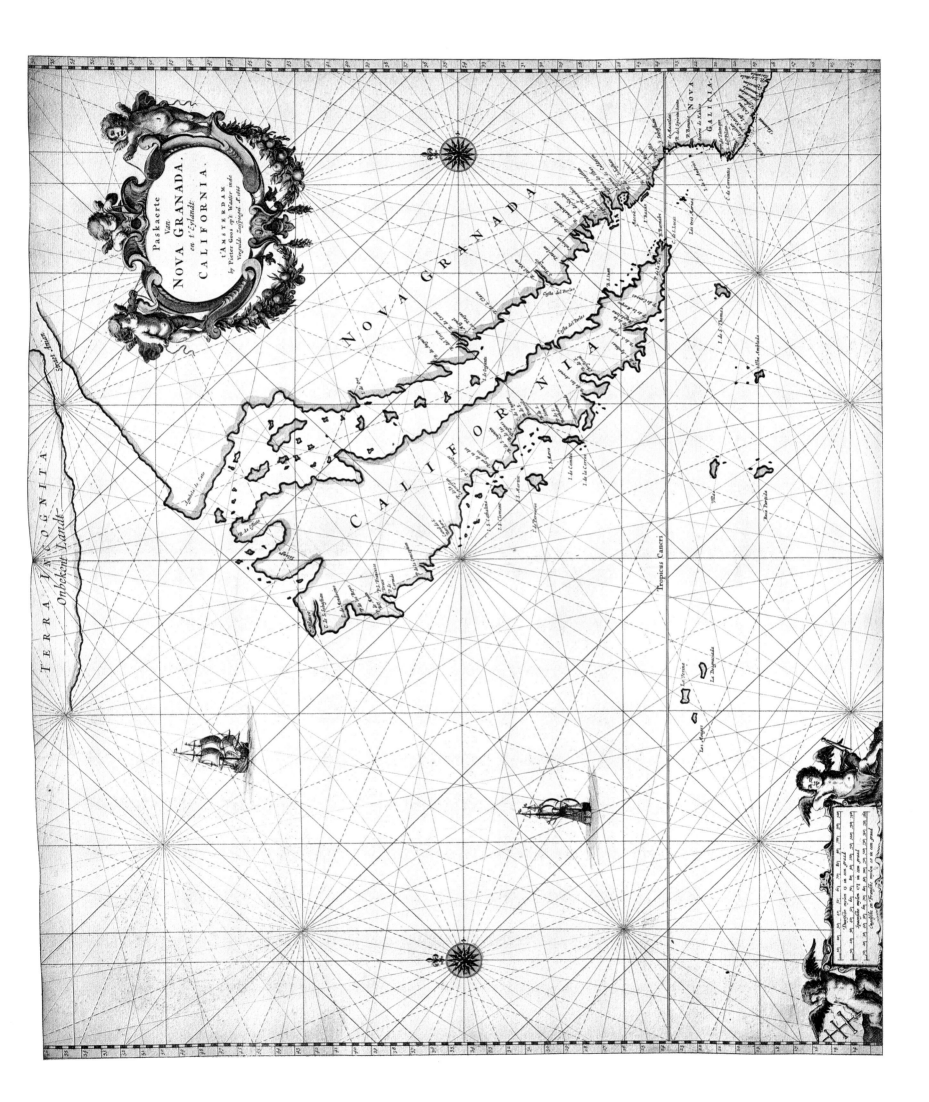

Paskaerte
Van
NOVA GRANADA.
en t'Eylandt
CALIFORNIA.
t'AMSTERDAM
by Pieter Goos op't Water inde
Vergulde Zeespiegel.

NOVA GRANADA

CALIFORNIA

TERRA INCOGNITA
Onbekent Landt

Sugt Anian

Tropicus Cancri

NOVA GALIIIA

MAP 38

Virginia

[Ogilby (John)] *Nova Virginia Tabula*. [Amsterdam, Johannes van Meurs, 1671, or London, for the Author, 1671–1672.]

This general map of Virginia appeared in both Arnold Montanus's *Nieuwe en Onbekende Weereld* and in John Ogilby's *America*. It is essentially reduced from the standard seventeenth-century Dutch maps by Blaeu and Jansson of the 1630s and later. These in turn owe their ancestry to the survey of Captain John Smith for the Virginia Company in 1612.

In all its variant forms, the map was the accepted view of the Chesapeake Bay region for most of the century.

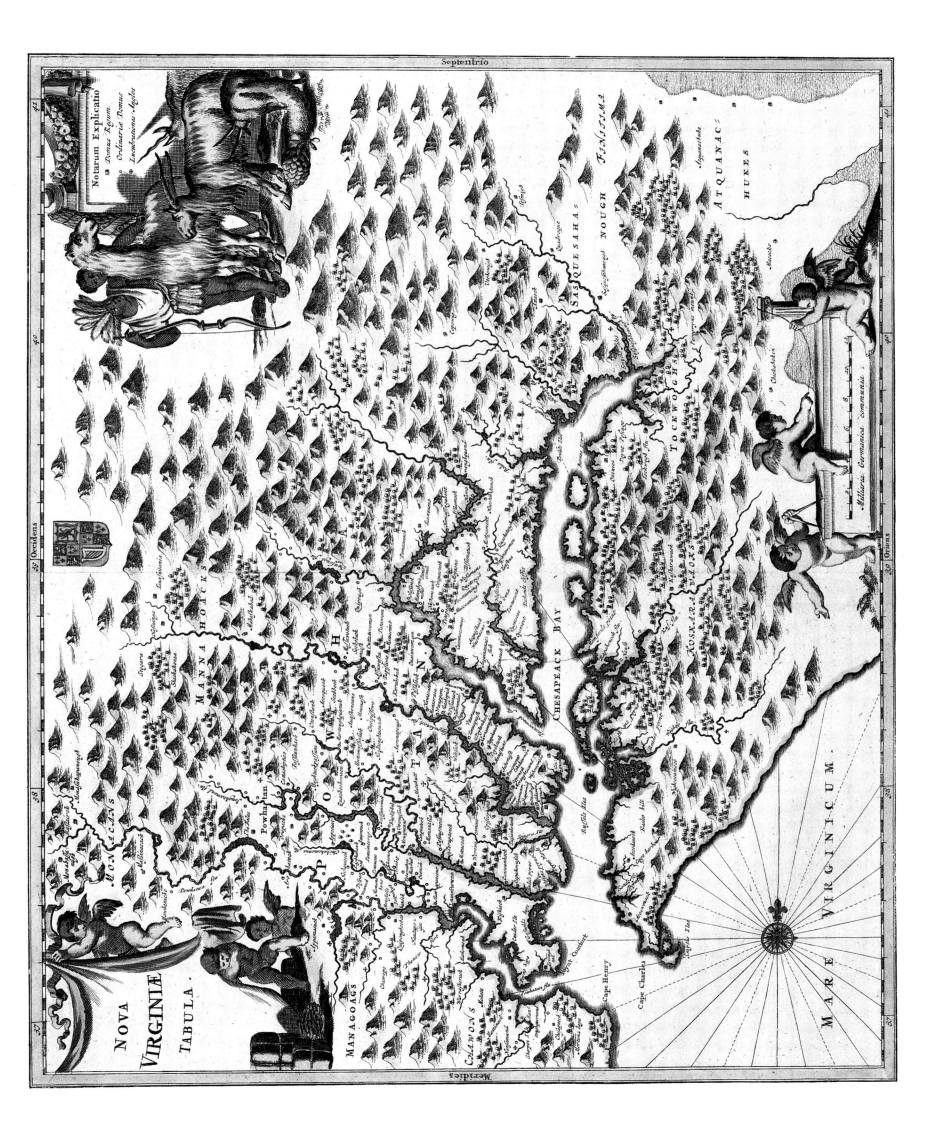

NOVA VIRGINIÆ TABULA.

MAP 39

Carolina

[Ogilby (John)] *A New Discription of Carolina By Order of the Lords Proprietors.* [London, for the Author, 1672.]

Engraved by James Moxon, published in some copies of Ogilby's *America*, a volume from his uncompleted *English Atlas* project. The map is also known as the 'First Lords Proprietors' Map', and was very likely used as publicity in promoting the new province, the first plantations having been established in Carolina on the Charles River in the spring of 1664.

This map of the new colony was given wide circulation in Ogilby's popular work, which was itself an English translation and augmentation of Arnold Montanus's *De Nieuwe en Onbekende Weereld*: the first encyclopaedia of America. Ogilby's map appears to have been based on official documents of the Lords Proprietors, for John Locke, secretary to Lord Ashley, the Earl of Shaftesbury, was approached on Ogilby's behalf with a request for information: 'Mr Ogilby who is printing a relation of the West Indies hath been often with mee to gett a map of Carolina wherefore I humbly desire you to gett of my lord those mapps of Cape feare & Albermarle that he hath.' Ogilby's map prints many of the names of the Lords Proprietors: *Craven River, Colleton River, Berkeley County, Ashley River, Ashley Lake, Cooper River, Cape Carteret, Clarendon County, Albemarle River*, and so on.

Other information comes from an extremely rare map by Robert Horne from the promotional work *A Brief Description of The Province of Carolina on the Coasts of Floreda*, published in London in 1666. There are persistent echoes still of Jacques Le Moyne de Morgues's map published in 1591 (see map 16) in the form of Indian village names in the south, together with John Lederer's more recent map of 1672 lending other topographical detail and names such as *Deserta Arenosa* and the lake at the southern end of the Appalachians.

Ogilby's map was much copied by subsequent mapmakers, including Francis Lamb who included a version of it in the final edition of John Speed's *Prospect* in 1676 (see map 25). Earlier copies of Ogilby's *America* had, instead of the present map, another based on much older Dutch sources which had been included in Montanus's original Dutch work; the present map was inserted in copies after about 1672, and sometimes *America* may be found containing both maps.

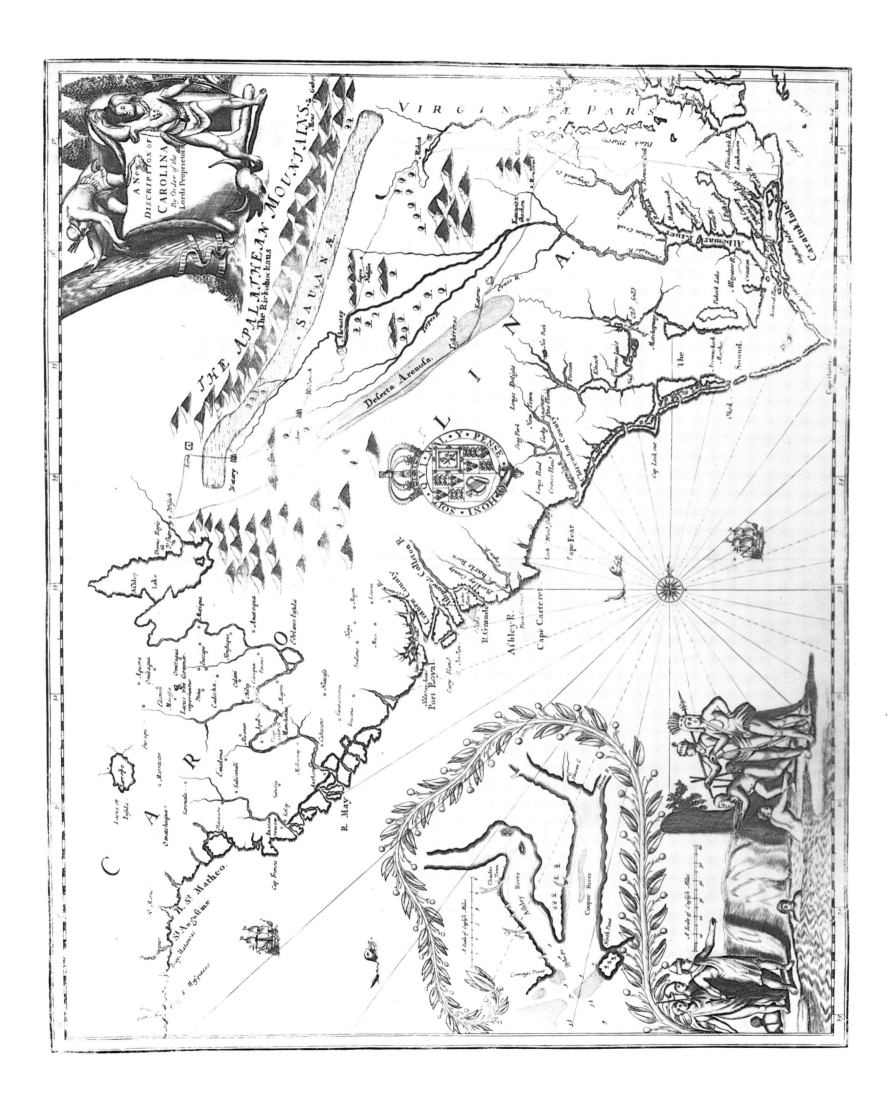

MAP 40

Virginia and Maryland

Lamb (Francis) *A Map of Virginia and Maryland*. London, Thomas Bassett and Richard Chiswell [1676 or later].

This striking map, engraved by Francis Lamb, appeared in the final, 1676, edition of John Speed's *A Prospect of the Most Famous Parts of the World*.

Based in part upon the John Smith map of Virginia of 1612, taking much of the topographical information from that source, place names and many feature names are taken from the much more recent 1673 map of the region by Augustine Herman, showing a more or less continuous pattern of settlement on the shores of the Chesapeake Bay area, but very little in the interior. This illustrates how little was as yet known of eastern North America beyond the Fall Line even after more than fifty years of English colonization and the waves of immigration from England and continental Europe between 1649 and 1660 during the Commonwealth.

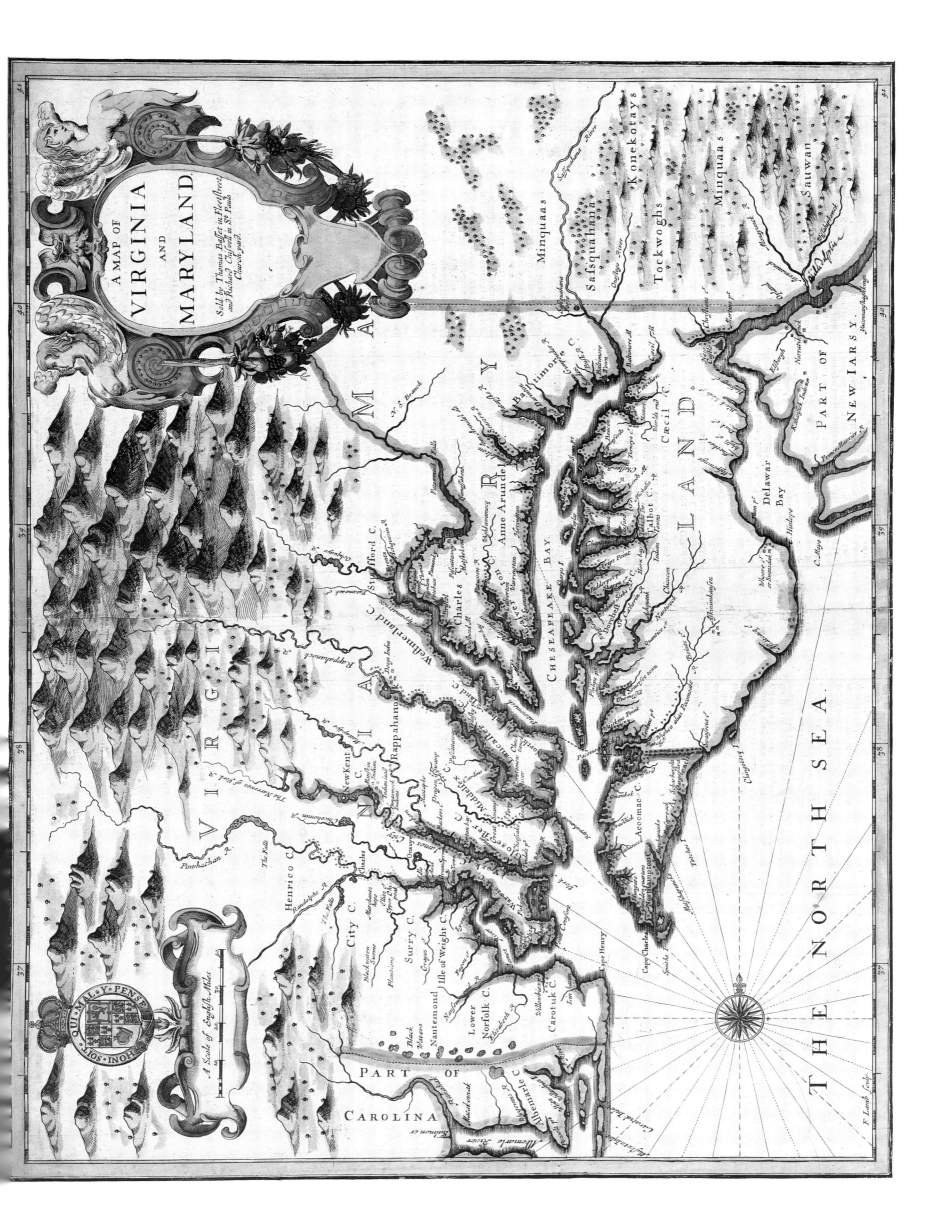

A MAP OF
VIRGINIA
AND
MARYLAND

Sold by Thomas Basset in Fleetstreet
and Richard Chiswell in St. Pauls
Church yard.

A Scale of English Miles

QVI MAL Y PENSE HONI SOIT

M A R Y L A N D.

V I R G I N I A.

CHESEAPEAKE BAY.

Konekotays

Minquaas

Tockwoghs

Minquaa s

Sauwan

Safsquahana

PART OF
NEW IARSY.

Delawar
Bay

Baltimore C.

Anne Arundel

Charles C.

Stafford C.

Westmerland C.

Rappahanock C.

New Kent

Cecil C.

Henrico C.

City C.

Surry C.

Isle of Weight C.

Nantemond

Lower
Norfolk C.

Carotuk C.

PART OF

CAROLINA

Albemarle C.

Albemarle River

Cape Charles

Cape Henry

Smiths I.

Acconac C.

T H E   N O R T H   S E A.

F. Lamb Sculp.

MAP 41

Carolina

Lamb (Francis) *A New Description of Carolina*. London, Thomas Bassett and Richard Chiswell [1676 or later].

Engraved by Francis Lamb this map, like that of Virginia and Maryland (see map 40), appeared for the first time in the final edition of John Speed's *Prospect*. Some of the detail is taken from John Ogilby's map of 1672(?), including some of John Lederer's misconceptions concerning the interior, for example the *Arenosa Desart* and the large lake at the southern end of the Appalachians (called by Lederer *The Lake of Usury*) and here shown as *Ashley Lake*. William P. Cumming commented, 'The errors that Lederer made lived after him and became fruitful, for they were laid down in fertile soil.'

Nevertheless, Lamb's map presents a useful contemporary picture of the settlement of the colony, particularly in the swampy areas around Albemarle, where in 1653 Virginia had established settlers to guard the southern flank, and Charleston, laid out in 1670 on the banks of the Ashley River.

A New
DESCRIPTION
OF
CAROLINA.

Sold by The Basset in Fleetstreet,
and Ric: Chiswell in St Pauls
Churchyard.

A Scale of Eightsiz Miles

MAP 42

New England

Seller (John) *A Mapp of New England by John Seller Hydrographer to the King And are to bee sold at his Shop at the Hermitage in Wapping And by John Hills In Exchange Alley in Cornhill London.* [1676 and later.]

This remarkable map shows the results of a war with King Philip of Mounthope, chief of the Wampagnoag Indians in the Plymouth area of New England, who led an uprising against the colonists in 1675. After some initial success, during which Swansea, Massachusetts, was destroyed, Philip gradually succumbed to the colonists and was trapped and killed in August 1676.

Philip's story became part of local folklore. To the right of the Connecticut River on Seller's map can be seen settlers firing at an Indian attack, presumably an illustration of the defence of Hadley on 1 September 1675.

At least three states of Seller's handsome map are known: this is a later state, showing the dedication to Robert Tomson completed to the immediate right of the title-cartouche, and with animals depicted near the Connecticut coast and a graticule (or grid) added to indicate latitude and longitude, as well as soundings in the waters off New York.

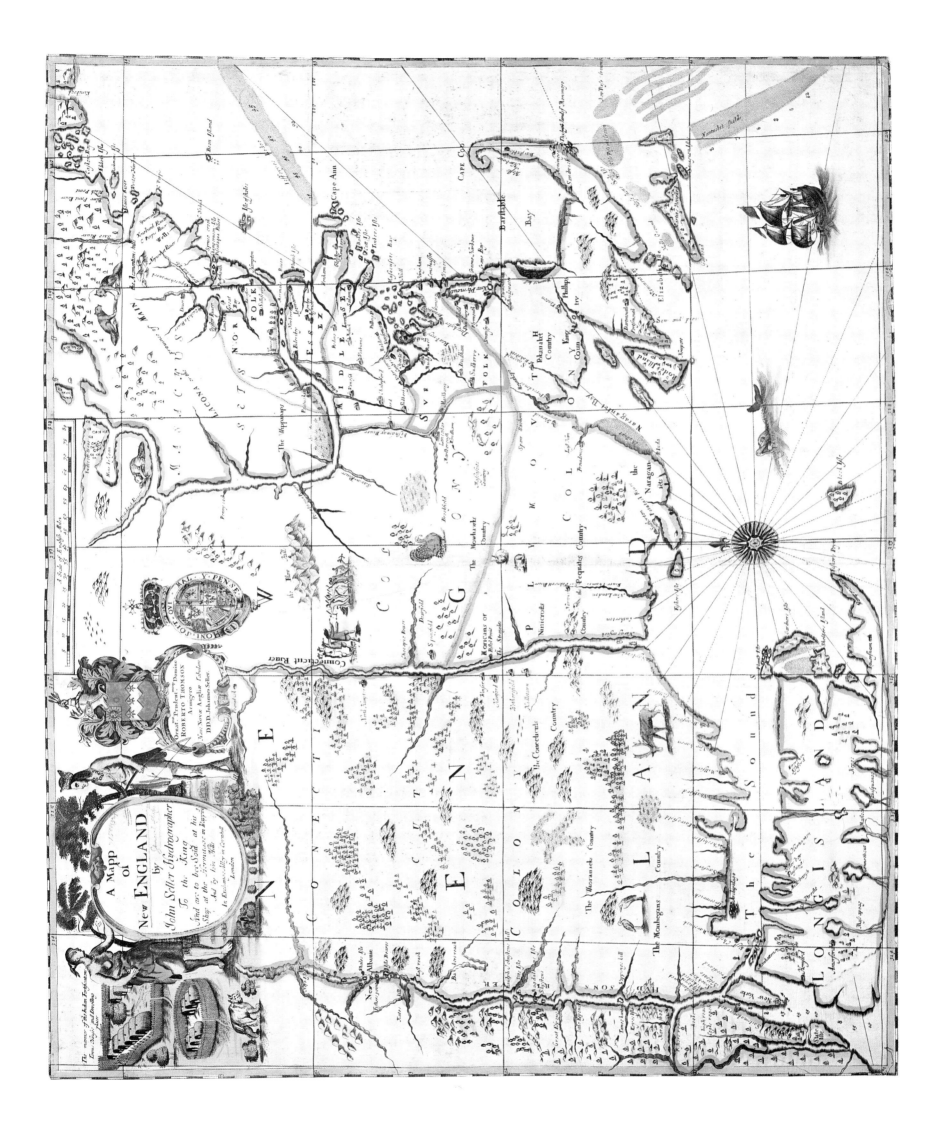

A Mapp of New ENGLAND by John Seller Hydrographer To the King And are to bee Sold at his Shop at the Hermitage in Wapping And by Iohn Hills in Exchainge Alley in Cornhill London

MAP 43

The Western Hemisphere

[Coronelli (Vincenzo Maria)] *Planisfero del Mondo Nuovo.* [Venice, 1688 and later.]

By the great Venetian mapmaker and publisher Vincenzo Maria Coronelli (1650–1718), founder of the World's first formally organized geographical society, the *Argonauti*, or *Accademia Cosmografo della Serenissima Republica*, this impressive map of the western hemisphere shows North America with California as a large island off the west coast.

It is an interesting mixture of fantasy and up-to-date geography: the favourite fantasy of California (albeit tempered by the thought that it may be a peninsula after all), the up-to-date in the form of the latest information pertaining to the Great Lakes from the Jesuit Relations, such as the accounts of La Salle, Jolliet, Franquelin and Marquette, with its delineation of the Mississippi valley based on La Salle and his report of the discovery of the mouth of the great river in 1682. Nevertheless, that great river is placed some six hundred miles too far to the west here.

This is one of the more attractive maps of North America of the late seventeenth century, and one of the very few of any geographical importance produced in Italy at the time.

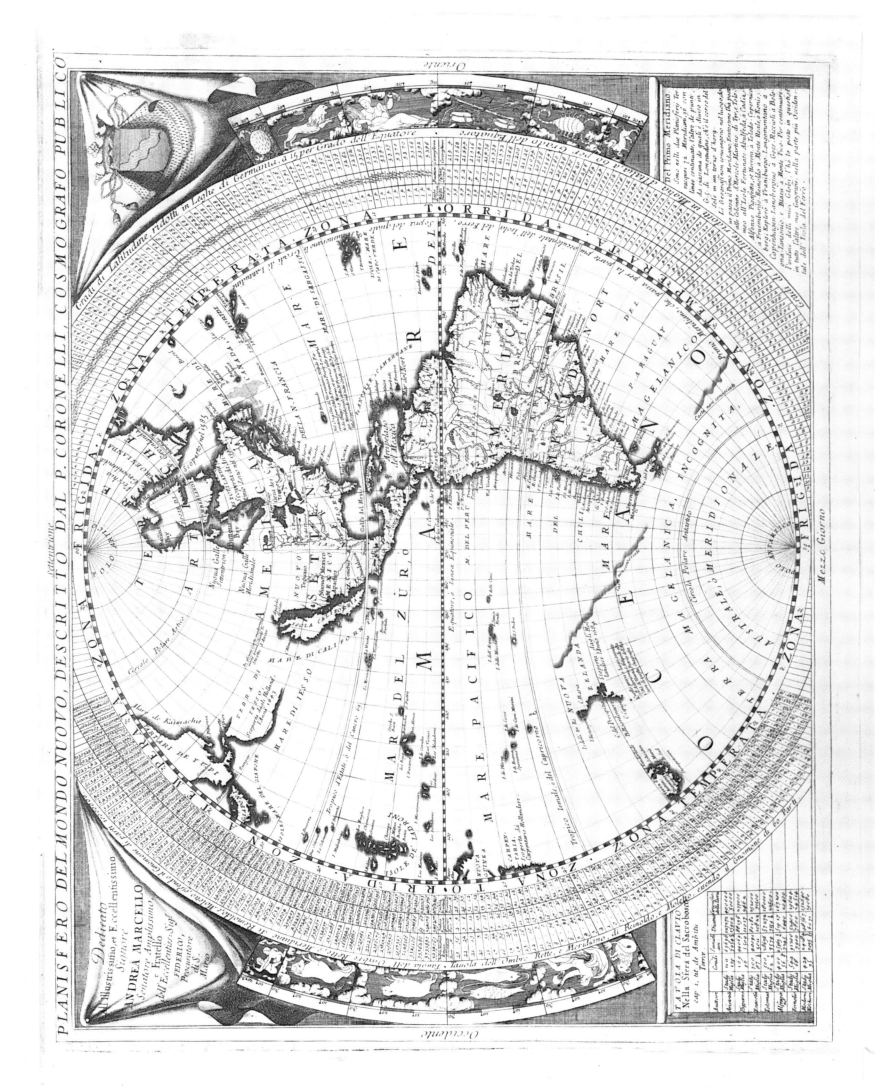

MAP 44

The Pacific Ocean

[van Keulen (Johannes)] Untitled chart of the Pacific Ocean and the western shores of North America. [Amsterdam, 1690 and later.]

Points of interest to note on this fine chart are the island of California, based on Sanson's outline of 1656 (see map 34), a hint of a possible Northwest Passage at its western end immediately to the north, and the large swathe of coastline stretching like a great land bridge from North America to Japan, after the reports of Dutch navigators in these waters in the 1640s.

The van Keulen family ran a large, highly organized firm publishing sea charts and chart atlases for some two hundred years, from the 1680s to the early 1880s. Many of their charts were reprinted several times over, the present chart appearing almost unchanged in their atlases until well into the 1760s.

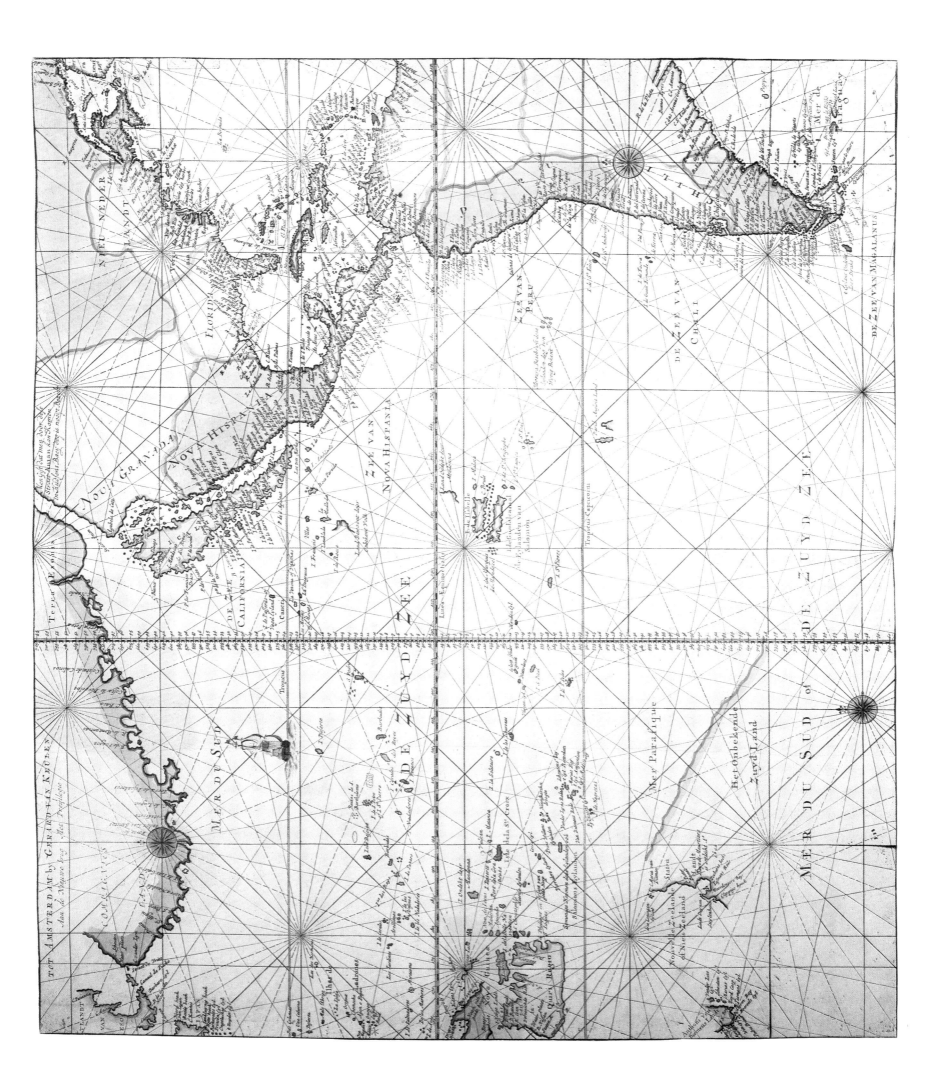

MAP 45

Louisiana

Coronelli (Vincenzo Maria) *La Louisiana, Parte Settentrionale, Scoperta sotto la Protettione di Luigi XIV, Rè di Francia, etc.* [Venice, 1695 and later.]

Coronelli's map of the northern part of the huge French trans-Appalachian territory of Louisiana gives a remarkably accurate outline of the Great Lakes. It is the best separate map of the five lakes published during the seventeenth century. It was based on the reports of French fur-traders and missionaries, such as the Jesuit fathers Simon le Moyne and Bréhaut de Galinée, and such printed maps as Jean-Baptiste–Louis Franquelin's map of 1681 or the so-called 'Jesuit Relation' map of 1672, which mapped Lake Superior in considerable detail.

The upper reaches of the Mississippi are here named as *F. Colbert, ò Mechissipi*, the name *Mechissipi* being derived from an Indian name used by Jacques Marquette in the text of his diaries of the explorations in 1672–1673. Farther south, below the Wisconsin River (here shown as *R. Ouisconsing*) is a short note stating that on 17 June 1673, Marquette and his companion Louis Jolliet were the first Europeans to sail into the Mississippi from the Wisconsin.

Although Coronelli's map is less decorative than many of its contemporaries, it is a much more important and informative map than most of its period.

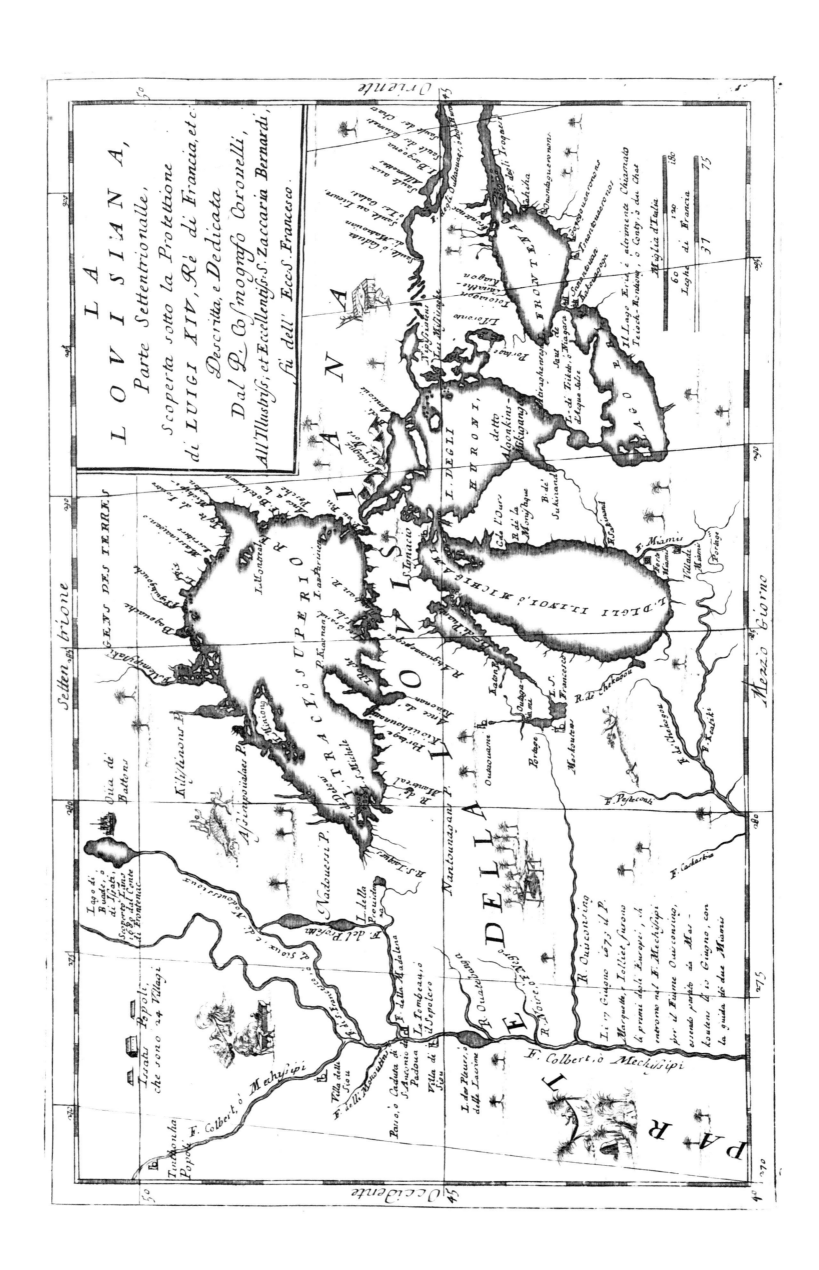

MAP 46

The Mississippi

[Hennepin (Louis, *SJ*)] *Le Cours du Fleuve Missisippi*. [1697, this issue Amsterdam, J.F. Bernard, 1737.]

This map shows Hennepin's claims in greater detail than his general map of North America (see map 47).

Here, although Hennepin manages to avoid too much inaccuracy in his depiction of the Mississippi, the river is still brought far enough west so that it flows near the mouth of the present-day Rio Grande in Texas, here marked as *Rivière de la Magdelaine*. The sources of the Mississippi are placed close together in the far northwest near a group of mountains and lakes, a concept—albeit erroneous—which had some longevity, remaining on maps of the region for many years afterwards. The correct positioning of the Mississippi had to await Guillaume de l'Isle's map *Carte de la Louisiane* of 1718 (see map 51 for a version of this).

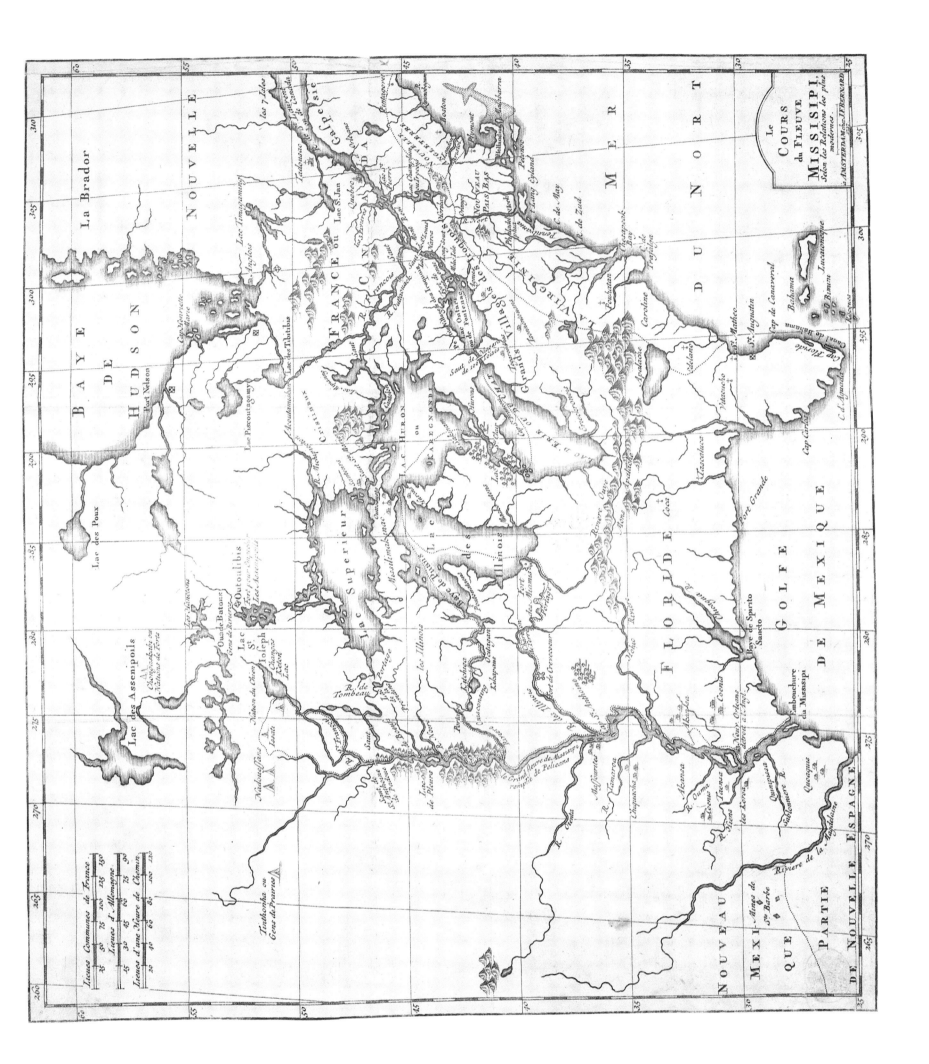

Le
COURS
du FLEUVE
MISSISIPI,
Selon les Relations les plus
modernes.
à AMSTERDAM chez J.F. BERNARD

MAP 47

North America

Hennepin (Louis, *SJ*) *Carte d'un tres grand Pays entre le Nouveau Mexique et la Mer Glaciale*. Amsterdam, A. van Someren, 1698 [this issue].

The Jesuit Father Louis Hennepin was an explorer and a missionary. He travelled with René-Robert de La Salle, a trader, who made a journey down the Mississippi in 1682 hoping to reach the Pacific, but instead achieving the Gulf of Mexico, thereby adding a large slice of North America to French claims west of the Appalachians, well away from the threat of British colonists.

Hennepin himself claimed to have been the first European to see and record Niagara. His account, *Nouvelle découverte d'un tres grand Pays situé dan l'Amérique*, first published in 1697, claimed also to be the account of his travels down the Mississippi to the Gulf coast. Hennepin had arrived in New France in 1675. He set off with La Salle in 1678. Although La Salle was forced to turn back in the first instance, Hennepin ventured farther up the Mississippi basin from Fort Crèvecœur (Chicago) and managed even to penetrate farther northwest than any European hitherto. La Salle's actual achievement was recorded in the continuation of Hennepin's book, the *Nouveau voyage d'un Pais plus grand que l'Europe*, published in 1698, and which also contains an account of the murder of La Salle in 1687.

During his short life (he was born in 1643), La Salle achieved much, discovering the Ohio River, and persuading the King of France to fund a project to establish a French colony in Texas, thereby bringing the mines of Spanish territory in Mexico closer to French hands. This scheme failed, and La Salle died in Texas at the hands of two members of his party as a result of a quarrel.

Hennepin, on the other hand, plagiarized many reports to write his works and to compile his map. The present map of North America shows the Mississippi—which he never navigated to the Gulf— placed too far to the west, and without a delta, hardly an accurate portrayal of one who claimed to have surveyed the river. It is doubtful, in fact, whether Hennepin really understood what he had heard about Louisiana.

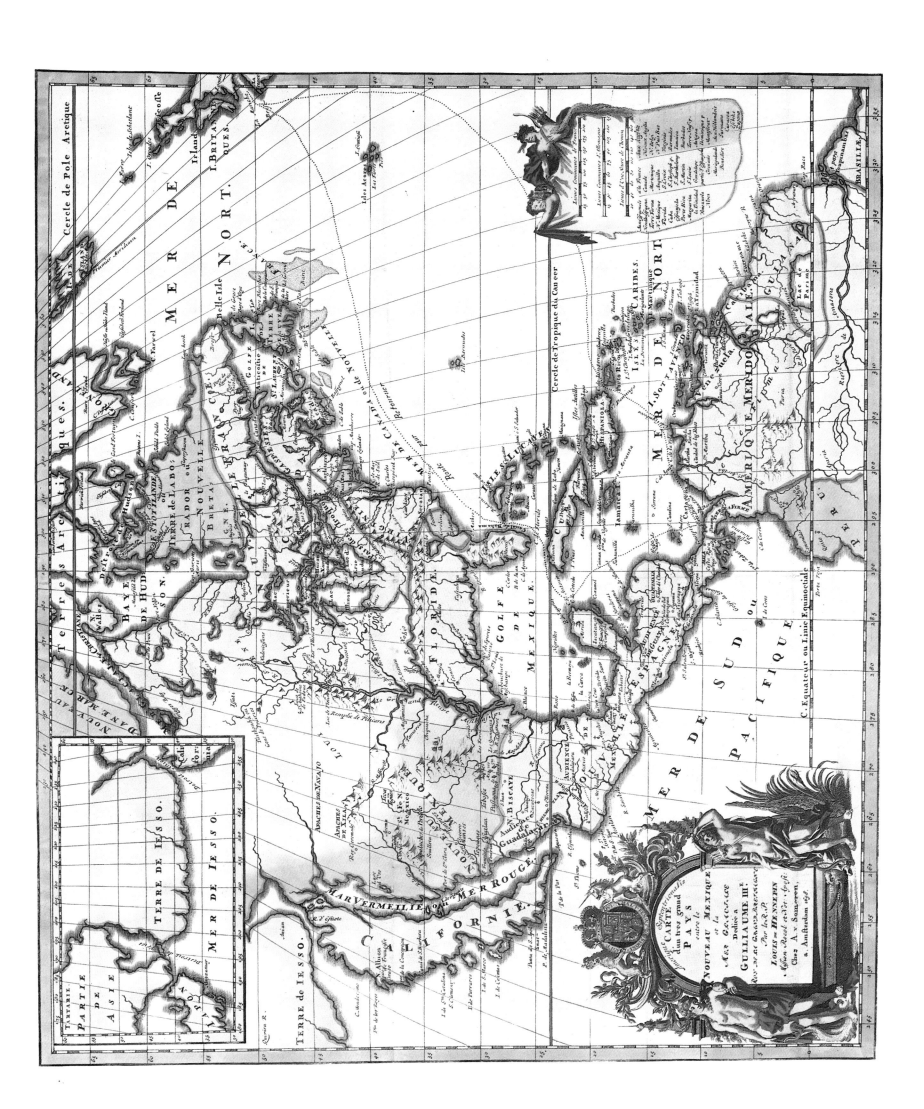

CARTE
d'un très grand
PAYS
entre le
NOUVEAU MEXIQUE
et la
MER GLACIALE
Dedié a
GUILLAUME III.
Roy. de la Grand. Bretagne.
Par le R.P.
LOUIS de HENNEPIN
Mißion. Recol. et Not. Ap. 1698.
Chez A. v. Someren.
a. Amsterdam 1698.

MER DE SUD ou PACIFIQUE

MER DE NORT.

BAYE DE HUDSON.

NOUVELLE FRANCE ou CANADA

FLORIDE

GOLFE DE MEXIQUE

NOUVELLE ESPAGNE

MEXIQUE

CALIFORNIE.

MER VERMEILLE ou MER ROUGE.

TERRE DE IESSO.

PARTIE DE ASIE

TARTARIE

MER DE IESSO.

Cercle de Pole Arctique

Cercle de Tropique du Cancer

C. Equateur ou Linie Equinoctiale

MAP 48

The Gulf of Mexico

de Fer (Nicolas) *Les Costes aux Environs de la Rivière de Misisipi. Découvertes par M'. de la Salle en 1683. et reconnues par M'. le Chevalier d'Iberville en 1698. et 1699.* Paris, 1702 [and later].

This map is based on French maps compiled by Jean-Baptiste-Louis Franquelin, Guillaume de l'Isle and others, in particular de l'Isle's manuscript of 1701, his *Carte des environs du Mississipi.* It shows Indian settlements found by Pierre le Moyne d'Iberville, founder of Louisiana, in early 1699 during his exploration of the hinterland on behalf of Louis XIV, spurred on by rumours of a rival English claim to the Mississippi valley.

The map also contains, slightly out of place, detail based on René-Robert de La Salle's expedition south from Canada in 1682 in his search for the mouth of the great river. In his report, La Salle was convinced that the river flowed close to the Spanish mines in Mexico, thus making them easy prey for exploitation by a gold-hungry king to boost his flagging finances.

It might be said that, armed with the knowledge contained in these discoveries, France was presented with a most remarkable opportunity to occupy and exploit the trans-Appalachian North American continent and from two directions—either by way of Canada, or by way of the Gulf of Mexico.

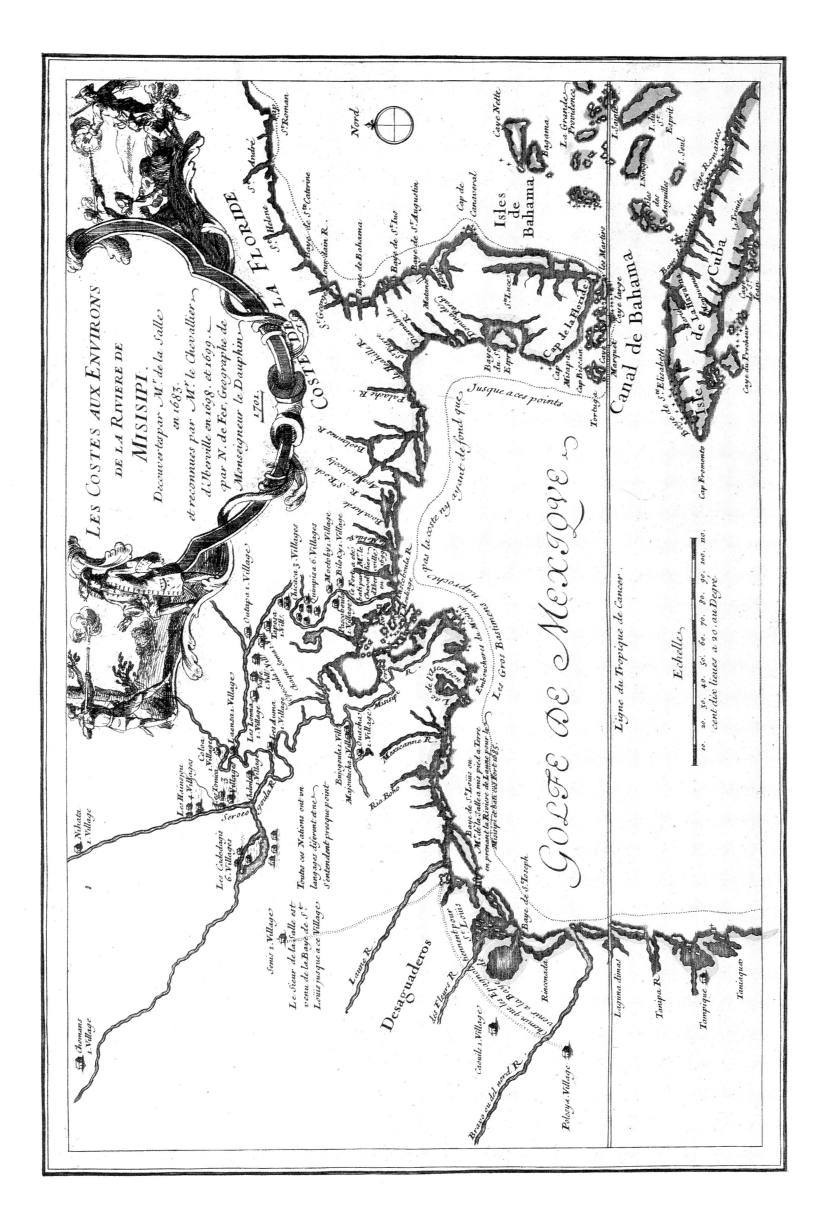

LES COSTES AUX ENVIRONS
DE LA RIVIERE DE
MISISIPI.

Decouvertes par Mr. de la Salle
en 1683.
et reconnues par Mr. le Chevallier
d'Iberville en 1698. et 1699.
par N. de Fer, Geographe de
Monseigneur le Dauphin.

1701.

COSTE DE LA FLORIDE

Nord

Isles
de
Bahama

Canal de Bahama

Isle de Cuba

GOLFE DE MEXIQUE

Ligne du Tropique de Cancer.

Echelle.

10. 20. 30. 40. 50. 60. 70. 80. 90. 100. no.
cent dix lieues a 20. au Degré.

Desaguaderos

MAP 49

The Mississippi Basin

Homann (Johanne – Baptist) *Amplissimae Regionis Mississippi seu Provinciae Ludovicianae à R.P. Ludovico Hennepin Francisc. Miss. in America Septentrionali Anno 1687 detectae.* Nürnberg [1714 and later].

This handsome map by the most famous German mapmaker of the eighteenth century follows closely Guillaume de l'Isle's map of 1718 (see map 51) and incorporates a scenic vignette of Niagara.

    That de l'Isle's map had so many imitators in the eighteenth century underlines the facts of French expansion in North America during the reign of Louis XIV; of the search for routes leading to California and Mexico; of the search for regions more habitable and hospitable than the cold valley of the St Lawrence River; of the search for lands beyond English influence; and of the ever-present search for gold and silver to replenish royal coffers emptied by wars in Europe.

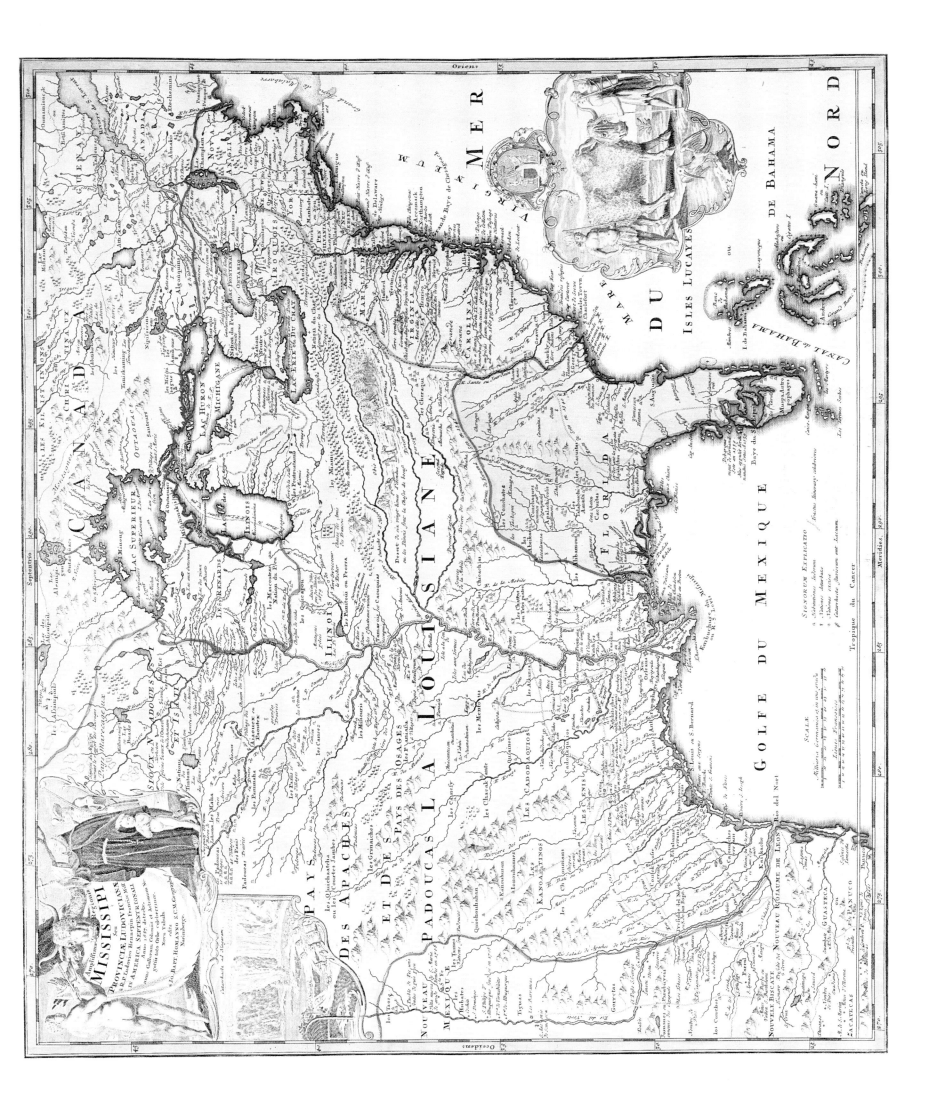

MAP 50

New England

Homann (Johann-Baptist) *Nova Anglia Septentrionali Americae implantata Anglorumque coloniis florentissima Geographice exhibita*. Nürnberg [1716 or later].

Homann's map was the standard eighteenth-century German atlas map of the Northeast, extending from New Jersey to the St John River, the latter forming the boundary between New England and New France.

The map is characterized by its large Lake Champlain—*Lac Champlain of Meer der Irocoise*—with its broad channel draining northwards into the St Lawrence; the location of two sizeable lakes in New York province—*Sennecaas Lacus* draining into the Delaware and *Groote Esopus* rivers, and *Lac Maquaas* nearby. Much other topographical detail is pure fantasy, with many of the interior and feature names confined to the immediate vicinity of the waterways. Note also that Cape Cod is shown as an island—a sort of cartographical counter to the island of California, perhaps.

The large title-cartouche at the lower right depicts Europeans engaged in bartering with the local Indians.

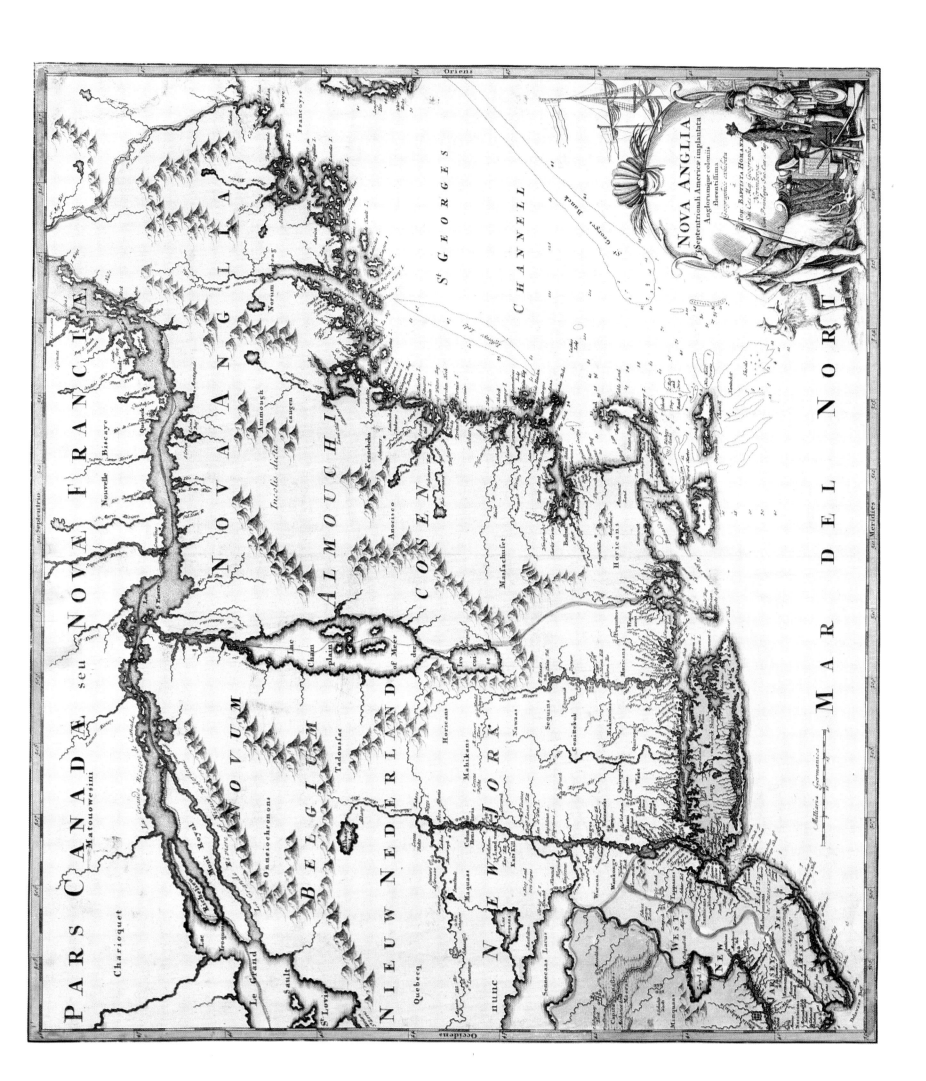

NOVA ANGLIA
Septentrionali America implantata
Anglorumque coloniis
florentissima
geographice exhibita
à Ioh. Baptista Homann
Sac. Cæs. Maj. Geographo
Norimbergæ
cum Privilegio Sac. Cæs. Maj.

PARS CANADA seu NOVA FRANCIA

NOVA ANGLIA

NOVUM BELGIUM

NIEUW NEDERLAND nunc NEW JORK

ALMOUCHIQUOSEN

St GEORGES CHANNELL

MAR DEL NORT

Oriens

Occidens

Meridies

Septentrio

MAP 51

Louisiana and the Mississippi

de l'Isle (Guillaume) *Carte de la Louisiane et du Cours du Mississipi.* [Paris, 1718: this edition Amsterdam, J. Covens and C. Mortier, *c.*1745.]

The French claims beyond the Appalachians and in Canada.

This map was first issued by Guillaume de l'Isle in 1718, the illustration showing a close copy published in Amsterdam during the 1740s. The detail of this Covens and Mortier issue is essentially unaltered from the original French issue and illustrates several important features: its accurate mapping of the entire Mississippi system, the chief authority, in fact, for half a century; the upper Mississippi and Ohio Rivers with their several tributaries; indications of the Missouri River, much of this information having been gathered direct from French explorers and fur-traders. Also indicated are Texas, shown by the *Mission de los Teijas* established in 1716; New Orleans, founded in 1718; an overview of Hernando de Soto's explorations in the Southeast in 1539–1542, Alonso de Leon's in 1689, as well as French travels in 1716 by St Denis.

De l'Isle's map caused angry English reaction on its first appearance. Note that France claims practically all of North America to the west of the Appalachians, the English seaboard colonies deliberately reduced in extent and scale by the pink colouring on this example. A little fantasy, however, creeps in by way of the Michigan peninsula, with the long range of mountains along its central area (see map 54).

Although new discoveries were made subsequent to the first publication of de l'Isle's map, the *Carte de la Louisiane* remained a great influence for many years and spawned many derivatives and imitators.

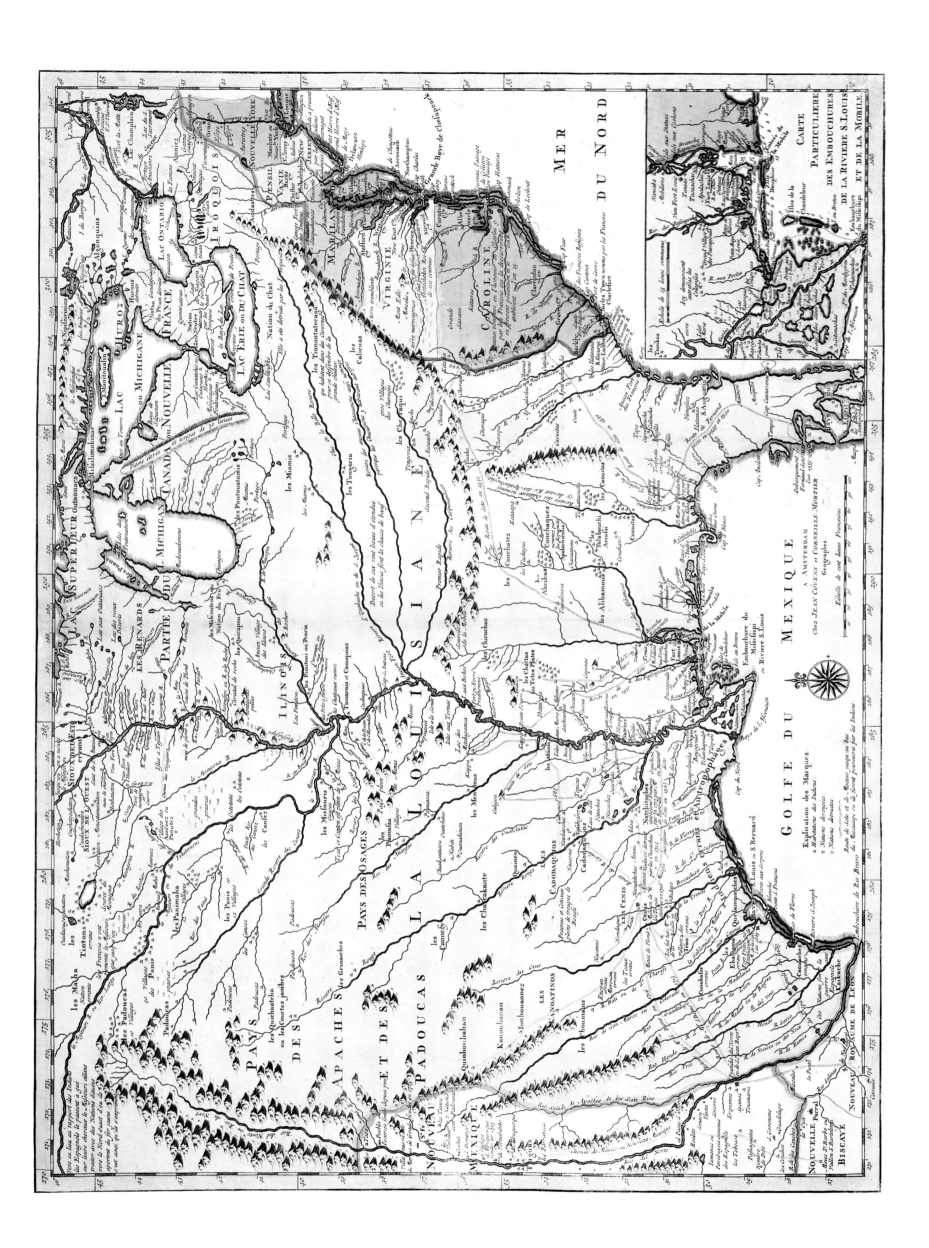

MAP 52

America

[Châtelain (Henri-Abraham)] *Carte très curieuse de la Mer du Sud, contenant des Remarques Nouvelles et très utiles non seulement sur des Ports et Îles de cette Mer, mais aussy sur les principaux Pays de l'Amérique tant Septentrionale que Méridionale, avec les Noms & la Route des Voyageurs par qui la découverte en a été faite.* [Amsterdam, l'Honoré & Châtelain, 1719 and later.]

From volume VI of Châtelain's *Atlas historique*, this is one of the most decorative and impressive maps of the Americas available. Printed on four large sheets, it is of wall-chart proportions and is a veritable pictorial encyclopaedia of the western hemisphere, including Japan and Australasia, North and South America and the western shores of the Old World.

Clockwise from the top left, the many vignettes include Niagara with beavers in the foreground and a hunting party, medallion portraits of explorers, fishing, the Straits of Gibraltar, the Cape of Good Hope, Vera Cruz, Rio de Janeiro, La Habana, Rio de la Plata, Concepción, an Aztec temple, Mexico, Valdivia, mining, Lima, the Mississippi delta, Canadian Indian customs, Panamá, and the Marianas in the Western Pacific. The routes of explorers, including Magellan (1520) and Schouten and Le Maire (1616) are also shown.

As is common to many maps of America published at this time, California is shown as a large island off the west coast. Here, it is based on Sanson's map of 1656 (see map 33). Many mission stations are shown here, probably derived from Nicolas de Fer's map of [1700]: *S. Marc, S. Mathieu, S. Rosalie, S. Juan, S. Bruno, S. Etienne, S. Jean,* and *S'. Innocents.* The Louisiana region is unlike that mapped in Châtelain's near-contemporary map *Mexique et Floride* (1719) which was published in the same atlas, based on Guillaume de l'Isle's map of 1703. Here, the Mississippi is located too far to the west and Robert de La Salle's discoveries of 1684–1685 are wrongly dated as 1683. The Ohio River is too far to the south, and is drawn in again as the Wabash to the north, comparable with Coronelli's maps of North America of 1689 and 1696 (see map 45).

Almost nothing of the discoveries of Louis de St Denis in the region in 1713 and 1716 or the discoveries in the Red River valley are shown. And in the Pacific, the Solomon Islands are put several degrees too far to the east, almost as if deliberately to fill what otherwise would be a large empty space.

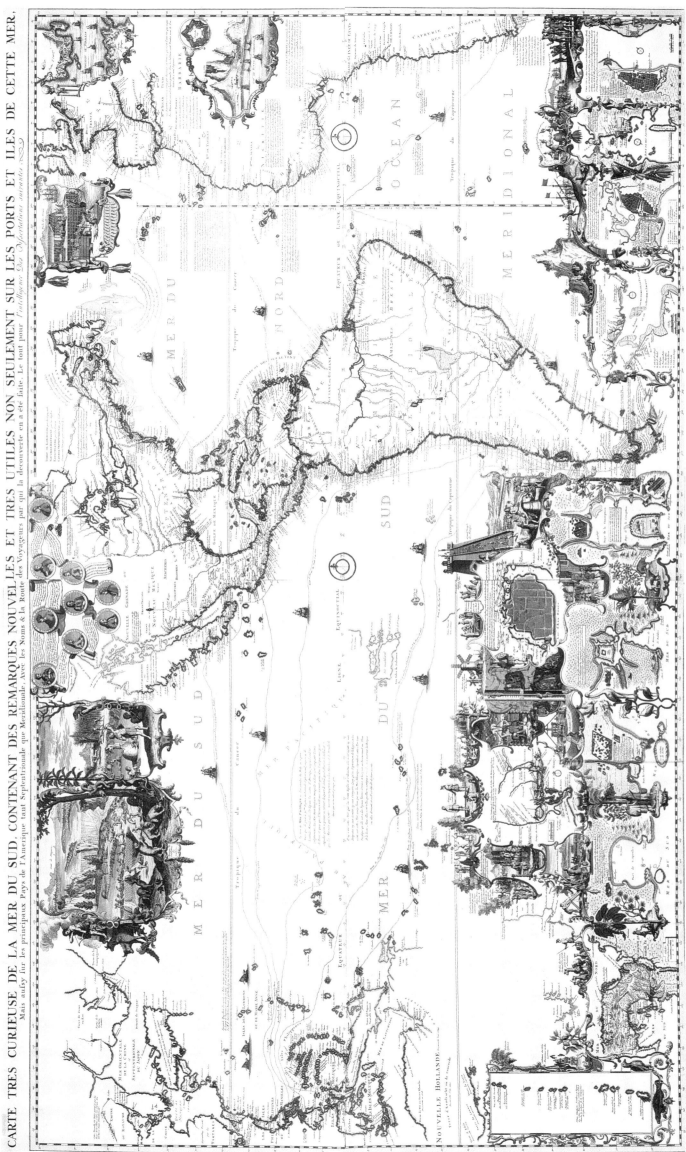

CARTE TRES CURIEUSE DE LA MER DU SUD, CONTENANT DES REMARQUES NOUVELLES ET TRES UTILES NON SEULEMENT SUR LES PORTS ET ILES DE CETTE MER,
Mais auffy fur les principaux Pays de l'Amerique tant Septentrionale que Meridionale Avec les Noms & la Route des Voyageurs par qui la decouverte en a été faite. Le tout pour l'intelligence Des Differtations fuivantes

MAP 53

North America

Moll (Herman) *To the Right Honourable John Lord Sommers . . . This Map of North America According to ye Newest and most Exact Observations is most Humbly Dedicated.* [London, 1720 and later.]

In 1718, the Frenchman Guillaume de l'Isle published his map *Carte de la Louisiane* (see map 51) which showed the French claims encompassing the whole of trans-Appalachian North America. Here, Herman Moll presents his counter-blast by reducing French Louisiana to south of the Ohio River and pressing English claims in Canada by labelling Labrador as *New Britain*, together with the territory ceded to Britain by the Treaty of Utrecht in 1713 in the form of Newfoundland, Acadia and the vast lands around Hudson Bay. As was so often the case where treaties attempted to codify and formalize vague geographical ideas, boundaries were not defined precisely, leading in later years to many disputes in the bay area and elsewhere in Louisiana, Carolina and Florida.

Note, too, that Moll continues with his favourite geographical myth, the island of California—here modelled on Sanson's map of 1656 (see map 34)—that wonderfully persistent notion which did not die out, cartographically speaking, until almost the very end of the eighteenth century.

As is often the case with Moll's larger maps, a fine pictorial title-piece is incorporated into the design, here showing Indians and Inuit paying homage to the crest of Lord Somers, President of the Privy Council, together with small insets illustrating the cod fisheries of Newfoundland, and detail plans of St John's, Boston, New York, Charleston, Port Royal, La Habana, Portobello, Vera Cruz, Cartagena, and Acapulco.

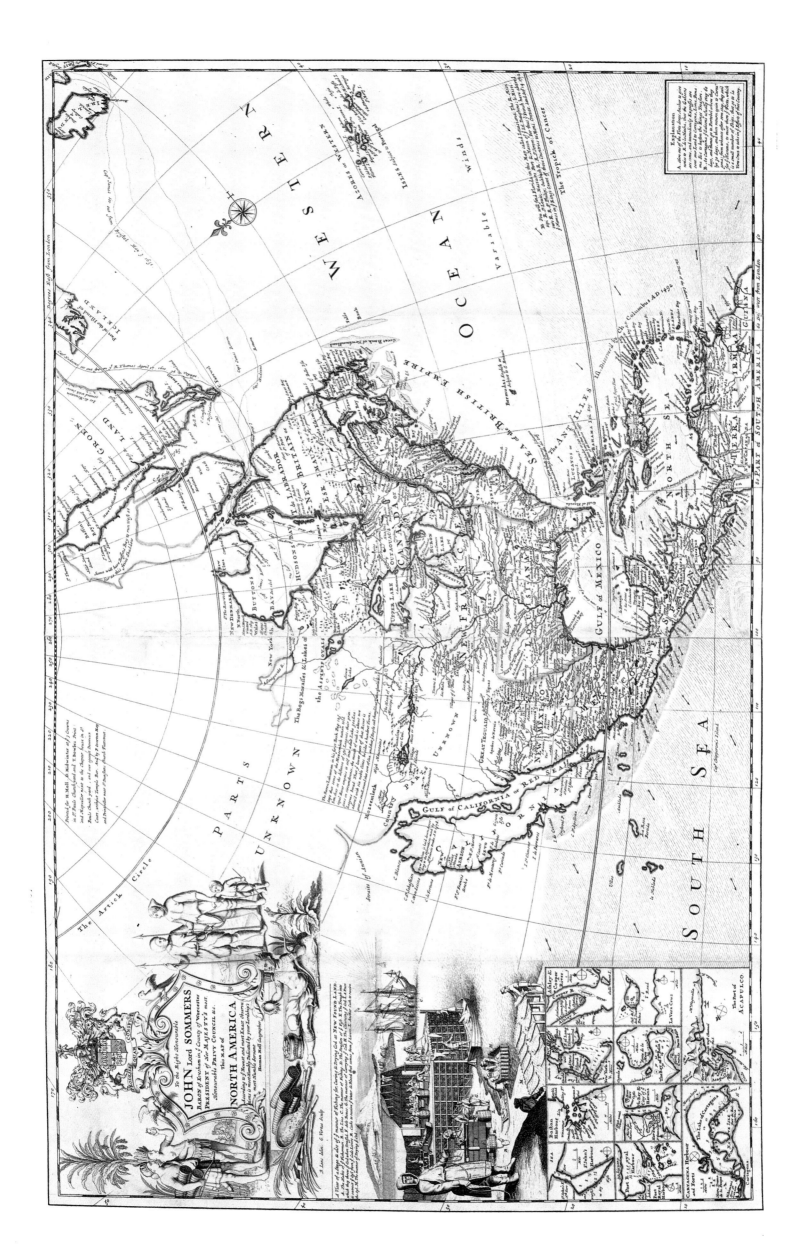

MAP 54

The English Empire in America

Senex (John) *A New Map of the English Empire in America viz Virginia Maryland Carolina New York New Iarsey New England Pennsylvania Newfoundland New France &c. Revis'd by Io. Senex 1719.* [London, Daniel Browne and others, 1721.]

Engraved by John Harris and published in this form in Senex's *New General Atlas*, this map covers the greater part of North America east of the Mississippi, extending from Hudson Bay to the Gulf of Mexico.

Senex's map has impressive origins. It makes available, almost unchanged, the map by Robert Morden and Christopher Browne, 1695(?), which itself closely follows a yet earlier map, that by Richard Daniel, of 1679. Like other maps of its kind, coverage extends to show interesting information beyond the area immediately called for by the title: in this case the Great Lakes as well as the Carolina and Florida regions. In the case of the Great Lakes, in central Michigan, there appears a long range of entirely fictitious mountains, connecting across the area of present-day Ohio with the Appalachians—'On the top of those Mountains is a Plaine like a Terras walk above 200 miles in length'—a 'geographical monstrosity' followed as late as the early nineteenth century by some mapmakers. Other information shown borrows from the 1672 Jesuit Relation map and other maps of French origin.

In the Carolina and Virginia Tidewater areas the features of Lederer's maps are still seen—the lake called *Ashley Lake* with its shoreline town of *Ushery*, the *Large Savana*, the *Desert Arenosa* and the triple-branched Appalachian range extending deep into the Florida peninsula. The gradual spread of colonial settlement, albeit some years advanced by the appearance of this map 'Revis'd' by Senex, encroaches along the seaboard below the Fall Line to New London and Carolina. *Charles Town* nestles comfortably at its new site at the confluence of the Ashley and Cooper Rivers.

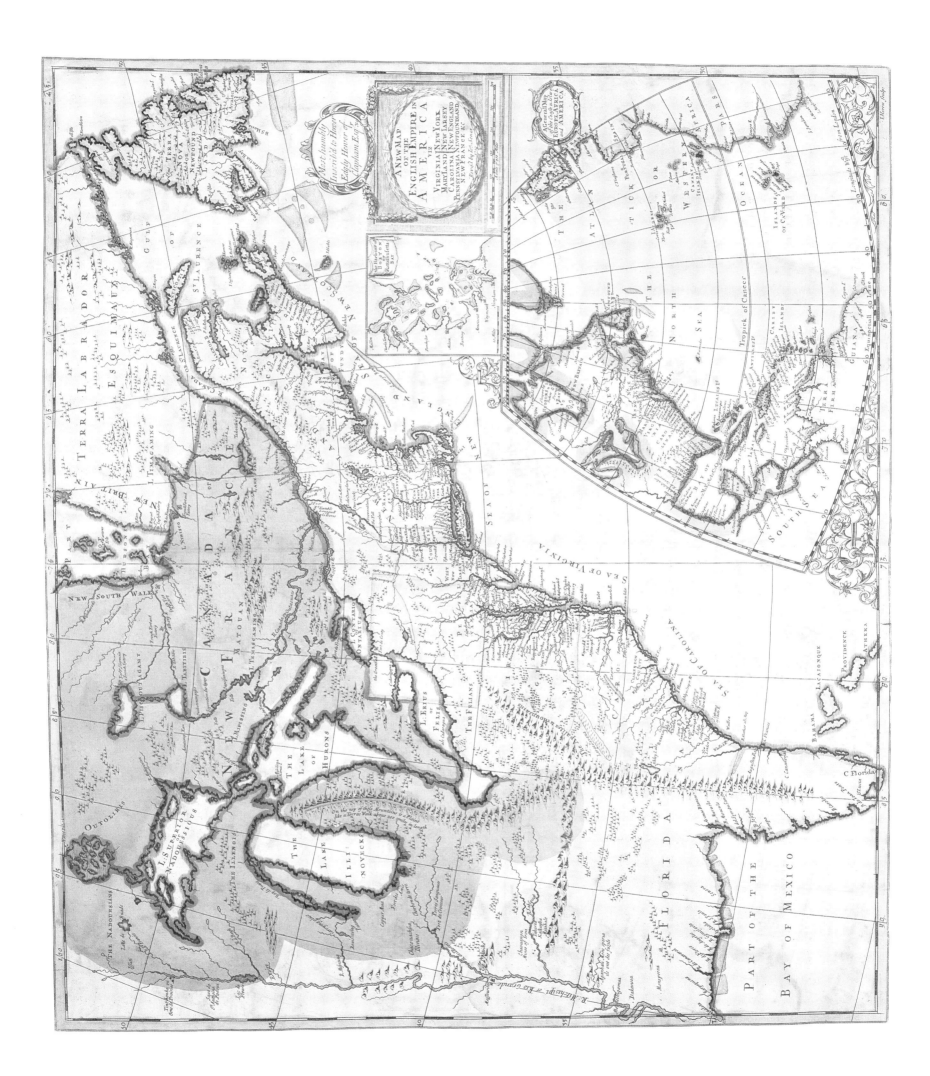

A NEW MAP
OF THE
ENGLISH EMPIRE IN
AMERICA
VIZ
VIRGINIA | NEW YORK
MARILAND | NEW IARSEY
CAROLINA | NEW ENGLAND
PENNSYLVANIA | NEW FOUNDLAND
NEW FRANCE &c.

Most humbly
Inscribed to Henry
Edgly Hevver Esqr.
of Popham Esqr.

The Harbour of
BOSTON in
Massachusetts
Bay

MAP 55

Eastern America

Popple (Henry) *America Septentrionalis. A Map of the British Empire in America with the French and Spanish Settlements adjacent thereto.* London, 1733.

Engraved by William Henry Toms. This single-sheet map forms the index to Henry Popple's twenty-sheet survey of North America, the earliest large-scale map published during the colonial period, and the first English map to name all Thirteen Colonies.

Henry Popple published his map during a time of conflict between the English and French in the north in Canada, and in the west in Louisiana, and between the English and Spanish in the south in Florida. In effect, therefore, the English colonies of the eastern seaboard found themselves entirely surrounded.

Increased French exploration and the activities of fur-traders in the Mississippi valley heightened English fears in this respect, since France claimed not only Canada, but also all the territories drained by the Mississippi and its tributaries—in practical terms, an area of half the continent. England and France disputed for many years the fishing rights off Nova Scotia and the Grand Banks. Added to these problems was the constant threat of attacks on colonists' settlements by Indians allied to the French, leading to the establishment of several frontier forts in the Ohio valley region.

Popple's map, published in atlas form, was issued under the aegis of the Lords Commissioners of Trade and Plantations with an endorsement by Dr Edmond Halley, seen at the lower right: 'I have seen the above mentioned Map, which as far as I am Judge, seems to have been laid down with much Accuracy, and to shew the Position of the different Provinces & Islands in that Part of the Globe more truly than any yet extant.'

So, by the time of publication, many old and widely held misconceptions concerning the interior of North America had been dispelled: the coastal regions, the Great Lakes, most of the Mississippi system and large parts of the southern Midwest and Texas were now known.

A series of inset vignette views and small detail maps and plans adds to the comprehensiveness of the survey, including a view of New York (after William Burgis, 1720), Québec (after J.-B.-L. Franquelin, 1688), Niagara (after Louis Hennepin, 1698), Boston, New York and Charleston, and islands held by the colonial powers in the Caribbean—the English, French, Spanish and Dutch.

A MAP
of the *BRITISH EMPIRE* in
AMERICA
with the *FRENCH* and *SPANISH*
SETTLEMENTS adjacent thereto
by *Hen. Popple*

MAP 56

The Great Lakes

Bellin (Jacques Nicolas) *Carte des Lacs du Canada dressée sur les Manuscrits du Dépost des Cartes, Plans et Journaux de la Marine et sur le Journal du RP. de Charlevoix*. [Paris, 1744 and later to *c*.1800.]

This map, by the famous French map- and chartmaker Jacques Nicolas Bellin, was published in 1744 in Fr Pierre François-Xavier de Charlevoix's *Histoire et description générale de la Nouvelle France*, which is one of the best eighteenth-century descriptions and accounts of North America.

Charlevoix travelled to Canada in 1720 to inspect the Jesuit missions there. He journeyed throughout New France and Louisiana and down to the Gulf of Mexico via the Illinois and Mississippi Rivers in 1721–1722. He described in his work the possibilities and great beauty of the land he saw, especially near Natchez, mentioning such products as cotton, indigo and tobacco.

Bellin had access to official journals, sketches, maps and charts of the earlier explorers, using such sources with great care and discrimination to produce some of the finest mapping of French America available in the eighteenth century. It is qualities such as these which result in the high esteem with which much of Bellin's mapping is still regarded by the late twentieth-century collector.

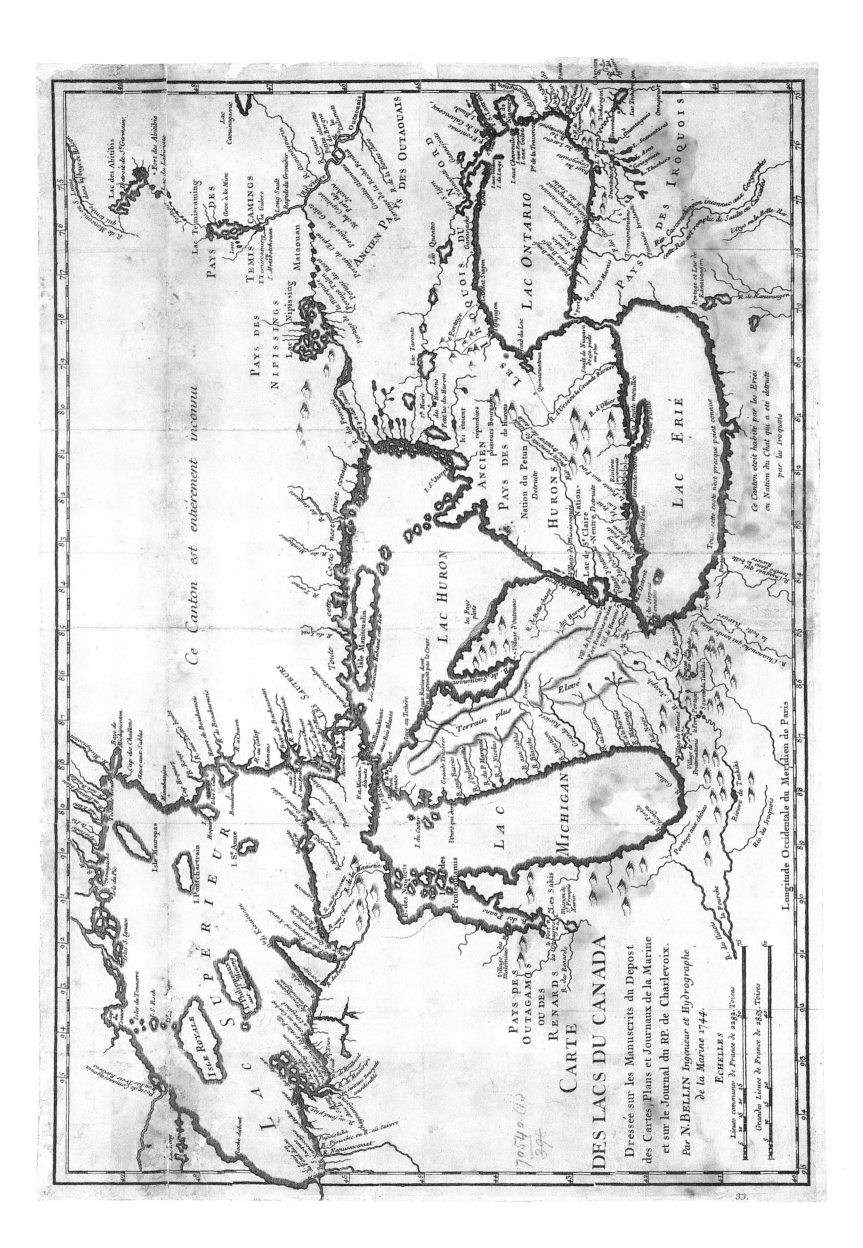

CARTE
DES LACS DU CANADA

Dressée sur les Manuscrits du Depost
des Cartes, Plans et Journaux de la Marine
et sur le Journal du R.P. de Charlevoix.
Par N. BELLIN Ingenieur et Hydrographe
de la Marine 1744.

ECHELLES

Lieues communes de France de 2424. Toises

Grandes Lieues de France de 2853. Toises

Longitude Occidentale du Meridien de Paris

Ce Canton est entierement inconnu

Ce Canton etoit habité par les Eriés
ou Nation du Chat qui a été detruite
par les Iroquois

MAP 57

Virginia and Maryland

Fry (Joshua) and Peter Jefferson *A Map of the most Inhabited part of Virginia containing the whole Province of Maryland with Part of Pensilvania, New Jersey and North Carolina. Drawn by Joshua Fry & Peter Jefferson in 1751.* [London, Robert Sayer and Thomas Jefferys, 1754; this issue 1775 and later.]

A highly influential map of the colonies of Virginia and Maryland, showing the hinterland and valleys of the Allegheny and Appalachian ranges beyond the Tidewater, with a good indication of the ridge-and-valley topography of the region. It was drawn up in 1751 and published for the first time in 1754.

By order of the Lords Commissioners of Trade and Plantations, dated 19 July 1750, the Thirteen Colonies were required to commission an accurate survey of their lands. Joshua Fry was Professor of Mathematics at William and Mary College, and Peter Jefferson was a surveyor, also father of the future President of the United States. Having already made surveys of the boundary of Virginia and North Carolina in 1749, Fry and Jefferson submitted their draft of the present map in 1752. Their survey of 1751 used surveys by earlier mapmakers and surveyors, as well as their own original detailed work. The work of John Dalrymple in the western reaches of the province contributed to the mapping of that part and the Fry–Jefferson map saw extensive dissemination in Thomas Jefferys's important and influential *North American Atlas* in 1775–1776.

The map is the basic cartographic document for Virginia in the eighteenth century. Thomas Jefferys is believed to have engraved the geographical detail himself, while the distinctive pictorial title-cartouche at the lower right was engraved by Reynolds Grignon after Francis Hayman, the whole representative of the best in cartographic engraving in England in its time.

A Map of
the most INHABITED part of
VIRGINIA
containing the whole PROVINCE of
MARYLAND
with Part of
PENSILVANIA, NEW JERSEY and NORTH CAROLINA

MAP 58

The Middle British Colonies

Evans (Lewis) *A General Map of the Middle British Colonies in America*. [London, Carington Bowles, 1 January 1771 and later.]

This map first appeared in 1755 to illustrate an essay, *An Analysis of the Middle British Colonies*, printed by Benjamin Franklin at Philadelphia, with contemporary printings in London. It also saw service in numerous later atlases, considerably revised, up to as late as 1814.

Evans shows the British Colonies and the Ohio valley. His map rivalled John Mitchell's famous map of 1755 (see map 59) in its authority. Evans himself wrote in 1756: 'Although we have many copies of Mitchell's map, nobody pretends to look into them for any places in our borders.'

In 1750, Lewis Evans was commissioned by the Philadelphia Assembly to survey and map the region. Because of rival claims by France to this part of North America, particularly in the Ohio valley, much of his work had to be done in secret. It took Evans four years to complete his task. Publication, together with his essay, took place in 1755. In the *Analysis*, Evans underlined the necessity of permanent settlements in the border areas rather than mere trading posts in order to establish and uphold the legitimacy of any British claims.

Evans's map, in all its various forms, has been hailed as superior to English maps of the time, and was quoted as an authority in boundary disputes. It contributed in no small measure to informed knowledge of the Ohio region.

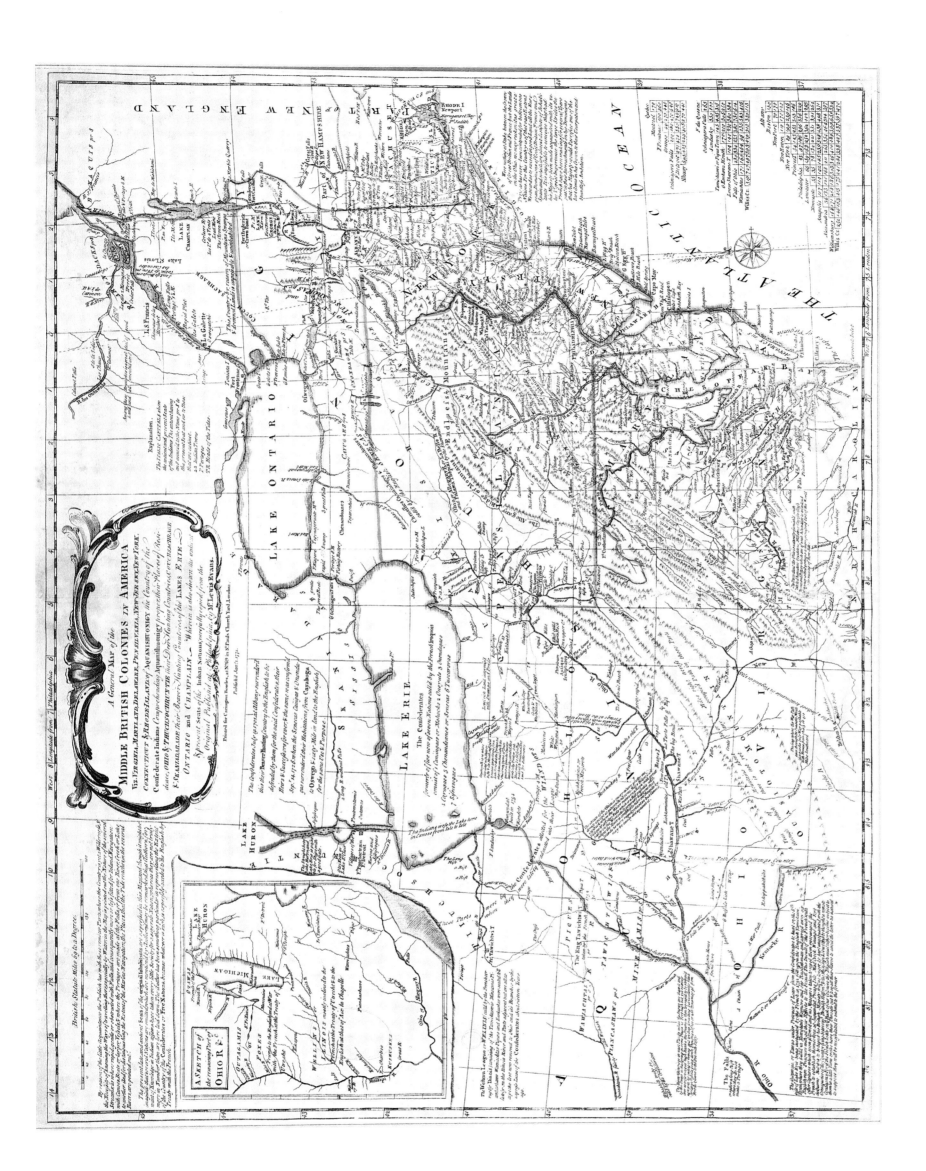

A General Map of the MIDDLE BRITISH COLONIES IN AMERICA.
Viz. VIRGINIA, MARYLAND, DELAWARE, PENSILVANIA, NEW JERSEY, NEW YORK,
CONNECTICUT & RHODE ISLAND: of AQUANISHUONIGY the Country of the
Confederate Indians Comprehending Aquanishuonigy proper, their Place of Residence Ohio &
Thuchsochruntie their Deer Hunting Countries Couchsachraga
their Beaver Hunting Countries of the LAKES ERIE,
ONTARIO and CHAMPLAIN—Wherein is also shewn the antient &
present Seats of the Indian Nations corespondingly copied from the
Original Published at Philadelphia by Mr Lewis Evans.

A SKETCH of
the remaining Part of
OHIO &c.

THE ATLANTIC OCEAN

MAP 59

The British Colonies in North America

Mitchell (John) *A Map of the British Colonies in North America, with the Roads, Distances, Limits, and Extent of the Settlements, Humbly Inscribed to the Right Honourable The Lords Commissioners for Trade & Plantations.* [London, by the Author, And Andrew Millar, 1755, but 1775 and later.]

The single most important map in American colonial history. Diplomatically, it was the basis for territorial boundaries drawn up in the treaties concluding the French and Indian War and the American Revolution, and has even been cited as evidence in boundary disputes during the present century, as recently as 1932 in fact.

Geographically, it incorporated knowledge derived from the close analysis of reports, journals and maps held in the archives of the Lords Commissioners for Trade and Plantations. John Mitchell's close friendship with Argyll and George Montague Dunk, second Earl of Halifax (President of the Board at the time, also hailed as 'The Father of the Colonies'), allowed him access to many unpublished sources. The numerous notes engraved in the blank sea areas on the map still provide a reliable source for historical study—these were added to the second edition of Mitchell's great map.

Mitchell's was the map referred to in the negotiations for peace for the Treaty of Paris during 1782–1783. Benjamin Franklin himself stated, in a letter to Thomas Jefferson: 'I now can assure you that I am perfectly clear in the Remembrance that the map we used in tracing the Boundary [on 6 December 1782] was brought to the Treaty by the Commissioners from England, and that it was the same that was published by Mitchell 20 years before.'

The copy illustrated here (the fourth edition of 1785), formerly in the collection of King George III and now in the British Library, London, is called the 'Red-Lined Map', so called after the manuscript additions (*c.*1782) by Richard Oswald (1705–1784) to make the boundary of the new United States with her neighbours—France in Louisiana and Canada, and Spain in Florida. Oswald was in business for many years in the North American colonies. During the years of the Revolution, because of his close association and friendship with Franklin, Oswald frequently acted as an adviser and consultant on matters pertaining to North America. Although he signed the Preliminary Articles of Peace on 30 November 1782, he was not present to sign the definitive Treaty on 3 September 1783, by which Britain formally recognized the United States. Instead, Britain was represented by David Hartley, an intimate of Franklin who had strongly opposed war with the colonists throughout the Revolution.

Altogether, some twenty-one distinct editions and impressions of John Mitchell's map in three languages—English, French (these published in Paris and in Amsterdam), and Italian—were published between 1755 and 1781, sufficient testimony to its importance, some of which are relatively easily obtainable for the collector today.

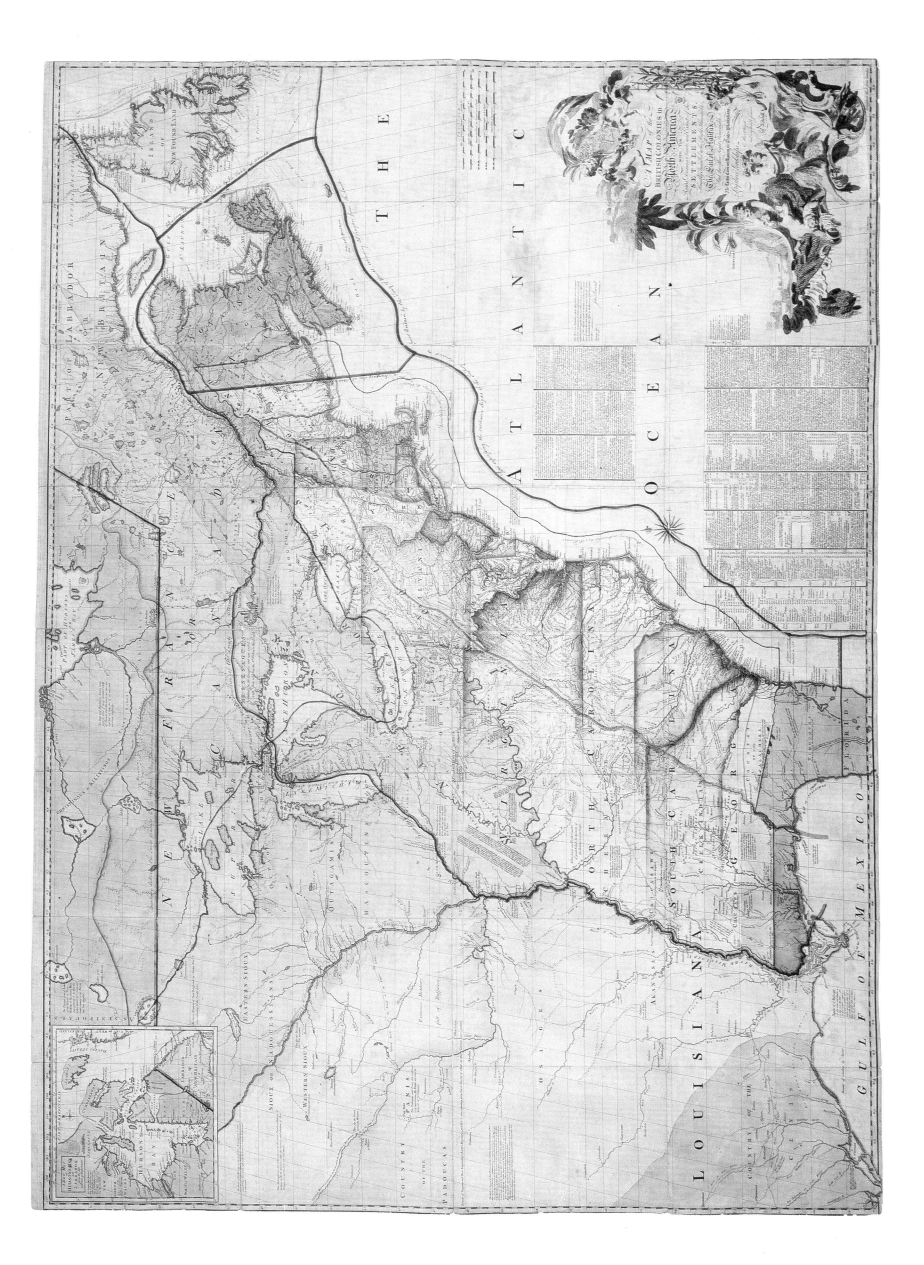

MAP 60

The Gulf of St Laurence

Jefferys (Thomas) *An Exact Chart of the River St Laurence, from Fort Frontenac to the Island of Anticosti . . . and all the necessary instruction for navigating that River to Quebec.* London, Robert Sayer, 1757 [and later].

This highly detailed, important survey of the St Lawrence, based on J.B.B. d'Anville's general map of 1755, with revisions from James Cook's survey of 1760, shows a series of insets including the river downstream from Lake Ontario to Orleans Island, together with enlargements of safe harbours and anchorages.

The map saw wide circulation through the editions of Jefferys's *North American Atlas*, and no doubt was used extensively following the confirmation of British government in the new province of Québec following the Royal Proclamation of 1763.

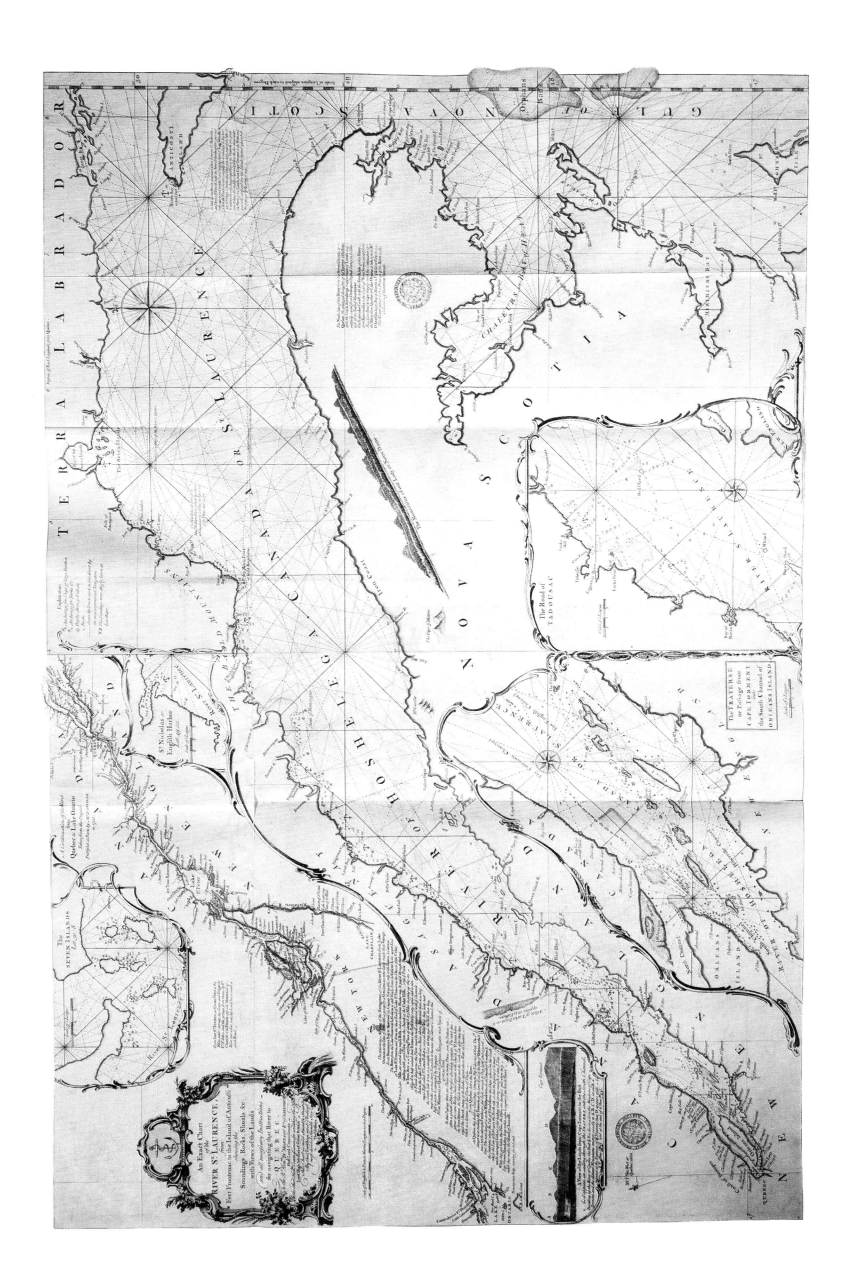

MAP 61

The Province of Quebec

Carver (Captain Jonathan) *A New Map of the Province of Quebec, according to the Royal Proclamation of the 2nd. of October 1763.* [London, Thomas Jefferys, this issue 1775 and later.]

The chief purpose of this map was to show the first boundaries of the new English province of Québec. When England came into the possession of French Canada by the Treaty of Paris of 1763, it was necessary to provide government and to establish defined boundaries for the new province. This was done by the Royal Proclamation mentioned in the title.

The map shows places visited by Carver—see also the detailed insets—during the recent French and Indian War. There were roads in existence on either side of the St Lawrence River running from Québec to Montréal, almost all of the original French settlement being concentrated in these two narrow riparian strips of territory.

Jonathan Carver was born in Canterbury, Connecticut, in about 1732. He served in the French and Indian War, narrowly escaping death near Fort William Henry. He was with General Wolfe at Québec in 1759, and was made up to captain in 1760.

Carver retired from the army later that year. Subsequently he travelled extensively throughout the northwestern parts of the colonies in 1766–1768, and left for England in 1769, where he lived until his death in 1780. His travels were published in his authoritative work, *Travels through the Interior Parts of North America,* in London in 1778.

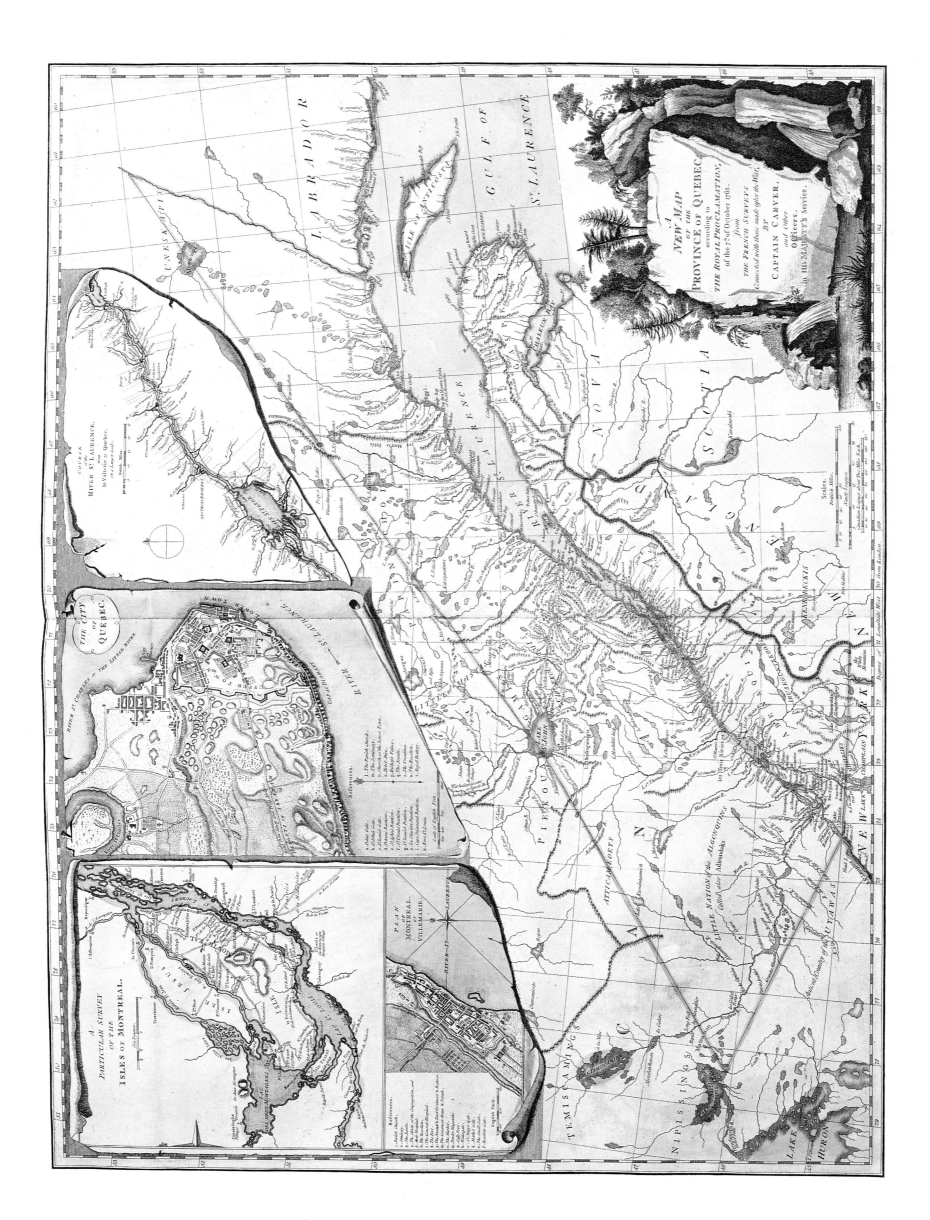

A NEW MAP OF THE PROVINCE OF QUEBEC, according to THE ROYAL PROCLAMATION, of the 7th of October 1763, from THE FRENCH SURVEYS Connected with those made after the War, BY CAPTAIN CARVER, and other Officers, in HIS MAJESTY'S Service.

COURSE of the RIVER St. LAURENCE, from In Valerie to Quebec, on a Larger scale.

THE CITY OF QUEBEC.

A PARTICULAR SURVEY OF THE ISLES OF MONTREAL.

PLAN OF MONTREAL or VILLEMARIE.

MAP 62

The Gulf of Mexico

Bellin (Jacques Nicolas) *Carte reduite du Golphe de Mexique et des isles de l'Amérique . . . Second Édition Année 17*. [Paris], Dépot de la Marine, [1764, this edition 1810 and later].

Jacques Nicolas Bellin (1702–1772), the most influential and most important chart publisher in eighteenth-century France, was responsible for a very large output of individual charts and chart atlases which were published for the use of the French navy, both royal and republican, and a little later, imperial.

His large chart of the West Indies straddles these historical periods: on first publication in 1764, France was a major colonial power in North America, holding vast territories in Canada and in the trans-Appalachian regions of the present-day United States. By 1810 however, those vast lands were lost to France, either by treaty or by purchase: Louisiana was sold to the United States in 1803 by Napoléon for less than 3 cents an acre. The area of some 828,000 square miles doubled the area of the United States and led to the opening up of the West.

Despite the somewhat fanciful rendering of the Florida Everglades on Bellin's chart, this was one of the best overall views of the West Indies available. When first published, it was available both as a separate chart as well as part of the *Hydrographie Français* chart atlas.

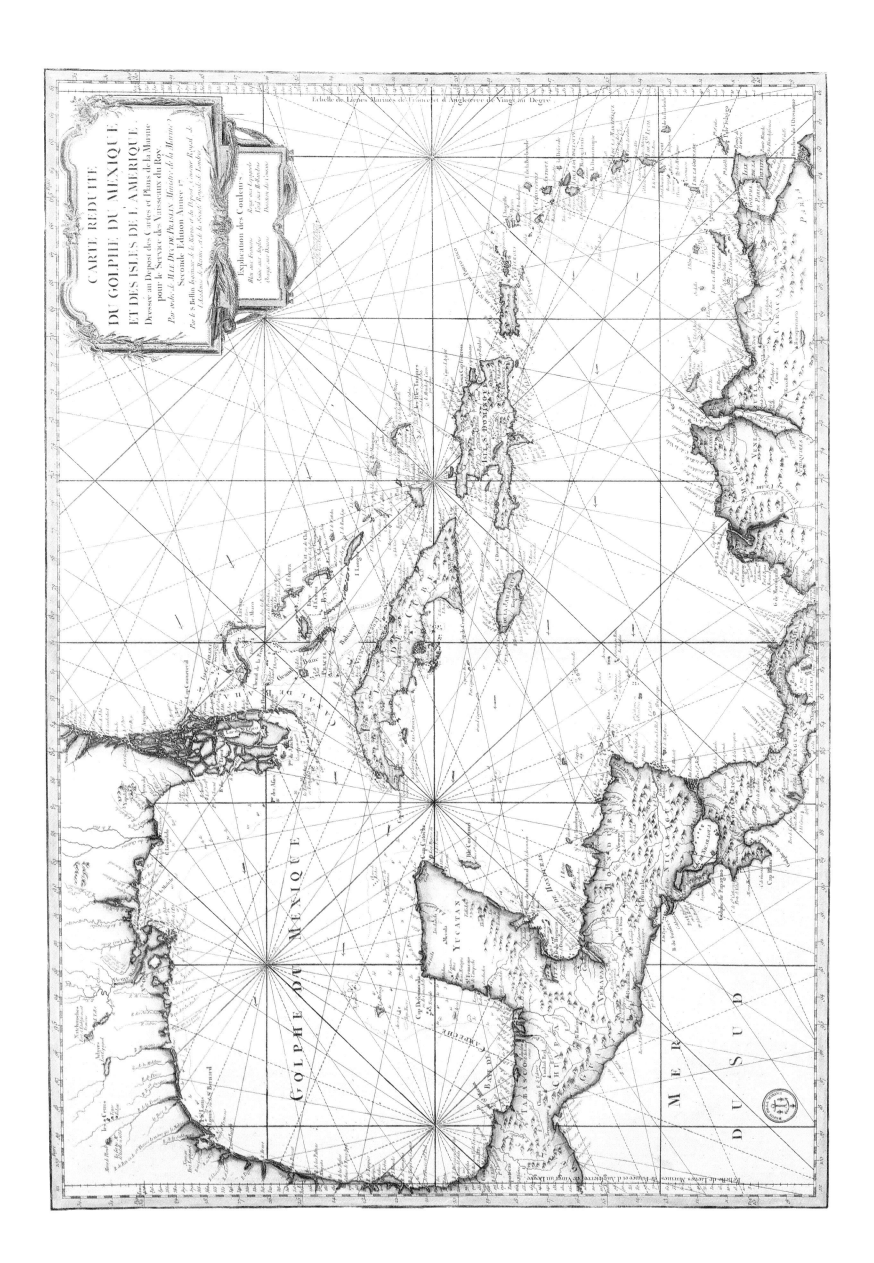

CARTE RÉDUITE DU GOLPHE DU MEXIQUE, ET DES ISLES DE L'AMÉRIQUE. Dressée au Dépôt des Cartes et Plans de la Marine pour le Service des Vaisseaux du Roy.

GOLPHE DU MEXIQUE

MER DU SUD

YUCATAN

ISLES DOMINGO

Echelle de Lieues Marines de France et d'Angleterre de Vingt au Degré

MAP 63

New Orleans

Tirion (Isaak) *Grondvlakte van Nieuw Orleans, de Hoofdstad van Louisiana; De Uitloop van de Rivier Missisippi; De Oostelyke ingang van de Mississippi, met een Plan van het Fort, 't welk het Kanaal beheerscht.* [Amsterdam, Isaak Tirion, c.1765.]

New Orleans was established on the east bank of the lower Mississippi in 1718 by Captain Celaron de Bienville at a point where the local Indians carried their canoes to Lake Pontchartain from the main river. The fort was laid out and built up by Le Blond de la Tour and Adrien Pauger in 1722. Having established their fort in order to control traffic on the Mississippi, the French then proceeded into present-day Alabama to counter the threat of rival British traders from the south-eastern colonies.

The plan shown here is a Dutch copy of a plan published by J-N. Bellin in 1764, forty or so years after the foundation of New Orleans. That it was founded at all may be as a result of Bienville's beliefs in the extravagant claims of the prosperity of Louisiana by financial promoters in Europe, such as John Law, whose *Compagnie de l'Occident* had received a charter from the French government.

As a capital city, New Orleans became a favourite settlement of the French, enjoying a considerable prosperity, with rich plantations laid out nearby. Even so, as late as 1797, not all of the land within the boundaries laid down by Bienville had as yet been built up.

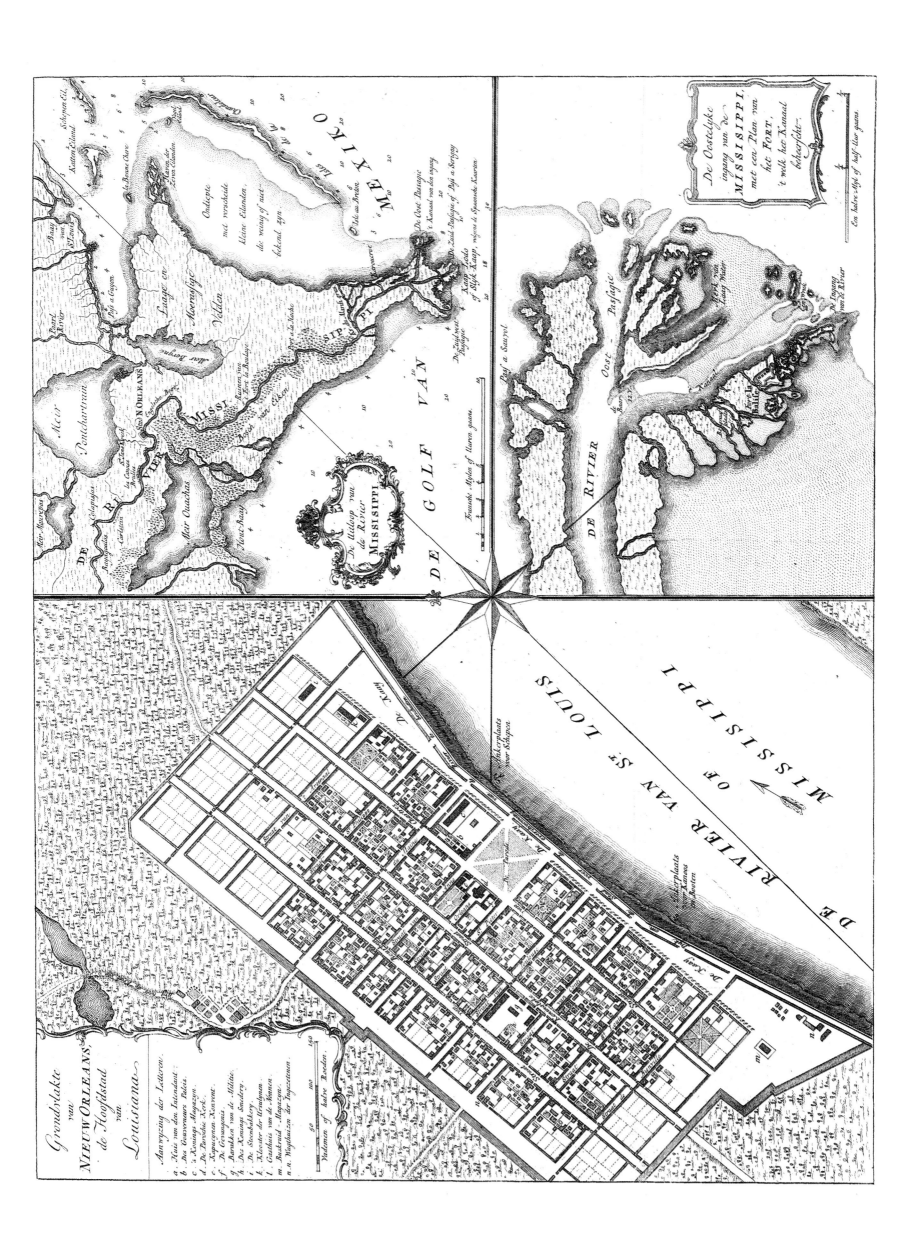

De Oostelijke
ingang van de
MISSISIPPI,
met een Plan van
het FORT,
't welk het Kanaal
beheerscht.

Een halve styd of half Uur gaans.

DE GOLF VAN MEXIKO

DE GOLF VAN

Fransche Mylen of Uuren gaans.

De Uitloop van
de Rivier
MISSISIPPI

DE RIVIER

Oost Passagie

DE RIVIER VAN St LOUIS of MISSISIPPI

Grondvlakte
van
NIEUW ORLEANS,
de Hoofdstad
van
Louisiana

Aanwyzing der Letteren.

a. Huis van den Intendant.
b. Das Gouverneurs Paleis.
c. 's Konings Magazyn.
d. De Parochie Kerk.
e. Kapucynen Konvent.
f. De Gevangenis.
g. Barakken van de Militie.
h. Des Konings Smidery.
i. De Steenbakkery.
l. Klooster der Ursulynen.
l. Gasthuis van de Konnen.
m. Bouwkruid-Magazyn.
n. n. Wagthuizen der Inspecteuren.

Vademen of halve Roeden.

MAP 64

The British Dominions in America

Kitchin (Thomas) *British Dominions in America.* [London, 1770 and later.]

This map is based largely on Kitchin's *A New and Accurate Map of the British Dominions in America*, published in 1763. It is here presented in the form published in Guthrie's *New Geographical Grammar*, showing the extent of the British claims in North America east of the Mississippi—thereby relegating the French claims in Louisiana to the relatively insignificant portion across the river, as this map would appear to show it.

Territorial disputes between England and France over their respective American claims and colonies finally came to a head during the 1750s, but a commission held in Paris in 1763 came to nought, having had to be abandoned during 1755 when the two countries became engaged in war in North America.

The province of Québec is here shown within the boundaries declared in 1763 (see also map 59) after England came into the possession of French Canada by the Treaty of Paris of that year, as well as the former Spanish settlements in Florida—here shown as East and West Florida.

Here, East Florida extends far to the north of the 31° parallel. This boundary was the subject of a separate dispute between Britain and Spain, Florida reverting to Spain once more in 1783.

Note also the names and locations of many Indian tribes and nations, particularly in the south and west, away from the more populated areas of European settlement.

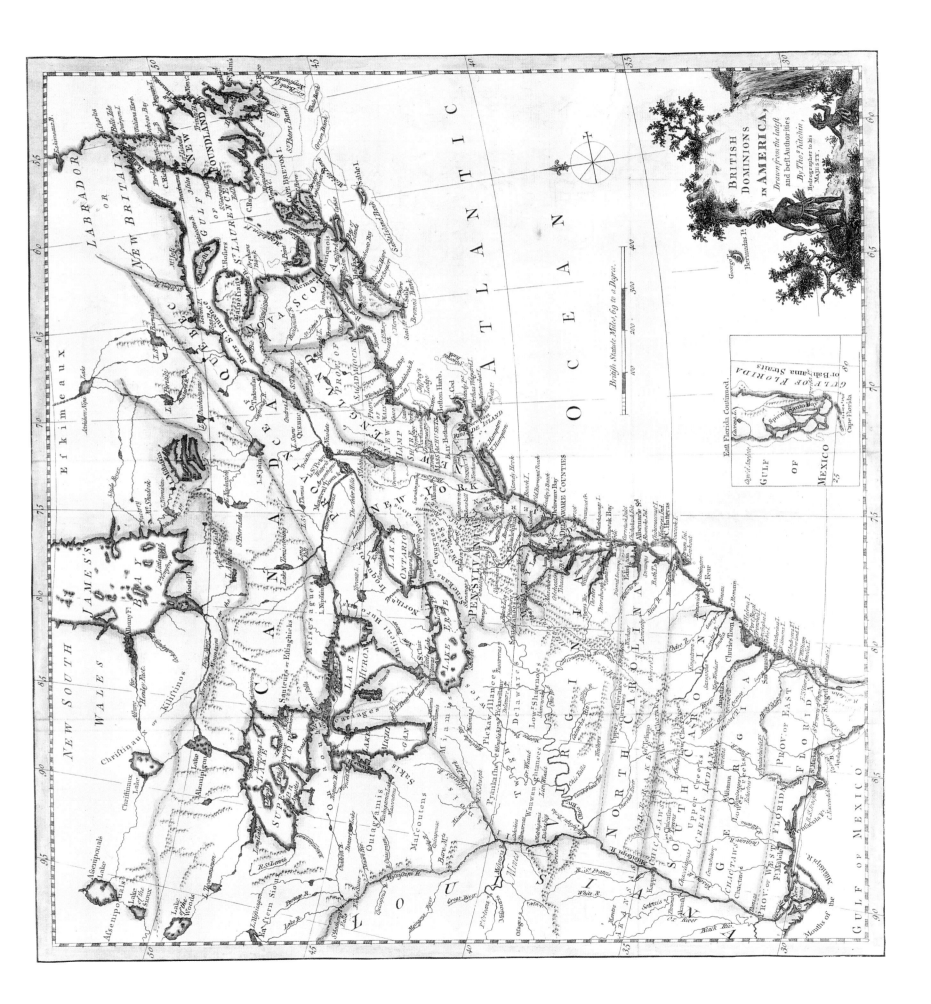

BRITISH
DOMINIONS
IN AMERICA,
Drawn from the latest
and best Authorities
By Thos. Kitchin,
Hidrographer to his
MAJESTY.

Georgy
Bermudas Is.

British Statute Miles, 69 to a Degree.
400 300 200 100

East Florida Continued.
GULF OF FLORIDA
or Bahama Streights

GULF
OF
MEXICO

Cape Florida
Spiritu Santo Bay

ATLANTIC

OCEAN

LABRADOR
OR
NEW BRITAIN

Erkimeaux

NEW SOUTH
WALES

JAMES'S
BAY

CANADA OR

QUEBEC

NEW
FOUNDLAND

GULF OF ST LAURENCE

NOVA SCOTIA

PROV. OF NEW ENGLAND

MASS.

NEW YORK

LAKE ONTARIO

LAKE ERIE

LAKE HURON

LAKE MICHIGAN

LAKE SUPERIOR

PENSILVANIA

RHODE ISLAND

C. Cod
C. Hatteras

MARYLAND
DELAWARE COUNTIES

VIRGINIA

NORTH CAROLINA

SOUTH CAROLINA

GEORGIA

PROV. OF EAST FLORIDA

PROV. OR WEST FLORIDA

LOUISIANA

GULF OF MEXICO

Mouths of the Mississippi

MAP 65

The Northwest Coast of America

Bowles (Carington) *A Map of the Discoveries made by the Russians on the North West Coast of America. Published by the Royal Academy of Sciences at Petersburg.* London, 1771 [and later].

This unusual map of the Northwest had its origins in a map published at St Petersburg in 1758 by Georg Friedrich Müller. It shows the results of the Bering and Chirikov explorations in 1741: the Shumagin, Aleutian and Kurile Islands, for example. The map demonstrates that there was still considerable uncertainty about the nature of the Northwest, for it neither proved nor disproved the existence of a Northwest Passage. But as an exercise in connecting disjointed portions of a coastline, the map remained the standard cartographic picture of the region for many years. Müller himself noted that his work had been 'no more than to connect together, according to probability, the coasts that had been separated in various places'.

Nevertheless, the map provided the best view of the Alaskan coastline and the far northern reaches of California between the Drake and Vizcaino voyages of the late sixteenth century and those of Captain James Cook in the North Pacific some two hundred years later. From time to time, the Spanish had attempted to put down settlements this far north, but without success—and even almost going to war with Britain in the mid eighteenth century over fur-trading settlements—most activity being confined to the occasional Russian fur-trading sorties along the coastal region, rather to the cost of the native seal population.

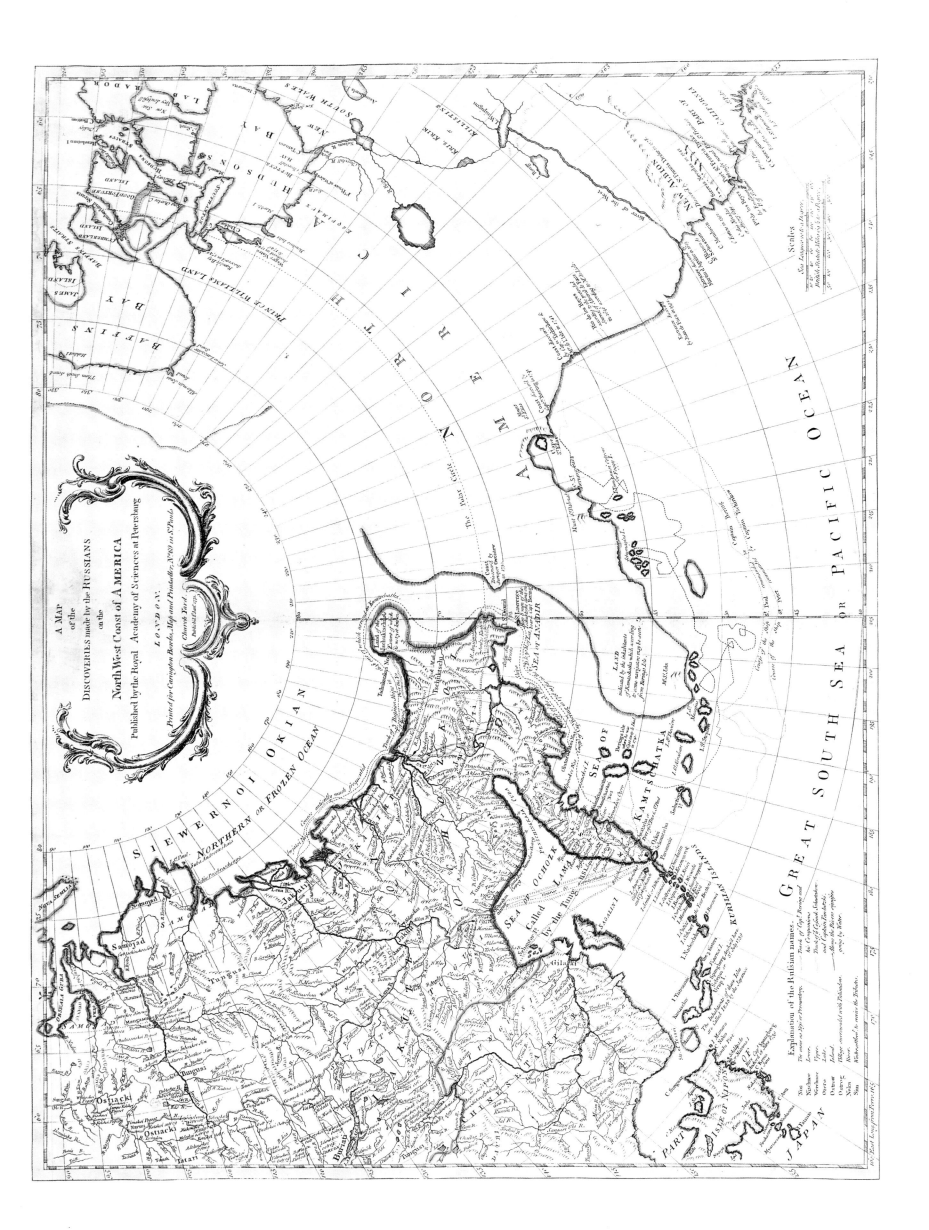

A Map
of the
DISCOVERIES made by the RUSSIANS
on the
North West Coast of AMERICA
Published by the Royal Academy of Sciences at Petersburg

LONDON:
Printed for Carington Bowles, Map and Printseller, No 69 in St Pauls
Church Yard.
Published Jan.t 1771.

MAP 66

New England

[Jefferys (Thomas)] *A Map of the most Inhabited part of New England; containing the Provinces of Massachusetts Bay and New Hampshire, with the Colonies of Connecticut and Rhode Island, Divided into Counties and Townships . . . November 29th. 1774.* [London, 1774 and later.]

Published in two large folding sheets in Jefferys's *North American Atlas* (1775), this detailed map of Connecticut, Rhode Island, Massachusetts, upstate new York, New Hampshire and part of Maine includes Long Island and part of New Brunswick.

It is the first detailed large-scale map of New England, at a scale of about seven miles to the inch. The surveyor's name is not given, but it is very likely that the map was the work of the Irish-born Braddock Mead, alias John Green (born *c*.1688), who edited several maps for Jefferys and others, as well as a series of books for Thomas Astley called *A new General Collection of Voyages* (1745–1747). A careful and meticulous editor, Green contributed much to scientific cartography and raised the standard of English mapmaking under Jefferys.

In this large map, we can observe some of those standards for ourselves—the emphasis on astronomical observation to establish the position of a town or feature, the citing of numerous authorities, and explanations of geographical terms (seen here at the right-hand side of the upper sheet). The finished map supplied information on the individual colonies, giving one of the earliest printed maps of Connecticut, for example. Detail insets show Boston and Boston Harbour.

The large vignette beneath the title-cartouche depicts the allegorical figure of an Indian bartering with European colonists.

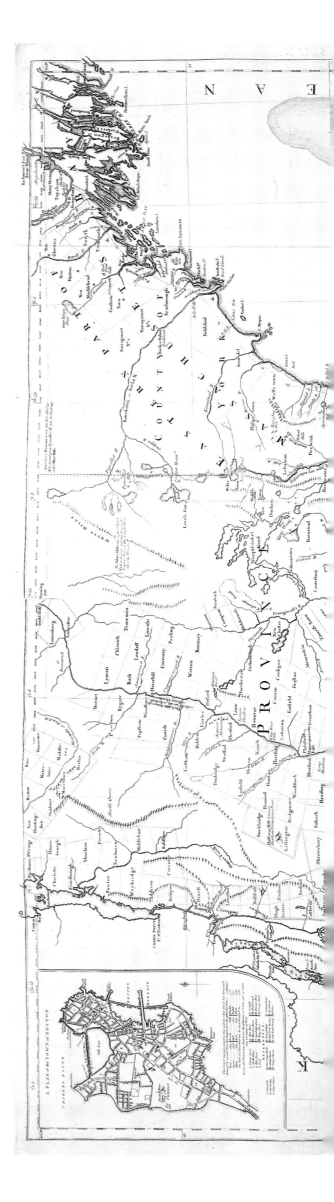

MAP 67

The Mississippi

Ross (Lieutenant John) *Course of the River Mississippi, from the Balise to Fort Chartes; Taken on an Expedition to the Illinois, in the latter end of the Year 1765. By Lieu^t. Ross of the 34th. Regiment: Improved from the Surveys of that River made by the French.* London, Robert Sayer, 1 June 1775, [and later].

Published on a scale of about one inch to fourteen miles, this map is the most detailed British military survey of the greater part of the Mississippi River, below the Ohio-Mississippi confluence. It is based in part upon Jean Baptiste Bourguignon d'Anville's large map of 1746 and his *Carte de la Louisiane* published in 1752.

   Fort Chartres in the north was the main centre of French administration, such as it was, in the Illinois region. Also shown is Fort Kaskaskia (built in 1756). These two forts were finally passed over to British administratin under the terms of the 1765 Treaty.

COURSE
OF THE
RIVER MISSISSIPI,
from the BALISE to FORT CHARTRES;
Taken on an EXPEDITION to the ILLINOIS,
in the latter end of the Year 1765.
BY
Lieut. Ross of the 34th Regiment:
IMPROVED
from the Surveys of that River made by the French.

LONDON
Printed for Robt. Sayer, No. 53 in Fleet Street
Published as the Act directs 1 June 1772.

CHIKASAWS

CHACTAWS
or
Flathead Indians

NATCHEZ

LAKE PONTCHARTRAIN

GULF OF MEXICO

MAP 68

North America

Dunn (Samuel) *A Map of the British Empire, in North America . . . improved from the Surveys of Capt. Carver.* [London, Robert Sayer and John Bennett, 17 August 1776, this issue.]

This map provides a general view of the situation in North America following the settlement of 1763, by which French Canada passed into British hands, cutting off Louisiana from the Great Lakes region and the east of Canada.

British territorial claims east of the Mississippi are shown, as well as the first established boundary of the new province of Québec, the subject of Jonathan Carver's fine map of 1753 (see map 61).

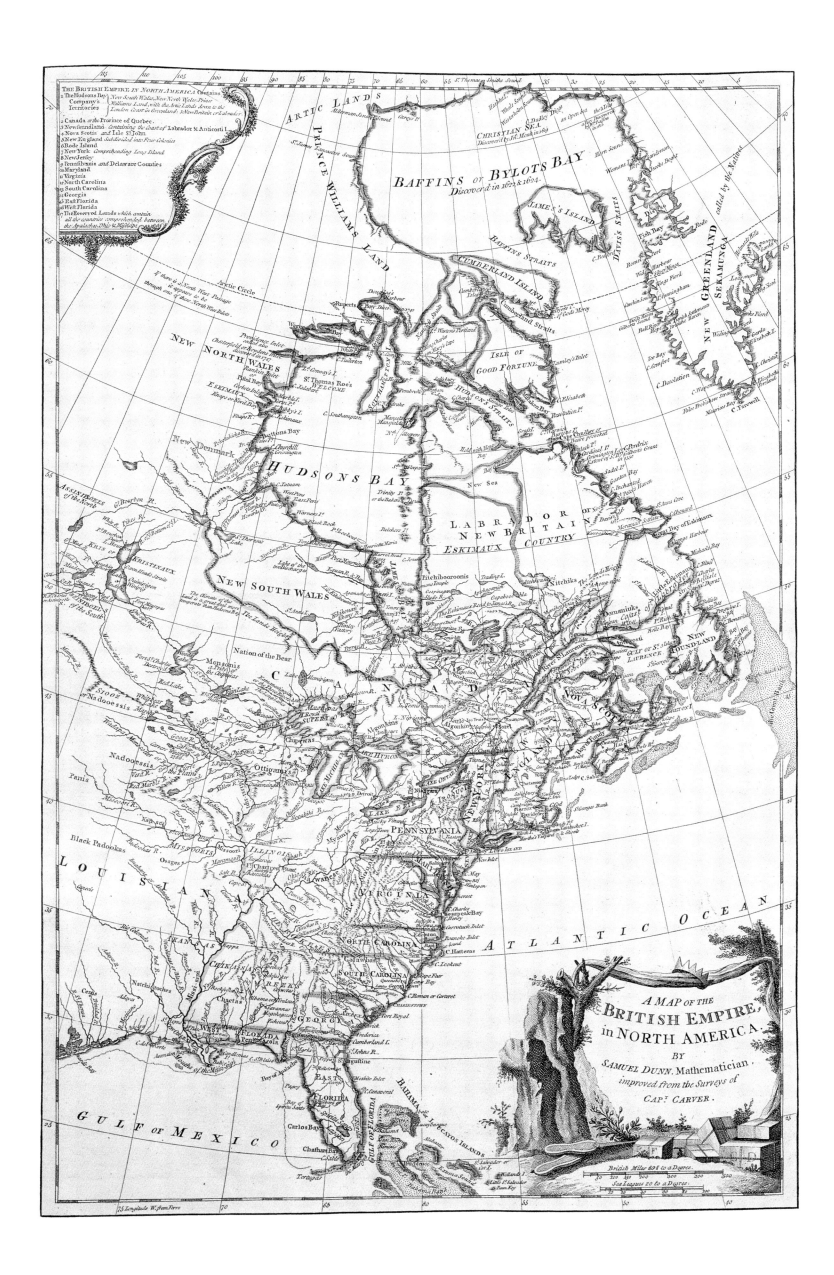

A MAP OF THE
BRITISH EMPIRE,
in NORTH AMERICA.

BY
SAMUEL DUNN, Mathematician,
improved from the Surveys of
Capt. CARVER.

MAP 69

New York and New Jersey

Holland (Major Samuel) and Thomas Pownall *The Provinces of New York, and New Jersey; with part of Pensilvania, and the Province of Quebec*. [London, Robert Sayer and James Bennett, 1776 and later.]

With its inset details showing the mouth of the Hudson River, New York and Perth Amboy, this is the last of several states of the Holland and Pownall survey which was disseminated in the *North American Atlas* of Thomas Jefferys. In this form, the British authorities had at their disposal a series of maps, plans and charts essential for the conduct of the military campaigns in the North American colonies.

The area shown on the Holland and Pownall map saw several British victories—at the Battle of Long Island in August 1776, for example. The detail includes such features as individual land owners in what is now upstate New York, and individual counties laid out almost as far as the Canadian border to the east of Lake Champlain.

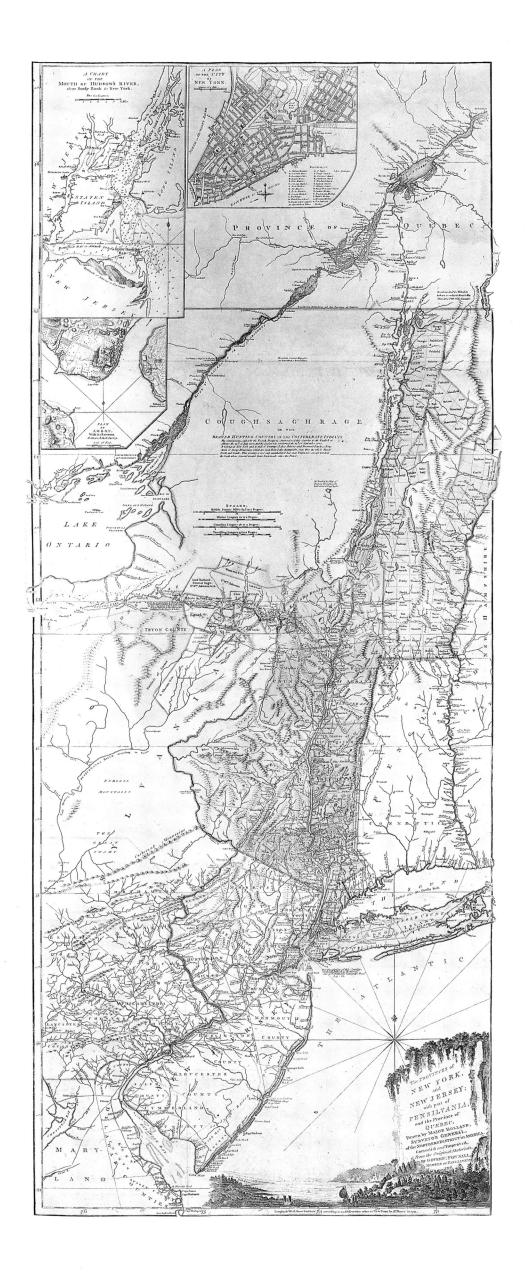

MAP 70

Map of America

Arrowsmith (Aaron) *Map of America*. London, 1804 [and later].

This large map of America, of wall-chart proportions, of which we show the
northern half, was one of a series of similar maps of the continents issued by Aaron
Arrowsmith at the turn of the eighteenth and nineteenth centuries. Arrowsmith
was the founder of a dynasty of mapmakers: Aaron junior, followed by Samuel and
John, nephew of Aaron, active until the late 1860s. The Arrowsmiths produced
maps and atlases of remarkable quality and accuracy, the *London Atlas* (see map 75)
in particular being constantly revised and updated.

This general map was compiled from several sources. Among these were the
results of Alexander Mackenzie's explorations in the Rocky Mountains and the
Canadian Arctic. In 1789, Mackenzie had been sent out on an exploring expedition
in the Northwest by the North-West Fur Company of Canada, rival of the Hudson
Bay Company in this region. Arrowsmith's map shows the river which bears
Mackenzie's name. Mackenzie's tour of some 2,990 miles was achieved in the most
remarkable time of 120 days, from Great Slave Lake to the Arctic shore and back,
resulting in a report of great accuracy. The atlas which was published with the
account of Vancouver's Pacific voyages in 1798 provided much of the coastal detail
for western Canada and Alaska.

Arrowsmith's map gives a summary picture of North America prior to
Alexander von Humboldt's researches, which appeared sporadically in print from
1805 onwards, and his surveys in New Spain in 1811. Later editions of
Arrowsmith's map incorporated this information in great detail.

Like most wall-maps, Arrowsmith's large maps are now hard to find in good
condition. They were published for sale separately, either in sheet form or
mounted and dissected as folding maps on linen. Very occasionally it is also
possible to find his large maps bound up as an atlas of large sheets, and when so
found, the maps can command high prices.

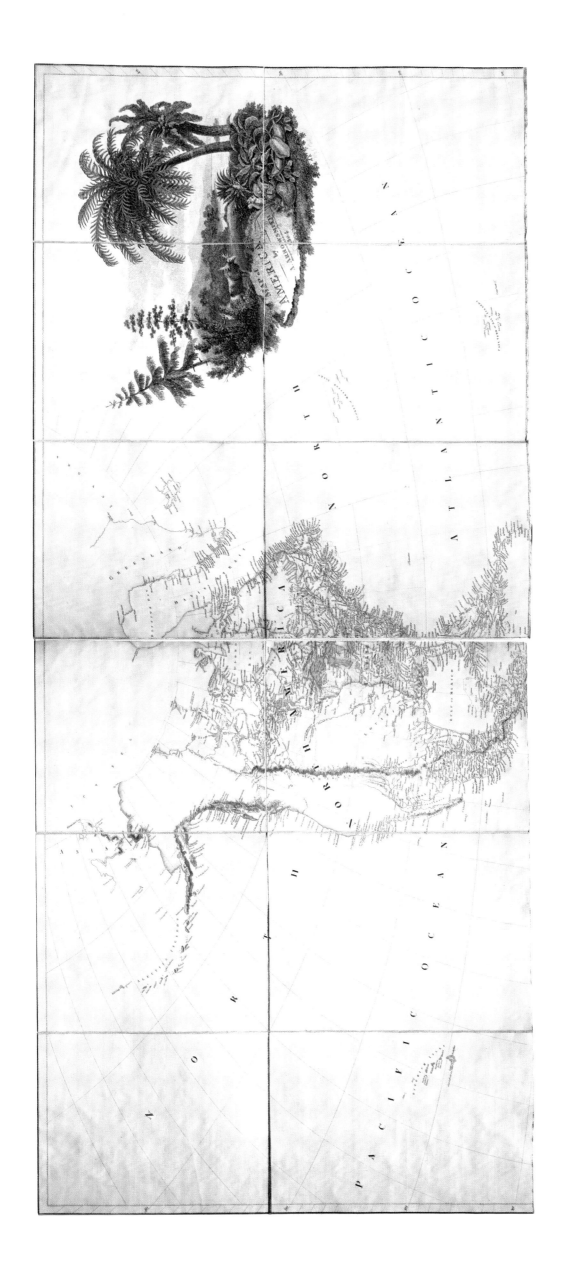

MAP 71

The United States of America

Faden (William) *The United States of North America with the British Territories and those of Spain . . . 1809*. London, 1809 [and later].

Like those of his contemporary John Cary, William Faden's maps are a model of clarity. Typical is this map of the United States, a relatively early example of its kind to name the country as such, despite official recognition in 1783. It shows the remaining British North American territories and the neighbouring Spanish possessions in Florida, Spanish again since the 1783 Treaty, but soon to change hands again, this time as West Florida in 1812, and East Florida in 1819 under the Presidencies of James Madison and James Monroe respectively.

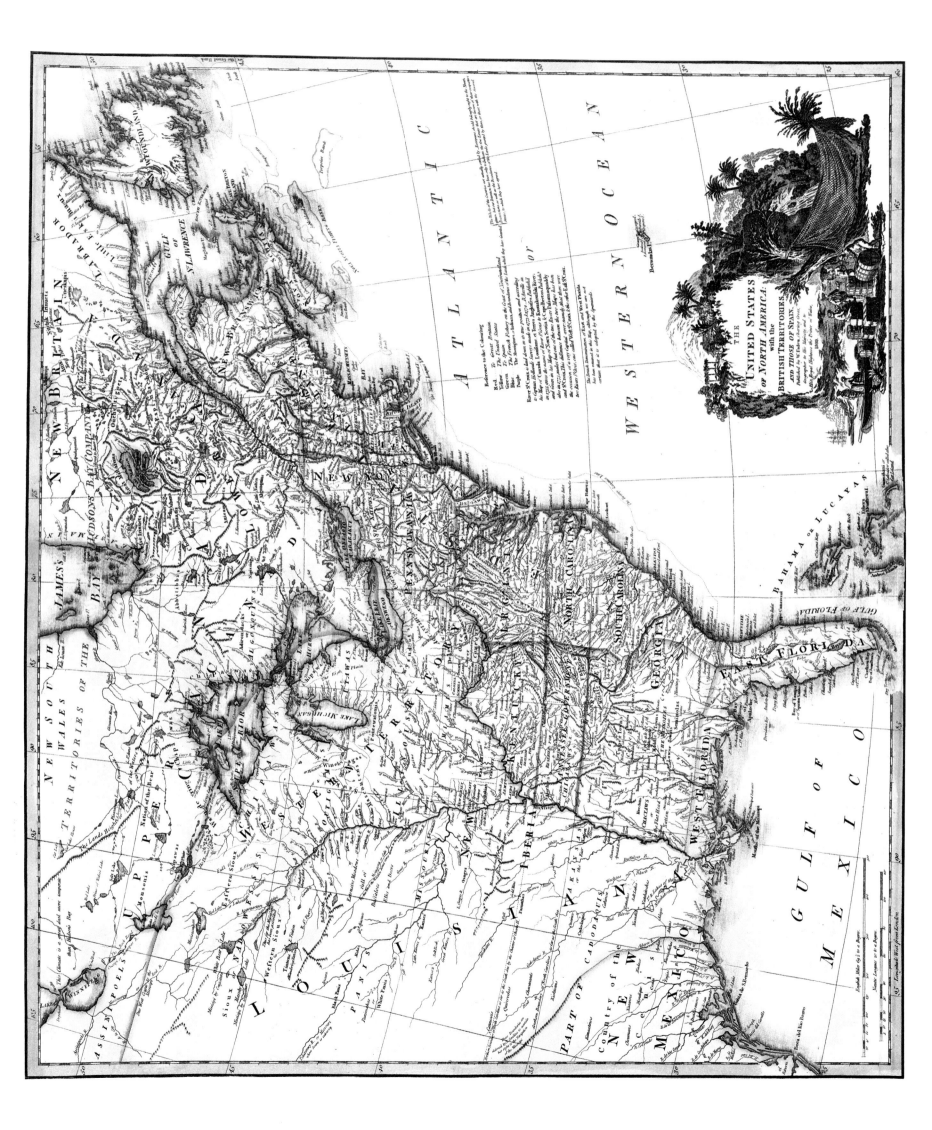

THE
UNITED STATES
OF NORTH AMERICA,
with the
BRITISH TERRITORIES,
AND THOSE OF SPAIN.
Published by W. Faden, Charing Cross,
Geographer to His Majesty and to
His Royal Highness the Prince of Wales,
1806.

WESTERN OCEAN

ATLANTIC OCEAN or

Bermuda Islands

Reference to the Colouring.

Red . . . . . To Great Britain.
Yellow . . . The United States.
Green . . . To Spanish Dominions.
Blue . . . . The French Territory.
Purple . . . The Shawanese

NEW BRITAIN

LABRADOR

NEW FOUNDLAND

the Grand Bank

GULF OF ST. LAWRENCE

NEW BRUNSWICK

NOVA SCOTIA

JAMES BAY

HUDSON'S BAY COMPANY

NEW SOUTH WALES

TERRITORIES OF THE

NEW YORK

PENNSYLVANIA

VIRGINIA

NORTH CAROLINA

SOUTH CAROLINA

GEORGIA

EAST FLORIDA

BAHAMA OR LUCAYAS

GULF OF FLORIDA

UPPER CANADA

WESTERN TERRITORY

LAKE MICHIGAN

KENTUCKY

TENNESSEE

WEST FLORIDA

LOUISIANA

MISSOURI

ASSINIBOELS

SIOUX NAD WESSOUR or Western Sioux

NEW MEXICO

GULF OF MEXICO

PART OF CANADA

Country of the
NEW MEXICO

MEXICO

English Miles 69 to a Degree

Longitude West from London

MAP 72

North America

Cary (John) *A New Map of North America. From the Latest Authorities.* London, 1811 [and later].

By the end of the eighteenth century and the early years of the nineteenth, maps gradually became less decorative. That is not to say, however, that mapmakers were no longer producing visually attractive work, for the maps of the London mapmaker John Cary are examples of very fine engraving and attractive lettering in the art and science of cartography.

Cary's *General Atlas* was an important publication in its day, attempting to bring before the public new information. His general map of the United States shows European (now independent American, of course) settlement still concentrated east of the Appalachians, and a large number of Indian tribal names in the Mid-South. His delineation of the Mid-South region is more accurate than that of most of his contemporaries, showing accurate courses of the Tennessee and Cumberland Rivers, for example.

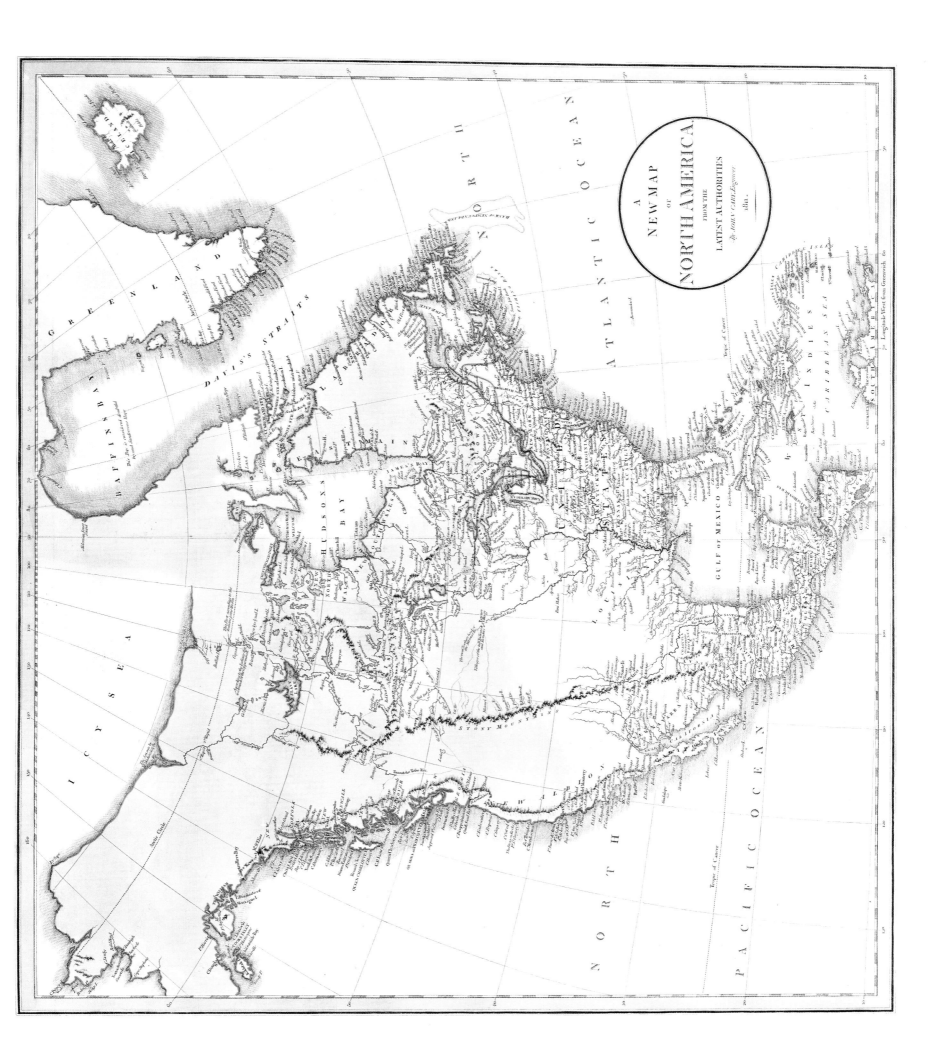

A
NEW MAP
OF
NORTH AMERICA,
FROM THE
LATEST AUTHORITIES
By JOHN CARY, Engraver
1811.

MAP 73

Virginia, Maryland and Delaware

Tanner (Henry Schenck) *Virginia Maryland and Delaware*.
Philadelphia, 1827 [and later].

With the publication of Henry Schenck Tanner's *New American Atlas* in 1823,
Philadelphia became the centre of American map production. Before Tanner,
mapmakers relied upon old surveys of the colonial era, or maps by Aaron
Arrowsmith (see map 70), Matthew Carey, and others. But Tanner managed to
acquire previously unavailable material, such as classified War Department
manuscript maps and charts, British Admiralty charts and surveys, topographical
maps and other documents, together with captured source materials.

Tanner's maps are characterized by fine engraving, bright 'mathematical'
hand-colouring and careful assessment of his source materials, all of which go to
produce handsome maps that are well in advance of their time. His early maps
were engraved; subsequently, in the 1840s, Samuel Augustus Mitchell acquired
Tanner's plates and made lithographic transfers of the plates for his own *Universal
Atlas* of 1849 and later (also see map 74).

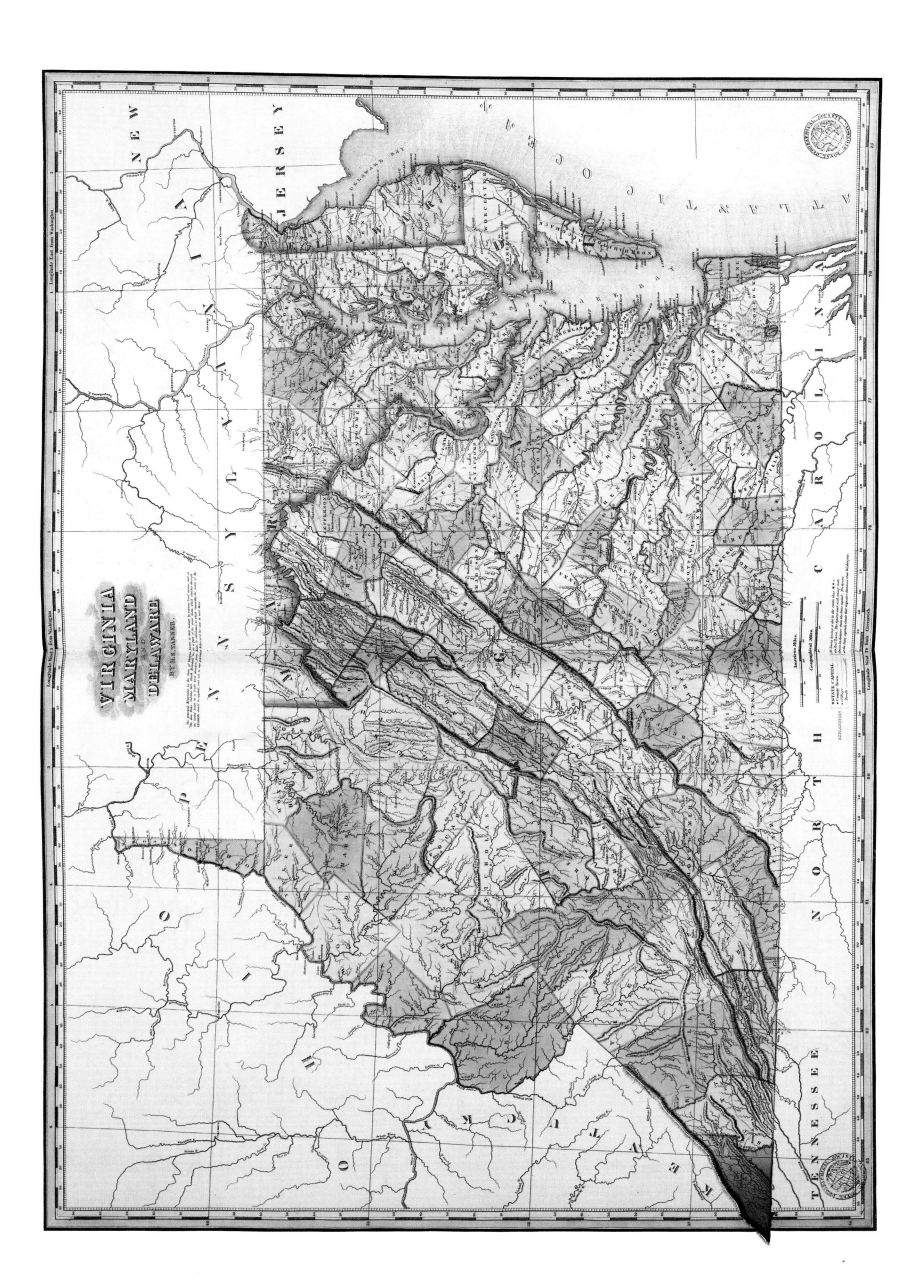

VIRGINIA
MARYLAND
AND
DELAWARE
BY H.S. TANNER.

MAP 74

Kentucky and Tennessee

Tanner (Henry Schenck) *Kentucky and Tennessee.* Philadelphia, 1827 [and later]
(see caption for map 73).

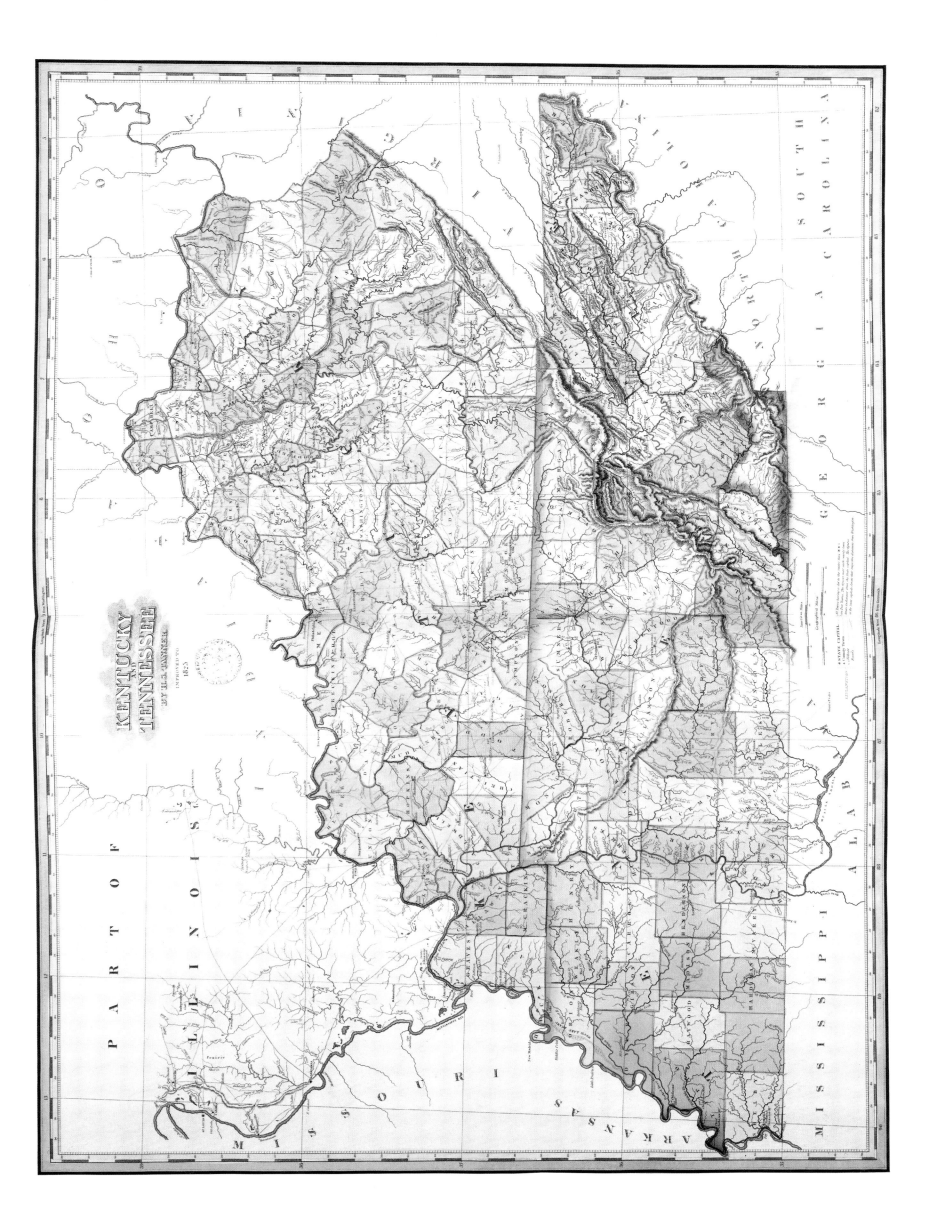

KENTUCKY
AND
TENNESSEE
BY H.S. TANNER
IMPROVED TO
1825

MAP 75

Texas

Arrowsmith (John) *Map of Texas*. London, 1841 [and later].

When this fine map was issued, Texas was an independent republic, having broken away from Mexico in 1836. During its brief life—it was annexed by the United States in 1845—several maps of the republic were published with the aim of stimulating American immigration.

That such a detailed map of Texas should appear in a British atlas can be explained by the fact that Britain saw a need to maintain the existence of Texas as a potential market for British goods, free of the restrictions of US commercial tariffs, and as a source of cotton independent of the rival cotton-producing Southern States of the USA. Texas could only compete with the South with the aid of slave labour, to which Britain was strongly opposed.

British recognition of the new republic was therefore withheld until 1840 in the hope that slavery might be abolished in Texas, and that with emancipation a free Texas might be used as a base from which to undermine slavery in the neighbouring States of the USA.

This map is one of the rarest published by John Arrowsmith in his *London Atlas*; it did not appear in atlases following the annexation in 1845.

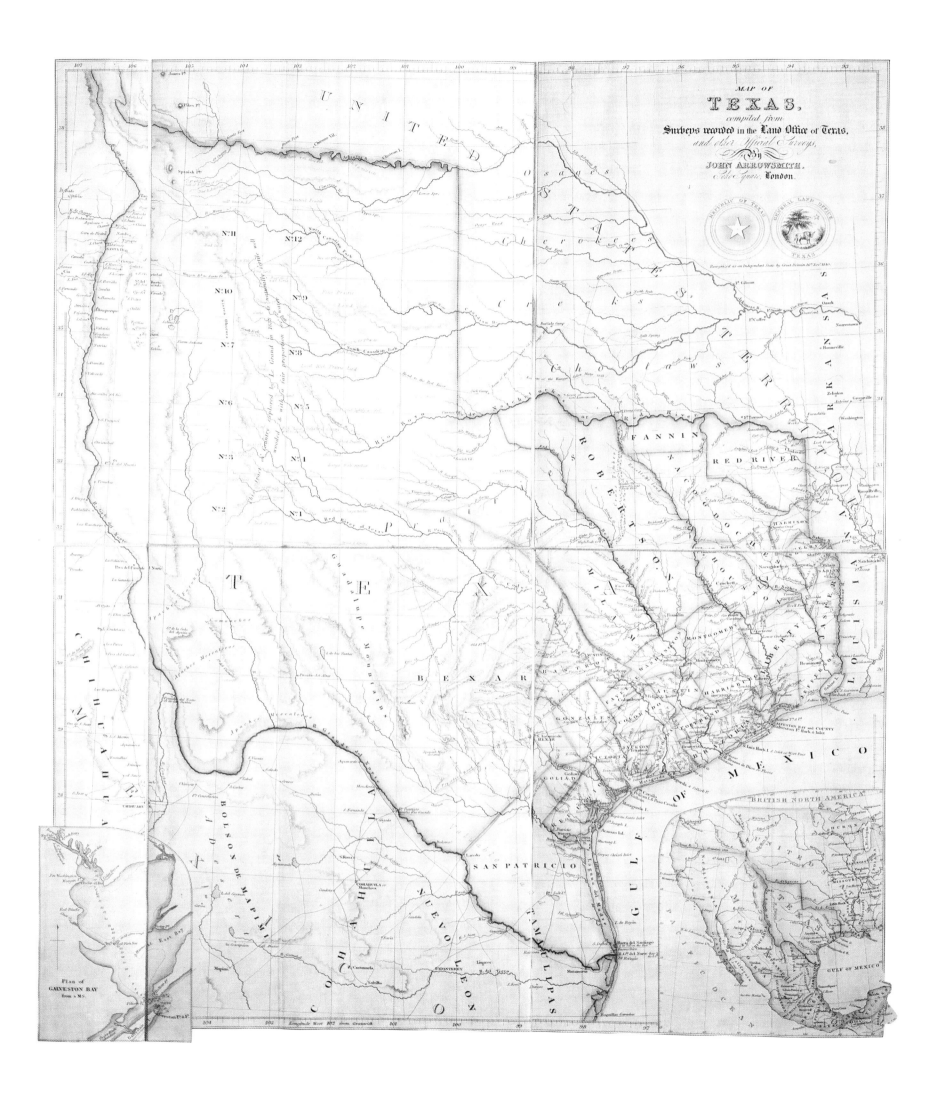

MAP OF
TEXAS,
compiled from
Surveys recorded in the Land Office of Texas,
and other Official Surveys,
By
JOHN ARROWSMITH.
Sohoe Square, London.

REPUBLIC OF TEXAS   GENERAL LAND OFFICE

Recognised as an Independent State by Great Britain 16th Nov. 1840.

Plan of
GALVESTON BAY
from a MS.

BRITISH NORTH AMERICA

GULF OF MEXICO

PACIFIC OCEAN

MAP 76

The United States of North America

Burr (David H.) *Map of the United States North America*. London, John Arrowsmith, 1842.

This map comes from The American Atlas exhibiting the Post Offices, Railroads, Canals . . . of the United States of America.

Davis H. Burr was Topographer of the United States Post Office during the 1830s, a post which enabled him to travel widely as a mapmaker. For the first time, he located all of the Post Offices in the United States on a series of maps intended for distribution to all postmasters. In 1839 he was appointed Geographer—still an official post today—to the House of Representatives.

Burr's rare and valuable atlas, with its plates engraved and published in London by John Arrowsmith (see also map 75), holds a position of high esteem among the collectors of individual State and territorial maps, for, in addition to every Post Office, four categories of roads are shown, together with canals and early railroads, all of particular importance to the postal service in those early years. For these reasons, Burr's maps are also of great interest to postal historians.

David Burr's general map of the United States is the most complete of its time, and his atlas was published at the then expensive price of $75.00, mounted on cloth, or $5.00 for individual maps so mounted. It is in the latter form that his maps are usually encountered. Ironically, since Congress had not authorized their production, despite the fact that they had been prepared under the auspices of the Postmaster General, individual postmasters had to buy their own copies at $5.00—a high sum in comparison with postal receipts at some of the smaller Post Offices at this time. This may account for the scarcity of Burr's maps today.

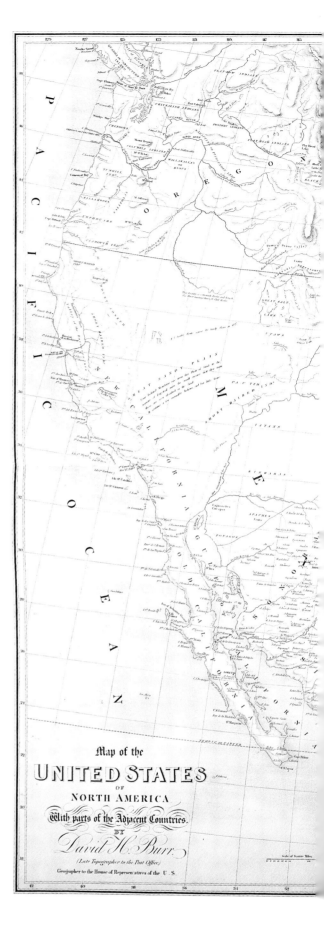

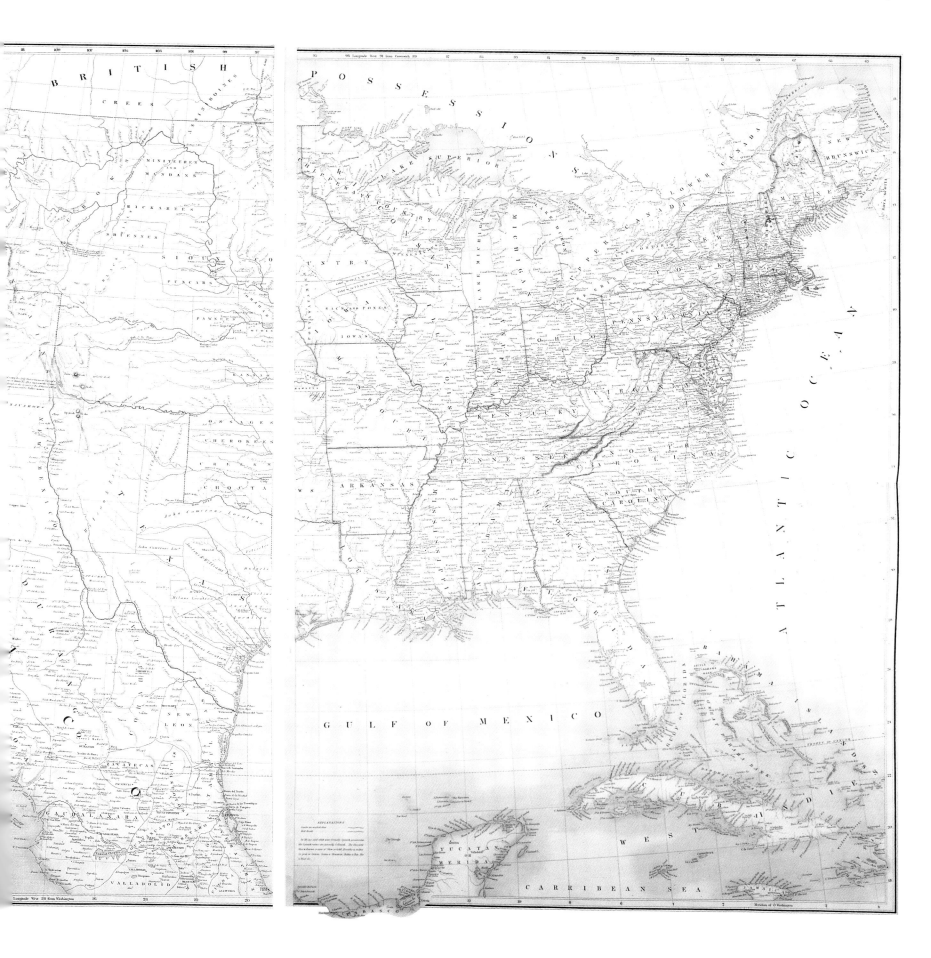

MAP 77

Oregon and Upper California

Frémont (John Charles) *Map of Oregon and Upper California*. Washington, DC,
Printed for the Senate of the United States, 1845 [and later].

The US Army Topographical Corps engineer, John Charles Frémont, explored
the country in and west of the Rocky Mountains between 1842 and 1844 with the
aid of mountain men such as Kit Carson. He travelled to the Great Salt Lake, the
Great Basin region, California and the Sierra Nevada range. The researches he
carried out were the first of their kind to be conducted on a systematic, scientific
basis, presenting for the first time a comprehensive view of the American West
from the Mississippi-Missouri system to the Pacific coast. This map assumed a vital
importance in the history of the West for settlers and railroad planners in the quest
for land and gold.

  The map was published in the *Report of the Exploring Expedition to the Rocky
Mountains in the Year 1842, and to Oregon and North California in the Years 1843–'44*. It
became a fundamental source used as a base on which to build cartographic
knowledge—despite its erroneous impression of the Great Basin. Frémont's maps
were published and read as official government documents, and widely regarded
as a guide to the American West. They won for him a national reputation as a
pathfinder, and this helped make him Republican presidential candidate in 1856.
But Frémont had always travelled with experienced mountain men, men who had
explored the same regions many years previously, but had not written reports of
their findings. In that sense, Frémont was merely the recorder and popularizer of
the achievements of the mountain men, those lone explorers of an earlier
generation. In later years, Frémont was to figure prominently in the political
history of California.

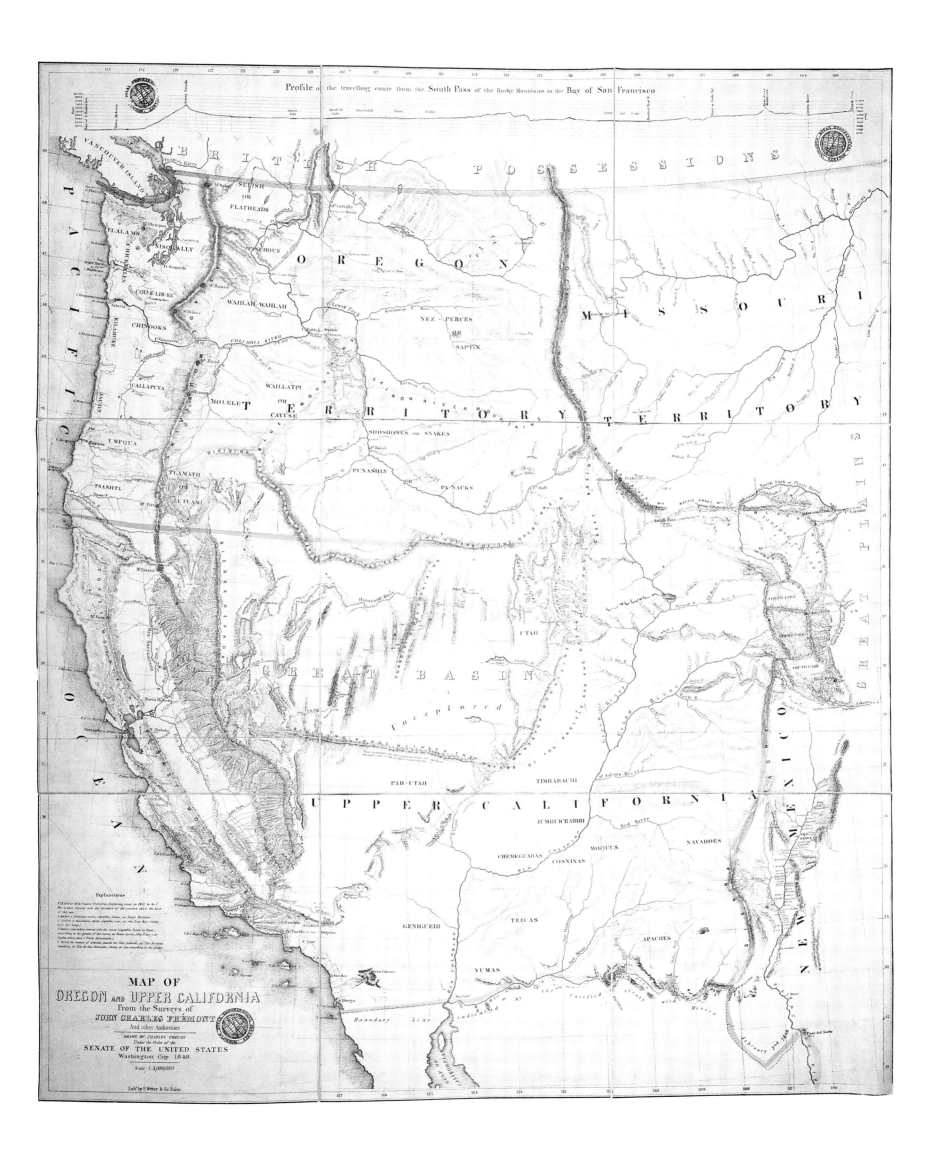

Profile of the travelling route from the South Pass of the Rocky Mountains to the Bay of San Francisco

MAP OF
OREGON AND UPPER CALIFORNIA
From the Surveys of
JOHN CHARLES FREMONT
And other Authorities
DRAWN BY CHARLES PREUSS
Under the Order of the
SENATE OF THE UNITED STATES
Washington City 1848.
Scale 1:3000000

MAP 78

The United States

Mitchell (Samuel Augustus) *A General Map of the United States with the contiguous British & Mexican Possessions*. Philadelphia, 1849 [and later].

This impressive map—note the particular detail of the Mississippi delta region (see map 79), for example—is typical of the high quality work put out by Mitchell in his earlier years, when he was issuing his own engraved maps as well as reprinting Henry Tanner's plates. Later editions of his atlases relied upon lithographic transfers which, although larger numbers of individual maps could be printed, meant also that a certain loss of aesthetic appeal resulted.

It has been estimated that Mitchell employed 250 staff at his Philadelphia works, and that more than 400,000 copies of his various atlases were sold over the years. However, owing to the often poor paper quality of these later atlases, relatively few have survived in fine condition, and collectable copies of his maps and atlases are now becoming quite scarce.

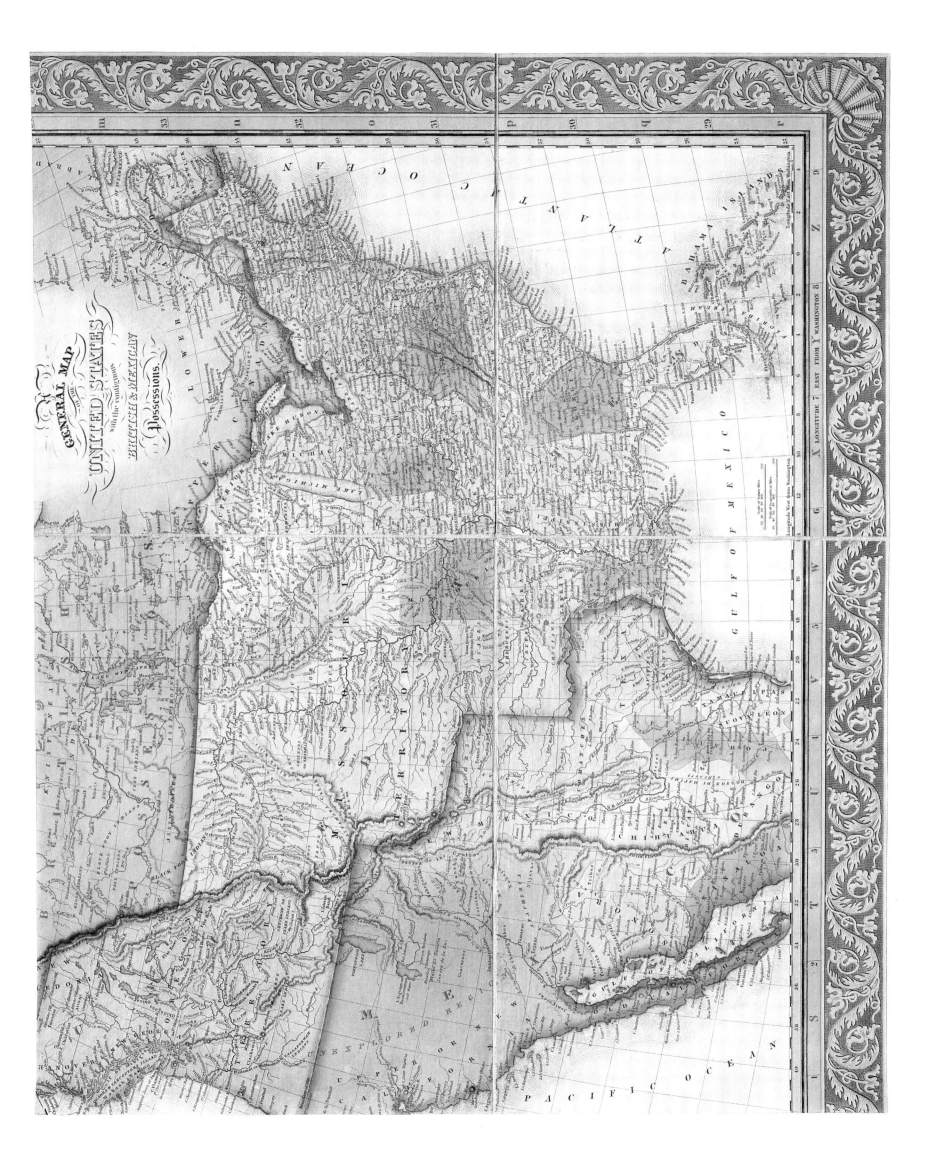

GENERAL MAP
OF THE
UNITED STATES
with the contiguous
BRITISH & MEXICAN
Possessions.

MAP 79

The Mississippi Delta

Mitchell (Samuel Augustus) A detail of the Mississippi Delta from *A General Map of the United States with the contiguous British & Mexican Possessions*. Philadelphia, 1849 [and later] (see caption for map 78).

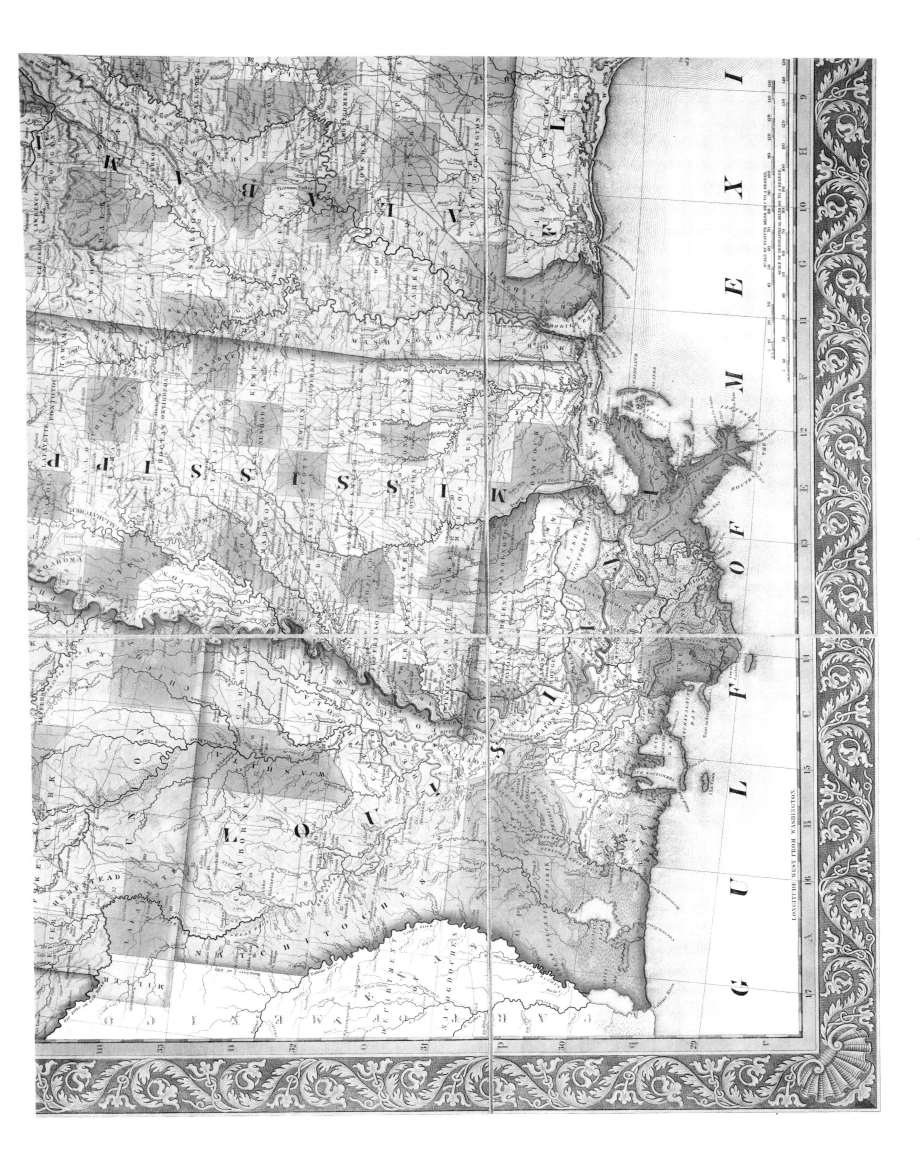

MAP 80

Mexico, California and Texas

Tallis (John) *Mexico, California and Texas*. London and New York, John Tallis & Co. [1851].

From *The Illustrated Atlas*, this map, drawn by John Rapkin, shows the Southwest on the eve of the great changes which would result from the breaking away of California from Mexico in 1848. In that year, California became part of the United States by the Treaty of Guadaloupe Hidalgo, and acquired statehood in 1850. Texas, formerly independent of Mexico from 1836, became part of the United States in 1845.

A hint of the economic importance of California is shown in the vignette at the left depicting gold-panning. Gold was discovered, merely days before California was ceded to the United States, by John A. Sutter, a Swiss immigrant of New Helvetia, on the American River, a branch of the Sacramento River in California, so marked. This discovery sparked off the Gold Rush of 1849. So many 'Forty-niners' left San Francisco in the hope of making their fortunes that one city newspaper editor was forced to comment on the sudden exodus from San Francisco in these terms: 'The whole country, from San Francisco to Los Angeles, and from the sea shore to the base of the Sierra Nevadas, resounds with the sordid cry of "gold!, GOLD!, GOLD!." While the field is left half planted, the house half built, and everything neglected but the manufacture of shovels and pickaxes.'

The vignette at the upper right shows Uxmal in the Yucatan as observed by John Lloyd Stephens and the artist Frederick Catherwood during the late 1830s, and recorded in their *Incidents of Travel in Central America, Chiapas and Yucatan*, published in 1841.

MEXICO, CALIFORNIA AND TEXAS

UNITED STATES

GULF OF MEXICO

T E X A S

M E X I C O

NEW OR UPPER CALIFORNIA

OREGON

NORTH PACIFIC OCEAN

GOLD WASHING

MEXICAN PEASANTRY

London, Published by J. Tallis & Co. Engraved by J. Rapkin.

MAP 81

New York

Tallis (John) *New York*. London and New York, John Tallis & Co. [1851].

From the *Illustrated Atlas*, the supplementary section which contains town plans, this handsome plan of New York City shows the southern end of Manhattan as far up as 42nd Street, together with Williamsburgh and part of Brooklyn. Three phases of development can be made out: the irregular streets of the first permanent settlement at the southern tip; the regular blocks of the next phase differently angled against each other as in Greenwich Village for example; and then the more regular rectangular blocks of the uniform pattern ordained by the Commissioner's Plan of 1811 which eventually were to extend the entire length of Manhattan to Harlem.

Monotonous as it may seem, the grid iron plan of nineteenth-century New York simplified engineering and municipal administration, the Commissioners remarking that 'a city is to be composed principally of the habitations of men, and . . . straitsided, and right angled houses are the most cheap to build, and the most convenient to live in . . . ' This certainly was a paramount factor in the later expansion of the city's population. The vignettes illustrate the view from Williamsburgh and Brooklyn.

NEW YORK.

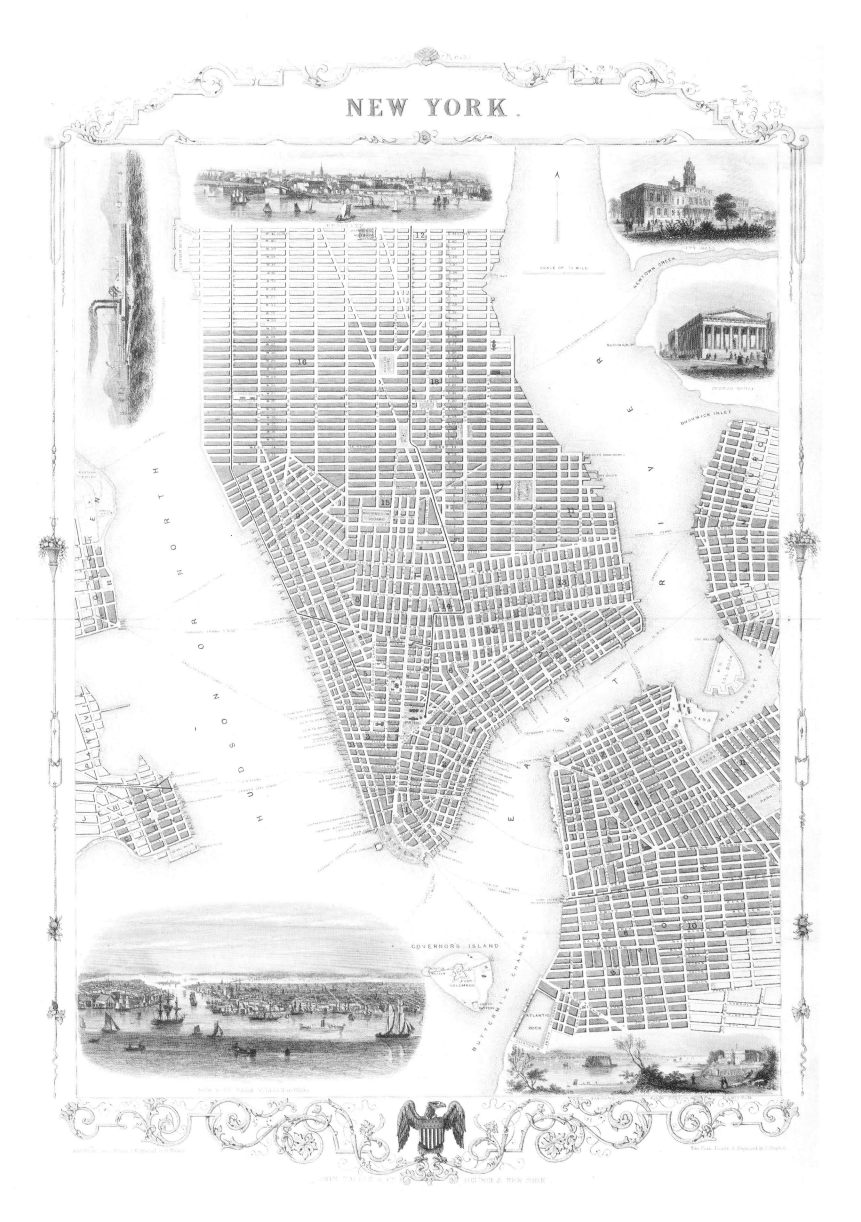

MAP 82

North America

Tallis (John) *North America*. London and New York, John Tallis & Co. [1851].

This is a fine general map of the United States, Canada and Mexico drawn by John Rapkin, showing the borders of the United States and Canada according to the 1848 settlement in the Oregon and British Columbia region, Upper California Territory rather than the State of California, Texas incorporated into the Union, and so on. Alaska is, of course, still Russian territory at this time: the great real estate deal was not to take place until 1867.

The vignettes are of interest here. Contemporary curiosity about the Indians of North America manifests itself in the illustration at the lower left, inspired by the work of the artist George Catlin and his celebrated *North American Indian Portfolio* of 1844, also Catherwood's view of an ancient Mexican monument nearby, together with illustrations of Inuit at the top and Niagara at the right.

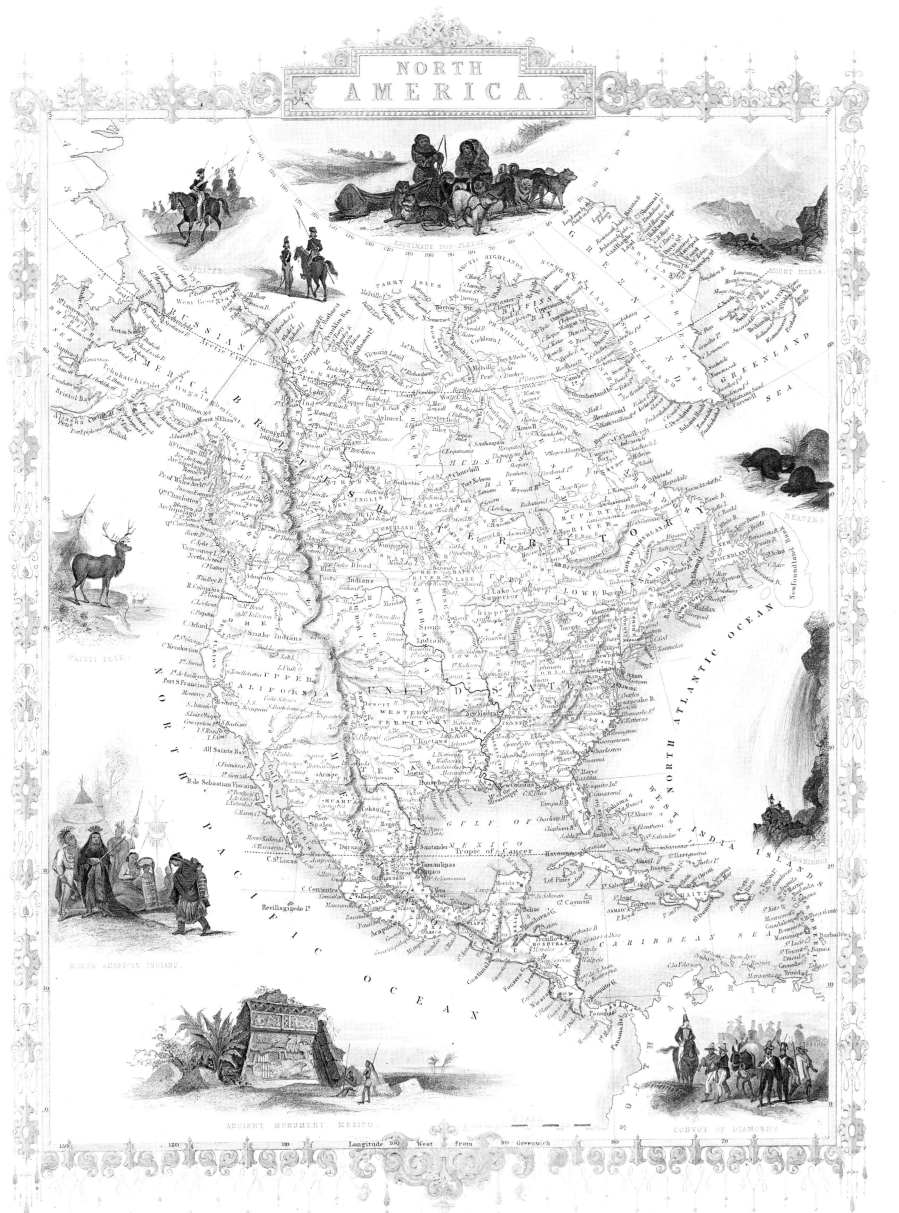

NORTH AMERICA.

ESQUIMAUX DOG-SLEDGE.

COSSACKS.

MOUNT HECLA.

BEAVERS.

WAPITI DEER.

NORTH AMERICAN INDIANS.

ANCIENT MONUMENT, MEXICO.

CONVOY OF DIAMONDS.

Longitude 100 West from 90 Greenwich

MAP 83

California and Nevada

Colton ([George Woolworth]) *Colton's California and Nevada*. New York, 1863 [and later].

This map was published during a transitional period in the history of the Nevada region. Expansion in the West, out of California as well as from the eastern States strengthened a demand for formalized government. A series of great mining successes had led to an influx of prospectors into the region around Virginia City during the early 1860s.

Congress, faced by the demands for territorial organization, set aside western Utah as the Nevada Territory in 1861. However, the fact that the mines here were producing at least 24 million dollars' worth of precious metal every year attracted still more settlers, and, with the prospect of increased revenues to Washington, Nevada was formally elevated to statehood in 1864.

In its first three decades, the new State enjoyed a boom unparalleled in the mining history of the West, a boom shared also by California (see map 80) from the days of the 'Forty-niners', and by the neighbouring Territory of Arizona, created in 1863 for the same reasons which had led to Nevada's status.

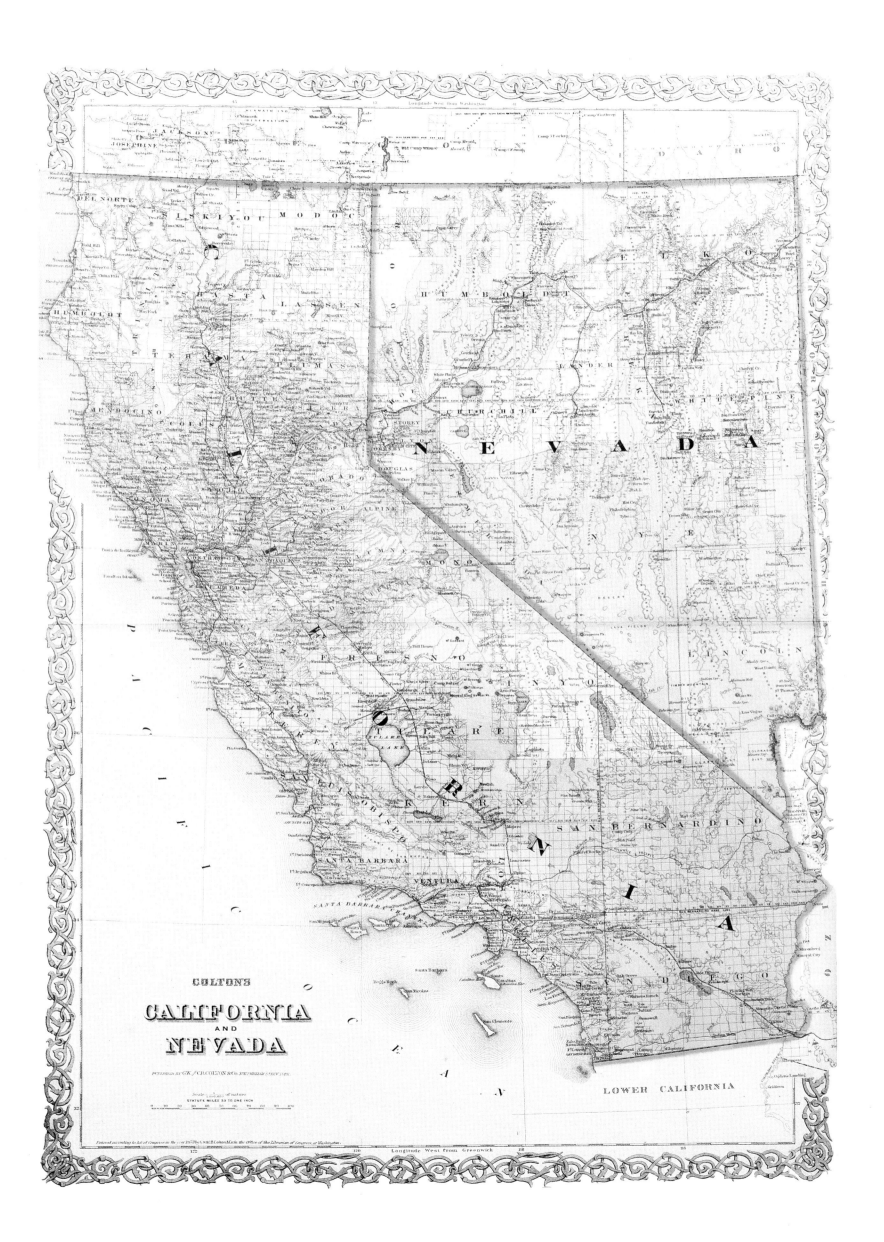

COLTON'S

CALIFORNIA

AND

NEVADA

Published by G.W. & C.B. COLTON & Co. N°.172 William St. New York.

Scale of Statute Miles 33 TO ONE INCH

NEVADA

LOWER CALIFORNIA

MAP 84

Texas

Johnson (A.J.) and Ward *Johnson's New Map of the State of Texas*. New York, 1863 [and later].

The State of Texas with its internal boundaries laid out. This is a lithographed map, typical of the style displayed in middle nineteenth-century American atlases. It shows counties, townships, sections, and so on.

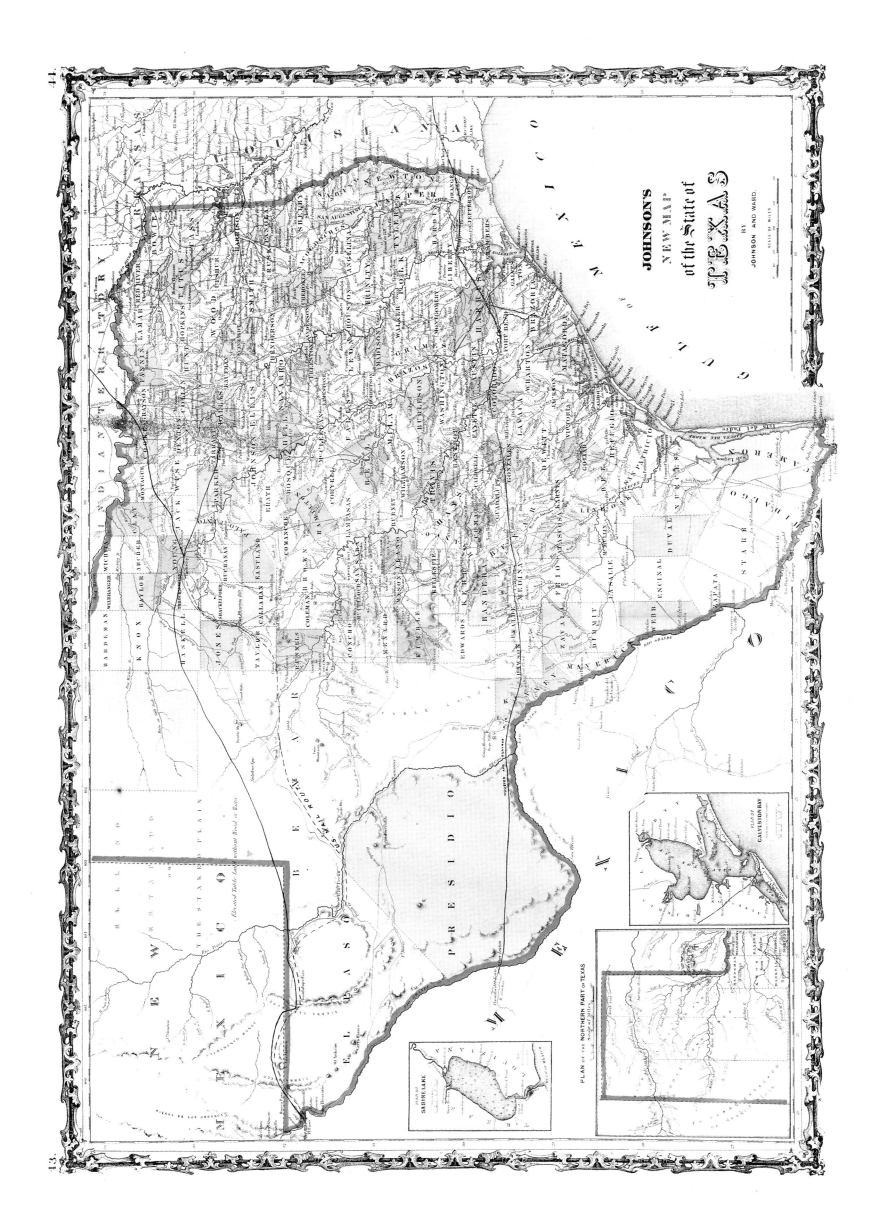

JOHNSON'S
NEW MAP
of the State of
TEXAS
BY
JOHNSON AND WARD.

SCALE OF MILES

PLAN OF
GALVESTON BAY

PLAN OF THE NORTHERN PART OF TEXAS

PLAN OF
SABINE LAKE

MAP 85

The United States

Bacon (George Washington) *Bacon's Map of the United States 1866*. London, 1866 [this issue].

By the middle of the nineteenth century, with the gradual rise in literacy and the spread of education to a mass public, the demand for maps of all kinds for ready reference rather than for merely decorative purposes increased to such an extent that the more traditional engraving processes found it hard to keep up. This example shows a lithographed map of the United States after the Civil War, produced quickly and cheaply, informative rather than aesthetically pleasing. Shown are the railroads in the course of being built.

Until quite recently, late maps such as this have been eschewed by most collectors and dealers alike: the preference, understandably enough, being for the more decorative items. But as we approach the twenty-first century, such mid- to late nineteenth-century maps are themselves approaching a century and a half in age, and it should not be forgotten that turn of the century railroad and other thematic maps can boast of having reached their century too. The ephemeral nature of many of these maps, Bacon's map included, means that many are already becoming rare and hard to find in good condition, even though they may have been produced in large numbers originally. The reader and the collector may draw his own conclusions.

Suggested Further Reading

ALDEN, J.R., *Pioneer America*. London, Hutchinson, 1966.

BILLINGTON, R.A., *Westward Expansion. A History of the American Frontier*. London, Collier Macmillan, 1974 edn.

CUMMING, W.P., HILLIER, S.E., QUINN, D.B., and WILLIAMS, G., *The Exploration of North America. 1630–1776*. London, Elek, 1974.

—— and RANKIN. H., *The Fate of a Nation. The American Revolution through Contemporary Eyes*. London, Phaidon, 1975.

——, SKELTON, R.A., and QUINN, D.B., *The Discovery of North America*. London, Elek, 1971.

FRANKLIN, W., *Discoverers, Explorers, Settlers. The Diligent Writers of Early America*. Chicago and London, University of Chicago Press, 1979.

GLASER, L., *America on Paper. The First Hundred Years*. Philadelphia, Associated Antiquaries, 1989.

HONOUR, H., *The New Golden Land. European Images of America from the Discoveries to the Present Time*. New York, Pantheon Books, 1975.

MERK, F., *History of the Westward Movement*. New York, Knopf, 1980.

NEVINS, A., and COMMAGER, H.S., *A Short History of the United States*. New York, Knopf, 1976 edn.

SCHWARTZ, S.I., and EHRENBERG, R.E., *The Mapping of America*. New York, H.N. Abrams, 1980.

SKELTON, R.A., *Explorers' Maps*. London, Routledge & Kegan Paul, 1958.